IRQ, DMA & I/O

3rd Edition

IRQ, DMA & I/O

3rd Edition

Jim Aspinwall

MIS:Press

An imprint of IDG Books Worldwide, Inc.

An International Data Group Company

Foster City, CA ■ Chicago, IL ■ Indianapolis, IN ■ New York, NY

IRQ, DMA & I/O, 3rd Edition
Published by
MIS:Press
An imprint of IDG Books Worldwide, Inc.
An International Data Group Company
919 E. Hillsdale Blvd., Suite 400
Foster City, CA 94404
www.idgbooks.com (IDG Books Worldwide
Web site)

ISBN: 0-7645-7519-8

Printed in the United States of America

10 9 8 7 6 5 4 3 2 1

3P/RS/QX/ZZ/IN

Distributed in the United States by IDG Books Worldwide, Inc.

Distributed by CDG Books Canada Inc. for Canada; by Transworld Publishers Limited in the United Kingdom; by IDG Norge Books for Norway; by IDG Sweden Books for Sweden; by IDG Books Australia Publishing Corporation Pty. Ltd. for Australia and New Zealand; by TransQuest Publishers Pte Ltd. for Singapore, Malaysia, Thailand, Indonesia, and Hong Kong; by Gotop Information Inc. for Taiwan; by ICG Muse, Inc. for Japan; by Norma Comunicaciones S.A. for Colombia; by Intersoft for South Africa; by Eyrolles for France; by International Thomson Publishing for Germany, Austria and Switzerland; by Distribuidora Cuspide for Argentina; by Livraria Cultura for Brazil; by Ediciones ZETA S.C.R. Ltda. for Peru; by WS Computer Publishing Corporation, Inc., for the Philippines; by Contemporanea de Ediciones for Venezuela; by Express Computer Distributors for the Caribbean and West Indies; by Micronesia Media Distributor, Inc. for Micronesia; by Grupo Editorial Norma S.A. for Guatemala; by Chips Computadoras S.A. de C.V. for Mexico; by Editorial Norma de Panama S.A. for Panama; by American Bookshops for Finland. Authorized Sales Agent: Anthony Rudkin Associates for the Middle East and North Africa.

For general information on IDG Books Worldwide's books in the U.S., please call our Consumer Customer Service department at 800-762-2974. For reseller information, including discounts and premium sales, please call our Reseller Customer Service department at 800-434-3422.

For information on where to purchase IDG Books Worldwide's books outside the U.S., please contact our International Sales department at 317-596-5530 or fax 317-596-5692.

For consumer information on foreign language translations, please contact our Customer Service department at 800-434-3422, fax 317-596-5692, or e-mail **rights@idgbooks.com.**

For information on licensing foreign or domestic rights, please phone +1-650-655-3109.

For sales inquiries and special prices for bulk quantities, please contact our Sales department at 650-655-3200 or write to the address above.

For information on using IDG Books Worldwide's books in the classroom or for ordering examination copies, please contact our Educational Sales department at 800-434-2086 or fax 317-596-5499.

For press review copies, author interviews, or other publicity information, please contact our Public Relations department at 650-655-3000 or fax 650-655-3299.

For authorization to photocopy items for corporate, personal, or educational use, please contact Copyright Clearance Center, 222 Rosewood Drive, Danvers, MA 01923, or fax 978-750-4470.

Library of Congress Cataloging-in-Publication Data
Aspinwall, Jim.
IRQ, DMA & I/O / Jim Aspinwall. -- 3rd ed.
    p. cm.
    ISBN 0-7645-7519-8 (alk. paper)
    1. Microcomputers. 2. Software configuration management.
I. Title.
QA76.5.A77432   1999
004.165--dc21   99--13150
                                                        CIP

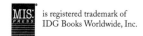

ABOUT IDG BOOKS WORLDWIDE

Welcome to the world of IDG Books Worldwide.

IDG Books Worldwide, Inc., is a subsidiary of International Data Group, the world's largest publisher of computer-related information and the leading global provider of information services on information technology. IDG was founded more than 30 years ago by Patrick J. McGovern and now employs more than 9,000 people worldwide. IDG publishes more than 290 computer publications in over 75 countries. More than 90 million people read one or more IDG publications each month.

Launched in 1990, IDG Books Worldwide is today the #1 publisher of best-selling computer books in the United States. We are proud to have received eight awards from the Computer Press Association in recognition of editorial excellence and three from Computer Currents' First Annual Readers' Choice Awards. Our best-selling ...For Dummies® series has more than 50 million copies in print with translations in 31 languages. IDG Books Worldwide, through a joint venture with IDG's Hi-Tech Beijing, became the first U.S. publisher to publish a computer book in the People's Republic of China. In record time, IDG Books Worldwide has become the first choice for millions of readers around the world who want to learn how to better manage their businesses.

Our mission is simple: Every one of our books is designed to bring extra value and skill-building instructions to the reader. Our books are written by experts who understand and care about our readers. The knowledge base of our editorial staff comes from years of experience in publishing, education, and journalism — experience we use to produce books to carry us into the new millennium. In short, we care about books, so we attract the best people. We devote special attention to details such as audience, interior design, use of icons, and illustrations. And because we use an efficient process of authoring, editing, and desktop publishing our books electronically, we can spend more time ensuring superior content and less time on the technicalities of making books.

You can count on our commitment to deliver high-quality books at competitive prices on topics you want to read about. At IDG Books Worldwide, we continue in the IDG tradition of delivering quality for more than 30 years. You'll find no better book on a subject than one from IDG Books Worldwide.

John Kilcullen
Chairman and CEO
IDG Books Worldwide, Inc.

Steven Berkowitz
President and Publisher
IDG Books Worldwide, Inc.

Eighth Annual
Computer Press
Awards 1992

Ninth Annual
Computer Press
Awards 1993

Tenth Annual
Computer Press
Awards 1994

Eleventh Annual
Computer Press
Awards 1995

IDG is the world's leading IT media, research and exposition company. Founded in 1964, IDG had 1997 revenues of $2.05 billion and has more than 9,000 employees worldwide. IDG offers the widest range of media options that reach IT buyers in 75 countries representing 95% of worldwide IT spending. IDG's diverse product and services portfolio spans six key areas including print publishing, online publishing, expositions and conferences, market research, education and training, and global marketing services. More than 90 million people read one or more of IDG's 290 magazines and newspapers, including IDG's leading global brands — Computerworld, PC World, Network World, Macworld and the Channel World family of publications. IDG Books Worldwide is one of the fastest-growing computer book publishers in the world, with more than 700 titles in 36 languages. The "...For Dummies®" series alone has more than 50 million copies in print. IDG offers online users the largest network of technology-specific Web sites around the world through IDG.net (http://www.idg.net), which comprises more than 225 targeted Web sites in 55 countries worldwide. International Data Corporation (IDC) is the world's largest provider of information technology data, analysis and consulting, with research centers in over 41 countries and more than 400 research analysts worldwide. IDG World Expo is a leading producer of more than 168 globally branded conferences and expositions in 35 countries including E3 (Electronic Entertainment Expo), Macworld Expo, ComNet, Windows World Expo, ICE (Internet Commerce Expo), Agenda, DEMO, and Spotlight. IDG's training subsidiary, ExecuTrain, is the world's largest computer training company, with more than 230 locations worldwide and 785 training courses. IDG Marketing Services helps industry-leading IT companies build international brand recognition by developing global integrated marketing programs via IDG's print, online and exposition products worldwide. Further information about the company can be found at www.idg.com.   1/24/99

Credits

Acquisitions Editor
Martine Edwards

Development Editor
Laura E. Brown

Technical Editor
Art Brieva

Copy Editors
Adam Newton
Nancy Rapoport

Production, Proofreading, and Indexing
York Production Services
IDG Books Worldwide Production

About the Author

Jim Aspinwall is a PC applications and networking consultant as well as a contributor to various computer and service industry magazines. He is one of the authors of the critically acclaimed, highly successful *Troubleshooting Your PC* published by IDG Books Worldwide, which is currently in its fourth edition.

To Kathy, with love

Preface

Welcome to the not-quite-pocket-size guide to quickly and easily creating and maintaining a clean, high-performance PC configuration. The focus of this book is on avoiding or, as needed, resolving resource conflicts within your system.

A considerable amount of education and experience has gone into writing this book, and it has served as an invaluable reference for both new and skilled technicians alike. The experiences behind the inception and delivery of this book may be comparable to the experiences you've had with PCs — a lot of tinkering, a lot of research, and a few opportune moments when more than a little light was shed on a particular subject at just the right moment. I hope the light you'll encounter as you go forward won't come as a blinding shock!

New to This Edition

The reason to update PC books is the same as the reason to upgrade our PC systems. Technology keeps changing and, as people want to try new things, they need new information.

The first edition of this book dealt mostly with legacy/ISA systems because that's about all PC users had back in 1995. Certainly MicroChannel, EISA, and even PCI were around, but many didn't have these systems. I couldn't deal too much with Windows 95 issues because that operating system was still in beta back then, it was buggy, and there was not a lot of experience to share.

The second edition of *IRQ, DMA & I/O* brought us Plug and Play and Windows 95. Both of these were significant changes to the PC landscape. It was an especially critical time to revise the book because we were all in the middle of remaining legacy issues, experiencing a lot of not-so-Plug-and-Play issues, and perhaps we needed to be reminded that Windows had only the hardware we gave it to work with.

This edition comes with over three years of experience with Windows 95, almost the same length of experience with Windows NT, a solid year of working with Windows 98, and quite a bit more experience helping others understand and develop products that take a lot of the mystery out of PCs. In this new edition, I introduce the Universal Serial Bus (USB), which fortunately hasn't created a lot of new technical issues, and perhaps even relieves us of some of them. The same may be said of FireWire/IEEE1394 and FibreChannel — technologies that have less effect on legacy and general configuration issues than they do on performance with high-end devices.

For all the new stuff, I don't slouch on stressing the history, principles, and realities behind the old stuff. The message is the same — if it doesn't start out configured right, you will have problems, and you'll need to fix them! There are still millions of PCs that have legacy/ISA and general configuration issues, which need to be dealt with, especially when upgrading to or adding new technology devices. I don't envision those millions of PCs vanishing suddenly and being replaced by 100 percent non-legacy systems. As far as I know, no 100 percent non-legacy systems are in existence yet anyway. Thus, legacy hardware will still be in service for at least a couple of years, while 100 percent non-legacy systems, if they ever appear, will likely comprise no more than 20 percent of the market.

Who You Are

If you are relatively new to PC technicalities, I hope you're at least aware of, if not vaguely familiar with, some of the basic aspects of PC systems. The learning curve here is not steep, so feel free to climb on up and enjoy.

If you are a moderately to highly skilled PC technician, you will be reading through a lot of information you probably wish you had a long time ago. This information should confirm your suspicions of one technical thing or another. Or you'll find things that you really didn't *want* to know, but *must* know in order to survive life or a career dealing with PCs. Still, I hope you find some new information or clarifications that will be of benefit.

In either case, feel free to skip ahead to what seems most important to you at the moment. At every step in the pages ahead, you will get a serious but easily digestible dose of techie stuff. If you've missed something along the way, you can always come back to the beginning.

What You'll Learn

The information provided in this book applies as much to the one- or two-user systems in the home or small office as it does to offices and enterprises with multiple PC systems. With this book, you learn how to:

- Determine your PC's present configuration
- Use the configuration information to determine what, if anything, to change
- Verify that your configuration is correct and functioning properly

You will be able to:

- Save several hours of frustration over each potential and real PC problem
- Avoid loss of productive time
- Avoid costly technical support calls
- Enhance the performance of your system
- Prepare your system for or correct an installation of Microsoft Windows 95, 98, or NT

Chapter Breakdown

This is a do-it-yourself guide. No complex tools, technologies, or skills are required to quickly and easily establish, upgrade, and maintain your PC system configuration. All the resources you need, with the possible exception of a common screwdriver or two, are contained within your system and this book, and aided by whatever information you can gather from your PC system board and add-in devices.

Here's a breakdown of the information contained in each chapter:

- Chapter 1, "The Legacy Lives On—The First Standards," contains important details about the past and some lingering PC designs.

- Chapter 2, "Progressions from Then to Now," covers PC design enhancements.

- Chapter 3, "Rules to Configure By," highlights PC performance and compatibility standards and issues.

- Chapter 4, "Configuration Management—What It Is and How to Do It," examines PC configuration management.

- Chapter 5, "Playing with Plug and Play," investigates the specifications and the reality of Plug and Play.

- Chapter 6, "Windows 95, 98, NT, and the Registry," looks at the interoperability of Windows and PCs.

- Chapter 7, "Progressing to PC99," looks ahead to PCs in the next millennium.

- Chapter 8, "Tools, Tips, and Tricks," helps you get it right.

- Appendixes A through D provide reference information galore.

You may get a lot of information that you never before wanted to concern yourself with. After all, computers and software are more powerful than ever. In fact, PCs do many things faster than they used to, but faster does not mean smarter or better unless the system is configured properly, and proper configuration requires information.

You simply may not want to deal with some aspects of PC configuration and hardware, and this book may help you recognize that this is the case and that you should wisely seek out the right kind of help from a friend, a service shop, or a technical support phone call. If you find this book to be the long-awaited relief from your PC nightmares, so much the better.

> **Note**
>
> Memory management configuration and conflict issues are best left to the software and other reference materials dedicated to the subject. This book focuses on hardware issues and the words *system* and *device* refer to hardware and the software or drivers that enable specific hardware. A system is the combined and cooperative interworkings of both software and hardware.

All the chapters are rich in reference information and experience on innovations ranging from the original IBM PC to the latest in high-speed Pentium technology, new data bus features, Plug and Play, and the Windows Registry. As you read further, you will learn about old and new configurations and standards, and the tools that are used in the process. You'll be alerted to inherent limitations of hardware, software, and technology implementations.

All this information is primarily for your benefit, and perhaps secondarily, to the benefit of jammed tech support phone lines. A few secrets are tucked away in here. The ultimate goal is for you to get the most out of your personal computer through an understanding of the discipline involved in having a smooth-running PC system.

A Few Rules

This book is also about rules. It refers to some very distinct and specific issues, some of which we're legally required to express and use properly. It also refers to other rules because they just plain make sense as they *should* be expressed rather than as they are commonly used, or too often abused. Someone has to keep them all straight. The context, premise, basic points, and useful information will come through for 99 percent of us. While I have technical editors and several thousand readers scour these pages, if I miss a point, feel free to respectfully make suggestions by e-mail.

We have a lot of terms to deal with as we walk, run, or trip and fall through PC configuration issues and the chapters ahead. Some of the terms refer to actual RAM memory and device addressing, BIOS, and various configuration items. All these technical terms and more are the language of PC configuration, and as they come along, I'll properly explain them.

There are also a lot of acronyms, trade names, standards, and often confusing terms to keep track of. For instance:

- Legacy — referring to the old but still prevalent PC architecture, ports and devices, and configuration issues.

- Plug and Play — a very precise definition of how I/O devices may be identified and automatically configured by the system BIOS, setup programs and, to some extent, tools available under the operating system. Perhaps the introduction to Plug and Play found on Microsoft's Web site says it best:

"Plug and Play is the technology that supports automatic configuration of PC hardware and attached devices. A user can just attach a new device such as sound or fax card ('plug it in') and start working ('begin playing') without having to configure the device manually. Plug and Play technology is implemented in hardware, in operating systems such as Microsoft Windows 95, and in supporting software such as drivers and BIOS."

If only it were really that easy!

Note

By the way, the proper expression is Plug and Play. It is abbreviated as PnP in the official specifications, and I believe that to be the only acceptable alternate form of indicating Plug and Play. Hyphenation and other abbreviations such as Plug n Play or Plug'n Play often indicate claims of functionality or compatibility that are at least misleading if not completely false. *Caveat Emptor.*

- MicroChannel, EISA, Local Bus, PCMCIA, PCI, USB, FireWire, and AGP — terms and acronyms referring to various PC I/O port and connection designs. Each will be defined in its own right and place as it evolves and affects system configuration.

- COM, LPT, A:, C:, and other logical names and labels — even very specific items are given somewhat less-than-specific labels. These labels are intended to make devices easier to identify, but they are often responsible for a lot of configuration confusion. We jump right into logical devices in Chapter 1.

Why I Wrote This Book

I fancy telling people "if you want to make toast, you have to know something about the toaster."

What does that have to do with PC configuration?

In principle, working with a toaster isn't much different from working with your PC. You should know what the pieces are, be able to hook it up, confirm that the pieces are what they say they are, and that the pieces are working properly.

While you may not want to design the toaster or make the bread or jam, you need to know that the toaster needs to be plugged in, where to put the bread, and how to make the toaster heat up. And since my toaster does not have a built-in setting for "Jim's Perfect Toast" (nor can it learn what that is on its own), then we need to know how to adjust it so the toast neither burns nor ends up as dried out lukewarm bread.

Unlike the toaster, my PC can't be randomly set up any old way and still come out working okay. Rather, I've learned that the computer must be set up to conform to many others' standards of PC perfection.

The toaster analogy is an oversimplification, but I use it to illustrate that neither using PCs nor making toast are things we just know as part of life. Neither are natural, instinctive functions. We havc a certain amount of responsibility to the task and to ourselves to become more aware of what we are dealing with. Effective use of both appliances takes a little good information, some time spent learning about them, and typically some trial-and-error until we get the results we want or need. If we learn enough, we'll go through fewer trials, and fewer errors will result.

PC configuration includes collecting and using information from your system and from your hardware and software manuals. Without accurate information, maintaining your system will be difficult at best. But too often the information you need is missing or misleading.

Note

I've included a valuable piece of software, a demo of Watergate Software's PC-Doctor, which provides the essential system information required to succeed in PC configuration. This program as-is will help you identify your system's hardware resources, and help uncover many unknowns and possible conflicts that could be preventing the most efficient use of your investment.

Okay, so why did I really write this book?

At least half of the PCs I hear about or am asked to support, whether as a favor to a family member or friend, through e-mail from readers, or as a primary career responsibility, are configured improperly. That's a lot of broken PCs for any one person. Ten percent would be a lot. Twenty percent would be a nuisance. Fifty percent is inexcusable.

The sad thing is that most users and support people may not be aware of this situation. Or they have intentionally set up their systems improperly, or they fail to associate some unusual system or application behavior problems with the possibility of a misconfiguration.

In early 1995, PC misconfiguration was indicated in the press as a significant cause of those expensive and frustrating tech support calls we all hate to make, and vendors hate to answer. We now call that part of the total cost of ownership, but we didn't know that then, nor did we know about or have Plug and Play. (Many argue that we still don't.) Thus, my impressions and experiences, and the message coming from the PC industry as a whole, were pretty well matched.

At that time I had been helping define PC diagnostic and information-gathering software, organizing various bits of system information, and trying to come up with *the* way to communicate to users and technical people how a PC should be correctly configured. The challenge was in how to express this, either in print or through software.

Since I don't really write code, expressing the information in print seemed like the only possibility. I had occasion to actually *meet* my publishers at the time (authoring is a truly virtual career) and by coincidence, luck, or being in the right place at the right time, they wanted to do a book that would address the configuration support issue. The match was obvious, and a book was created. Perhaps someday the code will come along, too.

Today we find that the PC is the same but different compared to 1995 and before. Until the PC is significantly re-engineered, and all old PCs vanish from use, we will still have significant configuration issues to deal with. Re-engineering the PC means removing all legacy devices, eliminating all interim progressions and odd-ball devices, and mating the resulting new hardware with operating systems and applications that don't care how devices exist, just that they do. Until that happens, this book, the information, and the tools it refers to, will still have life.

As you'll discover, PCs really do not have to be difficult to configure. All you need is good information and a little time to learn how and where to apply it. Information we have. I hope you'll arrange for the time!

Acknowledgments

There are dozens, perhaps hundreds, of people to thank for their assistance as I've been introduced to various technologies, absorbed them, been challenged by them, and found ways to share them:

- My parents, Bill and Joan, for everything
- My favorite user, Kathy, to whom I've dedicated the past two editions, for her love and patience
- To Kevin, Kathy's son, for testing a lot of what I know, and how well I could or could not share it
- Many close friends and supporters in and out of the computer trade
- My friends in amateur radio — past, present, and future — for pioneering and bringing technology to the masses before computers became popular
- My employers and coworkers at Curtin Call, Hycel, Finnigan, DiagSoft, CMG, LSI Logic, Vertisoft, TuneUp.com, National Semiconductor, Quarterdeck, and CST, among others for the opportunities to work on so many different projects and to gather the experience so critical to the topics in this book
- My first PC mentors and fellow authors, for their help, insight, and contributions to PC users and their PCs
- Brenda, Walt, Martine, Laura, Nancy, and the gang at IDG Books for taking *IRQ* one step further
- Leslie, Paul, Gloria, Rebekah, Bud, and everyone at M&T Books and MIS:Press for helping to make my words into something useful and presentable in the previous editions

- Dozens of online friends, acquaintances, and readers far and wide who have helped make all of my writing efforts and especially this book so worthwhile, and for making this hobby fun

- Ron and his students at B40 Junior High for the inspiration to convey knowledge of and access to computers to an inspiring generation of new computer users so they can carry on and exceed us

- The dozens of people I've come to know in the computer industry — from system board makers to disk drive engineers, BIOS authors to utility software authors — who have constantly challenged and constantly exceeded all my expectations of quality and performance

- All of my customers and the millions of PC users who need and want more knowledge and information to get through their lives and workdays

- The vendors who helped make this third edition of *IRQ, DMA & I/O* possible: Acer, ADi, ADS, AMD, Diamond Multimedia, Hewlett-Packard, Labtec, MSI Computers, Vista Imaging, and Xirlink. Without their USB products, Chapter 7 would simply not exist!

My most sincere thanks and appreciation to everyone!

Jim Aspinwall

"Windows Advisor," *Computer Currents Magazine*

E-mail: wb9gvf@raisin.com

Web sites: http://www.raisin.com
http://www.typc.com
http://www.bovine.org

Contents

Introduction

IRQ, DMA, and I/O are the root of the PC configuration evil we face, so let me define some basic resource names:

- **IRQ (Interrupt ReQuest signals).** IRQs are signal lines connected between a variety of devices, both external (through add-in cards) and internal, to your system board [containing the central processing unit *(CPU)*, or main computer chip, and the connections for built-in and external devices]. An IRQ assignment is expressed simply as IRQ3 or something similar. Via IRQ signals, devices such as the serial (COM) port, keyboard and disk drives, and some internal computer functions, signal the computer that an activity on that device needs the CPU's attention quickly in order to move data or handle an error situation.

  In PC and XT-class systems, there are only eight IRQ lines. A couple are reserved for internal system board use, leaving only IRQ 2, 3, 4, 5, and 7 to work with. In AT and higher class systems, there are 16 IRQ lines. Again, a few are reserved for internal system board use, leaving only IRQ 2, 3, 4, 5, 7, 9, 10, 11, 12, 14, and 15 to work with. IRQ 2 may or may not be useable, although it is available on the system bus, because it is used to tie the second IRQ controller chip to the first. IRQ 9 may or may not be useable, although it is available on the system bus, because it is the replacement for the otherwise occupied IRQ 2 line.

  As a practical example, let's say an IRQ is signaled for every block of data received into a serial/COM port, letting the CPU know that it needs to fetch this data before it is lost and new data replaces it. A *lot* of IRQs occur during online e-mail and Web page loading.

- **DMA (Direct Memory Access signals).** A DMA channel is a
  set of two signal lines, one line for *DMA request* (DRQ) and
  the other for *DMA acknowledgment* (DACK), assigned in corresponding pairs (as simply one DMA assignment), and is
  expressed simply as DMA3 or something similar. DMA
  channels are available with devices that have the ability to
  exchange data directly with system memory without going
  through the CPU (many disk drive functions and multimedia
  cards use DMA to speed data throughput).

  With a DMA channel, a device signals the computer or the
  CPU signals a device about the need for or status of direct
  access between two devices, one of which is usually system
  memory. DMA data transfer is performed under the control of
  the devices themselves. It is very fast — much faster than if the
  CPU and software handled the operation, although it does
  cause the CPU to stop processing memory operations for a
  short time, so DMA cannot control the system indefinitely.

  In PC and XT-class systems there are only four DMA lines.
  One is reserved for diskette drive use, leaving only DMA 0, 1,
  and 3 to work with. In AT or higher-class systems, there are
  eight DMA lines. One is reserved for diskette drive use,
  leaving only DMA 0, 1, 3, 5, 6, and 7 to work with. (DMA 4
  is usually not useable because it is used to link the second four
  DMA lines to the first DMA controller chip.) DMA 2 is
  always dedicated to diskette drives only.

  As a practical example, sound files sent to your PC's sound
  card and speakers use DMA to transfer large amounts of data
  from memory into the sound card, filling the sound card with
  information that it translates into smooth music, sounds, or
  voices. If your system cannot satisfy a lot of DMA activity,
  either because it has a slow CPU or because more data needs
  to be moved than there is allowable DMA time for, the audio
  will stutter and sound choppy.

- **I/O (Input/Output Addresses).** These are numerical representations of actual memory locations that are used for the data bus (the 8-, 16-, or 32-bit data lines that interconnect devices within the computer) or system RAM memory (from DOS or low memory, through the first 640K of RAM, to the upper memory areas through any and all extended memory).

  The Intel i8088 processor used in PC or XT-class systems can address memory ranges from 0 to 1MB (0–1024K, or 1,024,000 addresses). To maintain programmatic compatibility, both in operating systems and application programs, all Intel x86-based systems maintain some compatibility with this address limitation and use only 0–640K for the DOS operating system, applications, and data. Enhanced operating systems such as Windows 95, 98, NT and variations of UNIX can control the i80386 and better processors to access more memory, but that's a topic for entirely different discussions. The upper memory range from A000h–FFFFh is reserved for video, disk, and other accessory adapter data and ROM BIOS uses.

  I/O addressing is separate from memory addressing. It provides us a range from 0h–500h for use by physical I/O devices. Expressed most often in the form *378h*, indicating address 378 expressed in hexadecimal (*h* suffix) format, I/O addresses are used to uniquely identify the places in your system where data and control information can be written to or read from for the interactions between devices, the CPU, and system memory. Each device, such as a serial port or disk drive, is said to occupy a specific *address*, or location, in memory. Only data or commands specific to the device that occupies a particular address should be sent to or expected from its location.

  In practice, a device such as a serial or COM port really uses more than one full-byte address. While COM1's base address is 3F8h, it also uses every address inclusive from 3F8h to 3FFh (8 memory locations) for various data and control information. Some devices use only one address, others four, still others use sixteen or thirty-two addresses.

IRQ, DMA, and I/O are mutually exclusive in that one is not dependent on another (except for a few specific cases), and that they don't conflict with one another (IRQ1 doesn't conflict with DMA1, for example).

The Properly Configured PC

In the last three-and-a-half years, Plug and Play systems and devices, Windows 95, Windows 98, Windows NT, and their registry files, have received considerable attention as much for their successes as for their failures.

I hope that Microsoft and the system and device manufacturers have learned or been reminded of the same things I have — Plug and Play (PnP) often doesn't, thus making us rethink and adjust some of the methods we use when configuring new PCs or adding options to existing ones. The logic of PnP is not perfect.

Most of us still have legacy or non-PnP devices in our systems. With or without a mix of legacy and PnP devices, we're still required to obey the rules of the original and subsequent PC configuration designs and methods. Even when only PnP devices are in our systems, problems can arise. I'll talk about those problems and how to work around them as we go along.

You may have noticed that the introduction to Plug and Play on Microsoft's Web page refers to automatic configuration, but it says *nothing* about a proper configuration. Further, the Plug and Play specification itself says nothing about what the configuration of specific devices should be. It was never meant to do so, and thus leaves a lot to chance.

A properly configured PC is one in which there are no resource conflicts between system devices. These resources, as you'll see over and over again, are the IRQ, DMA, and I/O address items mentioned earlier, in addition to, or rather than, just the amount of RAM, free disk space, or resources left by the operating system and software.

The proper configuration and proper use of these resources depends on following standards established by others, at different times under different contexts, and in some cases, making legitimate preferential choices for some devices working within the standards.

A proper configuration is, for the most part, defined by original and subsequent PC system designs. These designs specify which system resources a particular device must or in some cases, can or should, use. Variances are not tolerated for most devices, but they may be allowed, with sufficient awareness and accommodations, in others.

A conflict within your PC system can be any occurrence of hardware and, in some cases, software that is configured in such a way that it is trying to use the same system resources as another device or program. Hardware may conflict if it is set up to use the same interrupt request (IRQ) signal, direct memory access (DMA) channel, or I/O address as another piece of hardware. Any one of these resources can be the cause of a conflict.

One symptom of a hardware conflict is the failure or inability to use one device coincident with the use of another. In such cases, either the entire system or just one or both devices may cease to operate. In some cases you may receive an error message from your software or from Windows that indicates that some device you expect to be functioning properly is unavailable for use.

Software may conflict with other software or the system by trying to use the same area of memory as another piece of software, which may result in overwriting the other program's data or program space. Software may also contain unknown or unresolved bugs or conflicts with DOS, Windows, or device drivers, which might cause the software to try to issue a command for an illegal or untimely operation to the microprocessor. Software may also be limited to working only within predefined rules, and otherwise acceptable variances may not be tolerated by a particular program.

Software conflicts may be signaled by error messages indicating insufficient memory, Exception 13, or Windows's infamous General Protection Fault dialog box. Exception errors and General

Protection Faults are indicated by memory management software or Windows, both of which monitor and attempt to maintain tight control over the computer's operations. If software tries to circumvent or improperly control these operations, Windows or the memory manager may warn you — or they may simply appear to freeze the system's operation.

While this is, strictly speaking, an operating system or environment configuration issue, software might be improperly set up to use the wrong device or the wrong address or IRQ or DMA channel for a device, consequently indicating a failure to locate or control a specific piece of hardware such as a sound board, COM port, or printer.

PC Standards and Their Evolution

A lot of history, tradition, logic, and reason are packed into the design and development of the PC and its various pieces. We are still using many items that were state-of-the-art technology circa 1981–1990. These items are the legacy of early PC development and are called *legacy devices* and *legacy systems*. Over time, PCs have become a hodgepodge of old and new technologies. Various attempts to create standards have been poorly or only partially implemented as work-around methods to try to fill in addresses or BIOS functions that IBM may have intended to use later on.

The following IBM documents form the functional and legacy foundation for all PCs to date:

- *The IBM PC Technical Reference Manual*
- *The IBM PC/XT Technical Reference Manual*
- *The IBM PC/AT Technical Reference Manual*

The following formal and *de facto* standards are all significant in the understanding and progress of the IBM PC and its subsequent enhancements:

- The PC, XT, and AT industry standard architectures in general
- IBM's MicroChannel PC system architecture
- EISA system architecture
- PCMCIA (PC Card) bus
- VESA Local Bus
- PCI system architecture

These standards are subsequently accounted for and affected by:

- Video Electronics Standards Association
- Plug and Play BIOS and hardware specifications
- Desktop Management Task Force
- Automatic Power Management and Energy Star
- Microsoft's PC95, PC97, and PC99 hardware specification initiatives
- Microsoft's Windows 95, Windows 98, and Windows NT operating systems

Considerable information may be obtained about the post-ISA architectures from online or membership sources referenced in the back of this book. The IBM reference manuals may be very hard to come by unless you find someone who is throwing out a set. They weren't cheap at $150 apiece.

All of these issues and developments affect the present-day PC to some extent. While VESA Local Bus is rarely if ever used in production systems these days, the VESA Video BIOS Extensions (VBE) are still quite important to video system compatibility. Of all of these, only ISA and PCI really concern us where PC hardware configuration resources are concerned, and often as not, PCI is not an issue, because it uses different signals from ISA devices.

The now outdated standard for the interworkings of hardware and software began with Microsoft's PC95 strategy. Microsoft and equipment vendors are now working toward new PC99 goals.

PC95, PC97, and PC99 are technical specifications that hardware makers are expected to build into their products and that software creators should accommodate. These standards encompass many aspects of the PC industry's Plug and Play specification, the PCI and PCMCIA/PC Card system bus, Intel's Pentium technology, new media and connection methods, and the functions of Microsoft's Windows family of PC operating systems.

For the PC9*x* standards to be effective, Plug and Play technology must be built into a PC's system BIOS (Basic Input/Output System software, which controls the booting up of your system). Plug and Play technology must also be built into all devices connected to a PnP-compliant PC and then used with a PnP-compliant operating system, such as Microsoft's Windows 95 or IBM's OS/2. (Windows NT up to and including version 4.0 does not support PnP.)

PnP must take into account and support both legacy and PnP-compliant hardware devices. Plug and Play exists in all new PC systems, and many systems built as early as 1994 (although systems built back then may not support the latest release of the PnP specification).

Note

The latest Plug and Play specifications are available from `http://www.microsoft.com/hwdev/respec/pnpspecs.htm`.

PnP is intended to detect and resolve, if not eliminate, PC configuration problems by providing automatic legacy and PnP device detection and automatic configuration of PnP-compliant hardware devices. PnP can only detect but not reconfigure legacy or non-PnP devices, so it is our responsibility to properly configure the legacy devices ourselves.

PnP does its job by detecting non-PnP hardware first. Then it works around the items it cannot change, fitting PnP-devices into what's left of system resources to provide an optimum configuration. Some of this PnP work is done during bootup, some of it occurs while the operating system is loading, and some of it is done as we use various programs and devices. PnP is not really an implementation of artificial intelligence, and sometimes it seems to be a reverse evolution, because it won't unlearn or change its behavior when things change.

The introduction of IBM OS/2, Microsoft Windows 95, Windows 98, Windows NT, multimedia, and general networking connectivity into the world of IBM-compatible personal computers presents us all with more system conflict challenges. While both OS/2 and Windows 95/98 provide significant improvements in simplifying first-time installation of these powerful yet complex environments, they still do little to help you detect hardware, report exacting device conflicts, or offer solutions to any problems encountered.

Since most of us are not fortunate enough to be able to scrap our existing systems, peripherals, and software and invest in all new PnP-compliant tools, we will have to learn, know more about, and deal with both old and new hardware issues.

The Old-Fashioned Way

Even with Plug and Play, we are still faced with the problems of setting up our existing PC hardware and software by the numbers that represent existing resources we are given. These numbers or resources include the addressing of input/output (I/O) devices, and the interrupt request (IRQ) and direct memory access (DMA) assignments common to all add-in devices.

To help you get your work done in the gap between legacy items and total PnP compatibility, there are many books, software tools, and old hands at this PC trade. You will be introduced to the information and foundation for them, and learn how to find the information you need, select which information is applicable, and make the most of it.

You will encounter a lot of discussion of both the jumpers and switches (hardware) of a typical PC configuration and the configuration files (software). These items are the implementation of the configuration rules and conflicts we are destined to work with until every PC system, peripheral device, and software application uses Plug and Play or better technology.

It is hoped that Microsoft and the system and device manufacturers have learned or been reminded of the same things I have — that Plug and Play (PnP) often doesn't, thus making us rethink and adjust some of the methods we use when configuring new PCs or adding options to existing ones. The logic of PnP is not perfect.

Most of us still have legacy or non-PnP devices in our systems. With or without a mix of legacy and PnP devices, we're still required to obey the rules of the original and subsequent PC configuration designs and methods. Even when only PnP devices are in our systems, problems can arise. I'll talk about those problems and how to work around them as we go along.

Over the course of the next few years, the PC industry will be working to eliminate all non-Plug-and-Play legacy devices. To redesign the PC, the industry will have to refine and follow its own standards very closely. Until then, and probably even when that day arrives, we will have to make our current tools perform the jobs we have to do today.

Chapter 1

The Legacy Lives On – The First Standards

IN THIS CHAPTER:

- Legacy devices
- What has to be configured?
- Addresses are in hexadecimal numbers

The term *legacy* is generally defined as something transmitted by or received from an ancestor or predecessor from the past. We might add the synonymous term "of historical significance." Perhaps we could simply say "the old stuff," but that's still not quite accurate.

When working with a PC, you are involving yourself with a piece of history. Unless your system is a very early original IBM model PC5150 or one of similar vintage, you probably don't have to worry too much just how ancient that piece of history seems to be — a PC weighing about fifty pounds, five pounds of which are "dust bunnies," ten pounds of which are the disk drives, another ten pounds of which are add-in devices, and the rest of the pounds comprised of sheet metal, screws, and discrete plastic or ceramic-encased chips.

If you can't wax nostalgic about the good old days of seventeen or more years ago, don't fret. You're not missing anything. Most of the good old days still exist, intact, right there in today's sleek 15-pound mini-desktop computer with the 8GB hard disk, 64MB of RAM, and considerably more computing power than was used to put astronauts on the Earth's only moon. The box got smaller, lighter, and thus better suited to the family den, and it displays a world of color, but it's still a PC and it always will be.

Today's PC still starts up looking for the same devices. It runs the same or similar internal self-checks; it tries to boot up an operating system off the same kinds of storage devices; and it uses memory the same way the original PC did. It just does it faster and with a few more internal and external complications. Even though we've already put out $3,000 to buy a system and software, we still have to go through certain rites of passage to print out our resumes, Christmas letters, and tax forms.

As much as we want our PCs eventually to just know how to set themselves up and take care of any problems by themselves, we have to face the fact that we are dealing with a distinctly and undeniably technical situation. The PC was designed by (and possibly for) engineers — people comfortable dealing with haywire prototypes, bare wires, and hot soldering irons. These are the type of people who feel that wire clippings all over the floor are a form of carpeting. Such was the state of the technology when the first PC was introduced in 1981. The engineers have based the PC's foundation on the goals, technology, and experience available back then. And although we as users no longer have to deal with bare wires and soldering irons, that foundation is the legacy we've been given.

This legacy carries with it certain rules — rules that have been designed in, wired in, programmed in, and otherwise fixed (perhaps "cast in silicon" is an appropriate metaphor?) when it comes to the computing device known as an IBM-compatible PC. Admittedly, we've come to both appreciate and dislike many of these rules by which a PC requires us to play.

The design team at IBM imposed some good rules that give some order to the world of PCs; and they imposed a few rules we wish we could rewrite. The rules are a little obscure at times, and they may not seem fair, but we have to play by the rules presented to us. Fortunately, many ingenious people inside and outside IBM have found ways to work with and around the rules; still others have bent the rules in our favor.

Unfortunately, a few other equipment designers have broken the rules or tried to make them up as they've gone along inventing new PC devices. This can cause us endless days and sleepless nights, until we dismiss the renegade devices to the trash can, having failed to resolve the conflicts they create for us.

Ideally we would address, by example, every possible system conflict that ever existed. Because there are millions of PCs, thousands of devices, and hundreds of BIOS revisions, neither you nor I have the time or space for the immense volume of configuration situations that have been encountered. Surely we'd miss one or two in the process. Instead, as the rules are examined in this and the following chapters, they will become clearer. We will not be able to work around all the existing rules (we can't always get what we want), but we can get nearly any PC to live up to the reputation and performance appropriate to the resources at hand.

Thus we enter the legacy of IBM-compatible computing. Our first encounter begins at the beginning (with the original IBM PC, PC/XT, and PC/AT) if only because you've already had enough surprises jumping into the middle of this world of technical details and frilly little wires.

After all is said and done, however, 99 percent of the problems we encounter can be fixed with a combination of a little shoulder shrugging, rolling up of our sleeves, deep breaths, and counting to ten with all our fingers crossed as we boot up to attempt to correct system conflicts.

Our adventure begins with explaining the bare rules as they have existed for many years. This sets the foundation for any and all developments, problems, improvements, and solutions we benefit from today as we go along. The premise here is to become aware of the rules, whether we like them or not, to take advantage of the structure and opportunity they provide us.

Legacy Devices

Legacy devices that are not preset or fixed in their motherboard or system board configuration require us to manually set jumpers (tiny connections between two protruding connector pins) or switches on system boards or I/O cards. These settings are usually accomplished in accordance with a table of possibly dozens of variations of settings, and in comparison to or in contrast with other devices in our PCs. Legacy devices typically do not lend themselves to automatic or software-driven reconfiguration, as may be possible with today's Plug and Play devices.

Among the legacy devices we have no configuration control over are:

- CPU and Numeric Processor using fixed addressing and IRQ 13
- Clock and timer resources using fixed addressing and IRQs 0 and 8
- Memory and device addressing chips using DMA channels 0 and 2
- Keyboard using fixed addressing and IRQ 1
- Diskette drives using known/expected addressing and IRQ 6
- Video display adapter using known/expected addressing

These listed devices are part of the system board or BIOS programming and, as with other devices we'll see, must remain as-is for a PC to function as a PC.

Almost all PC devices prior to implementation of the Plug and Play standard are considered legacy devices. These include add-in cards and other accessories, and to some extent, the basic PC system itself. Some recent devices may be configured through software settings rather than hardware jumpers, but they may not necessarily adhere to the new Plug and Play standard. Even MicroChannel, EISA (Enhanced Industry Standard Architecture), and VESA (the Video Electronics Standard Association) Local Bus devices, which provide enhanced configuration and performance features, may fall under the category of legacy devices. PCI (Peripheral Component Interconnect) devices have been designed with Plug and Play in mind, and most if not all of them will meet the PnP standard. PCI devices can also be used in some non-PC systems that support the

PCI bus, such as the new PowerPC systems, because these require automatic recognition and configurability of hardware devices. It will become evident and almost tedious to notice how many of the PC devices that we have used for years, and which we still buy and use today, have been influenced by IBM's original design. In 1981 when the PC was designed, it had one percent or less of the power and expandability it has now, and far fewer options and devices to attach to it. In fact, except for some critical low-level hardware and software constraints and basic functions, today's PC only vaguely resembles the original PC.

Perhaps no other invention has seen so much advancement, proliferation, and worldwide acceptance since its introduction as the IBM-compatible PC. Yes, personal computers in general have evolved from a half dozen or so attempts to provide small computers to the average person, yet only two of the original contenders in this market have flourished — Apple Computer products and IBM PCs and their descendants. If you consider (or have) a Silicon Graphics or Sun workstation or a personal computer, I'll certainly accept that and envy you.

For the past several years, while Apple Macintosh users claim to have merely plugged in new disk drives, keyboards, networking features, and document scanners (with multimedia features built into the basic Macintosh system), users of IBM-compatible PCs have struggled with dozens of different hardware and software configurations. Our struggle will probably continue for a few more years.

We fight minuscule hardware jumpers, illegible labels, and switches, interpreting SIO01 and PRT02, converting ones and zeros to ON and OFF or OFF and ON, and deciphering not just device addresses or identifiers, but IRQ and DMA settings. All because a system designed by engineers for engineering uses found fame and fortune in the hands of unsuspecting users.

For all the progress we've seen in computer system development, we must still at some point deal with the technical issues of PC system configuration. Even if we invest in a new Plug-and-Play-compatible PC system, we will probably still use many of our "old" non-PnP devices. Such will be the case for the next two to three years (the typical life span of a new piece of hardware) as we come to replace some or all of our systems and devices with 100 percent PnP devices.

For those of you still supporting even a small number of older-style PC, XT, and AT systems, legacy is your only option. It may seem easy for some to say that these systems should be replaced. However, several thousand of them abound in businesses, schools, churches, and homes that simply don't need or can't afford newer systems.

In any case, legacy devices present the bulk of the configuration and conflict issues we face in dealing with PCs. The next section addresses the most common types of add-in devices with which you could encounter configuration problems.

Logical Devices

The concept and application of logical devices seems to confuse many PC users. We expect computers to be logical, but admittedly this is not an easy topic to cover. Unlike their name, logical devices are not always logical, or the logic seems to change between device types and their assignments. Maybe there should have been an accommodation for literal versus figurative or representative devices, but we have to deal with the device naming conventions in terms of physical versus logical when we discuss PCs.

Your PC system consists of a lot of physical hardware devices with lots of technical names, numbers, and functions associated with them. This does not seem to make computers very personal does it? Well, people using DEC VAX, IBM mainframe, UNIX, or other systems weren't very comfortable either. Because of this, somewhere along the line, the technical folks gave aliases or more easily recognized names to commonly used devices in a computer system.

Names like LE0, DD1:, CON:, and PRT: don't seem very intuitive or logical, but it would have taken too long to write programs if you had to specify "Printer in Jack's Office" every time you wanted to send program output to a printer interface. ("Ah-ha," you say, "you can do that now under Windows 95/98." Patience, we're getting there, and we're just talking about raw hardware in your PC for now!)

We're spared a lot of the details of getting data from the CPU to a printer port, or taking data off the Internet into a serial port and onto a disk or screen. However, we still have to know that these various I/O devices exist, where they are, and what they are called or named, while leaving the lower level details to the system BIOS, the operating system, and programmers.

Because we just want to get our letters and reports out to a printer, not to some obscure technical system hardware address like 3BCh, a PC system offers us many named devices to interact with, whether we're writing or installing software, or configuring hardware.

Partially for our convenience, to eliminate the complexity of dealing directly with the cold, technical details of physical addresses, IBM provides logical or plain English translations of the technical complexities of addresses. So, we have at our disposal a means to gain access to devices by thinking of their function, rather than having to rewrite or configure each application for the hexadecimal addresses that an individual computer system uses. (Initially, IBM's logical translation from the technical nitty-gritty to more digestible terms also facilitated programming in the BASIC language.)

IBM provided for a handful of devices its developers believed we might have use for. These include:

- COM (serial) and LPT (parallel) I/O ports (which are probably the ones we're concerned with the most often)
- Disk drives (A:, B:, C:, and so on)
- Keyboard and Video output (combined as the CON: or system console)

This is a good list for the most part. Unfortunately, this list of common logical devices has not been expanded, except to add

LPT2:, LPT3:, COM3:, COM4:, and the occasional special hardware and software interfaces that give us other unique COM and LPT devices.

Note

In actual use with programs and DOS, these devices must be expressed with their numerical designation followed by a colon (LPT1:, for example, and COM2:), while generically, they may be identified as LPT and COM. Specifying only LPT or COM in DOS commands will result in an error message, and the desired command or operation will not occur. For the console and unique devices, there is no number. You may see CON, but the computer must use CON:.

It might be advantageous if we could invent some new logical device names for the pieces of our systems. It would be much easier if we could also refer to and use devices such as a sound card by calling it a new logical device SND:, or perhaps spell it all the way out as SOUND:. Or perhaps we could use MIC: or MIKE: for a microphone input, MSE: or MOUSE: for the mouse, MDM: or MODEM:, or even PHONE: for a telephone interface, and so on. To some extent Windows 95, 98, and NT do this for us.

The use of logical device names simplifies things for us in some ways, but ultimately, these plain English devices, services, and resources are still just labels for those physical memory addresses and their attendant internal signals. However, the internal rules used to determine where and what these devices are become confusing and seemingly contradictory between the hardware and BIOS in the system and the applications we use.

The new operating systems and environments—Microsoft Windows 3.x, 95, 98, and NT, and IBM OS/2—which strive to fill in where the BIOS and DOS could not by making the hardware easier for us to use, must work on top of the same, limited, complex, conflict-threatening foundation we are all dealing with—a PC, its BIOS, and thousands of add-in devices.

Logical Confusion

The logical assignment of parallel I/O (LPT) ports to specific hardware addresses is not as critical for most applications as is the assignment of serial I/O (COM) ports. Most software that uses the COM ports works directly with the hardware, bypassing the features built into the system BIOS (because doing so is much faster than using the BIOS features). Because most communications applications access the hardware directly, but make their own assumptions about logical names and physical addresses, the physical and logical device matching (in the order shown in Table 1-1) is expected and critical. Communications applications also require specific matching IRQ assignments to function properly.

Applications that use printers historically haven't dealt with the system BIOS services to access a printer, and may not make use of hardware addresses or interrupts. The more recent development of bi-directional parallel I/O ports, however, makes matching the physical and logical assignments of parallel ports with IRQ assignments essential for inter-system file transfers and obtaining information from new, "smarter" printers.

Consider Table 1-1, a listing of the most common physical and logical devices encountered in a PC system, to be a foundation set of rules for your system configuration.

Note

The issue of logical versus physical devices in a PC is not always an easy one to understand, much less explain. Yet this issue is one of the most significant rule-creating and binding aspects of a PC system, and the root of many conflicts.

The easiest way to deal with this issue is to simply follow the original rules that IBM defined for all of the devices in your system. In fact, that's what is advocated throughout this book — know the configuration rules and comply with them.

Table 1-1 *Logical Versus Specific Physical Translations for Common PC Devices*

Logical Address	Physical Address	IRQ	Device Name
COM 1	3F8-3FFh	IRQ 4	1st Serial I/O Port
COM 2	2F8-2FFh	IRQ 3	2nd Serial I/O Port
COM 3	3E8-3EFh	IRQ 4	3rd Serial I/O Port
COM 4	2E8-2EFh	IRQ 3	4th Serial I/O Port
LPT 1	3BC-3BFh	IRQ 7	1st Parallel I/O Port (on monochrome systems)
LPT 1	378-37Fh	IRQ 7	1st Parallel I/O Port (on color systems)
LPT 2	378-37Fh	IRQ 5	2nd Parallel I/O Port if LPT1: is at 3BCh
LPT 2	278-27Fh	IRQ 5	The accepted LPT2 device on color systems
LPT 3	278-27Fh	IRQ 5	3rd Parallel I/O Port

(*h indicates a hexadecimal number*)

During the Power-On Self-Test (POST), which runs when you boot up your system, the system BIOS performs a series of equipment checks, looking for specific devices at specific physical addresses in a specific order. As these devices are found, they are assigned sequential, logical port numbers. BIOS uses this information to refer to the I/O ports for any application that happens to rely on the system BIOS to provide access to these ports. Thus, when you are working directly with DOS or its applications, such as PRINT, and you send a file to be printed to LPT1:, DOS passes some control over the printing to the system BIOS, and the BIOS sends the file to the physical device associated with the name of LPT1:.

Problems arise because POST bases its naming strictly on a first-come, first-served basis. Although the logical and physical addresses are designed to be matched as shown in Table 1-1, and those addresses are what your system and devices will be looking for during operation, the actual order in which these logical devices are assigned may differ. Here's an oversimplified look at the programming logic for finding and assigning COM port labels to serial ports:

- POST will look for a communications port first at address 3F8h.

- The first serial device that POST finds becomes COM1:. If no serial device is found at 3F8h to assign as COM1:, POST continues the search at address 2F8h. If it finds a serial device at 2F8h, it becomes COM1:.

- The ports are assigned in the preprogrammed order of 3F8h, 2F8h, 3E8h, and then 2E8h.

- A port or logical assignment is not permanent — if a device addressed earlier in this order is added (before 2F8h, 3E8h, or 2E8h, depending on what already exists), the assignment shifts in order to have COM1: assigned to the first available device in this prescribed sequence after a subsequent bootup and discovery by the BIOS.

It does not matter to POST or the system BIOS services if the first serial device POST finds is at 3F8h, 2F8h, 3E8h, or 2E8h. But it matters a lot to your serial communications programs, since COM ports require properly matching IRQs. It is easier and proper to create a configuration by the given assignments and BIOS rules.

Subsequent logical port assignments are made as devices are found in the search process. If you have physical devices only at addresses 2F8 and 3E8, they become — to your system BIOS, and thus to DOS — logical ports COM1: and COM2:. This is contrary to the rules set forth in Table 1-1 in two ways. First, the hardware address is wrong. Second, the resulting IRQ assignment is wrong, according to what BIOS and our applications expect. To make matters worse, many serial port cards associate both the address and the IRQ together with each other, such that you may not be able to change the IRQ assignment.

parallel (LPT) ports, the logic is a little more straightforward, as follows:

- If there is a parallel I/O port device at 3BCh, it becomes LPT1:.

- If there is no parallel I/O port device at 3BCh, but there is one at 378h, it becomes LPT1:.

- If there is no parallel I/O port device at 3BCh or 378h, but there is one at 278h, it becomes LPT1:.

- If you subsequently add a parallel I/O port device at 3BCh or 378h, it becomes LPT1: and the device at 278h becomes LPT2:.

- If the device you added above was at 378h, and you then add a parallel I/O port device at 3BCh, it then becomes LPT1:, the device at 378h becomes LPT2:, and the device at 278h becomes LPT3:.

The apparent confusion and variable assignments for LPT ports (as noted in Table 1-1) begins with IBM providing a parallel port at 3BCh using IRQ7 on monochrome display video adapters. Any parallel port added to a system had to be at either 378h or 278h. When IBM introduced color systems (CGA, EGA, and PGA), it did not provide a parallel port on the card. Any parallel port provided with or added to these systems was configured for address 378h. Quite possibly this is because you could have both a monochrome display adapter and a color display adapter working at the same time in the same system. Subsequently, for a color system with an add-in parallel port at 378h, a second port was provided for at 278h.

All three ports can coexist, though the port at 3BCh and the one at 378h will be forced to share IRQ7. Since IRQs are not normally used for printing, this did not usually create a problem. This is a resource sharing conflict that is tolerated.

Tip

If you need a second non-conflicting parallel port, use 3BCh or 378h only as the first port, using IRQ7, and add a port at 278h using IRQ5 for the second port.

Note

Neither Windows 95 nor 98 assigns a port at 3BCh as a logical/LPT device at all. It merely indicates the presence of Printer Port in the Control Panel ➪ System ➪ Device Manager table. Thus, it is generally not possible to use this port at this address to assign printers under Windows 95/98. DOS programs that use logical/LPT designators will also not be able to use this port through Windows 95/98. DOS programs that address physical ports by directly addressing hardware may gain access to this port under Windows 95/98.

Logical Order, Please

Always keep in mind that the numeric designation indicates a logical ordering of devices. A good way to remember this is that in order to have a No. 2 or a second of something, you must have a No. 1 or first of something. You simply cannot reserve, save, or leave gaps in the logical numbering of the devices, as some people have wanted to do.

For example, we cannot leave the logical LPT2: assignment open or save it for a possible later expansion of the system by trying to force just an LPT1: (3BCh) and an LPT3: (278h) existence with the intent of filling in the gap later with an LPT2: (378h) device. BIOS and DOS simply will not allow this gap to happen. If there are two LPT port devices, they will become LPT1 and LPT2. Similarly, you can't have COM1: (3F8h), COM2: (2F8h), and (successfully try to have) COM4: (2E8h), leaving a gap at COM3:. BIOS will simply make the port at 2E8h into COM3:, which is technically a misconfigured system. If you later install a port addressed at 3E8h, the assignments will change such that it will become (properly) COM3:, and the 2E8h device that was COM3:

will (properly) become COM4. The configuration will be complete and correct.

I know that many who have tried to save device assignments, either for configuration planning or in anticipation of expanding the system later, have ended up with questionable or disastrous results. But this is a case where BIOS is too smart for us. It would be alright if all of our operating systems and programs referred to the physical device addresses so that the techies could play as they wanted (which would alienate about 95 percent of the PC user population from ever using PCs easily), but reality and standards dictate that it's easier to use the logical assignments as they were intended. Unfortunately, the BIOS is not equipped to evaluate or give us error messages concerning misconfigured COM and LPT ports.

The same logical assignment process is also used for detecting disk drives, video displays, and so on. At least the system BIOS is designed to give us error messages if there is a problem detecting the memory, keyboard, or video display, or if the disk drives aren't properly set up. Since all applications need the console (keyboard and display) and some means of loading the operating system, applications, and stored data (the disk drives), these critical items seem to warrant configuration warning messages about the video system being set wrong, a missing disk drive, or not finding a bootable device.

Because communications and printing are supposed to be handled by the system's BIOS and DOS services rather than having the applications circumvent these services, IBM didn't think it significant enough to provide error messages if the serial or parallel ports are not properly detected or configured.

For all of the more or less invisible help provided by the BIOS and DOS, neither one of them will tell you what your configuration should be, what conflicts exist, or how to fix them. Windows 95, 98, NT, and OS/2 lack significant detection or help tools in this regard. Windows 95, 98, and NT can tell you what resources are used, but they may not clearly indicate which device another conflicts with, and nothing short of opening the case and referring to the equipment manuals will actually tell you what the proper IRQ, DMA, or I/O address should be, much less what to do to fix the problem.

After all of this time and progress, it is amazing to me that no one, not IBM, not Microsoft, none of the many capable diagnostic companies, have created a configuration evaluation and reporting tool. Of the diagnostic and system information tools on the market, and even the Device Manager in Windows 95/98, while it tells you what conflicts and gives you detailed I/O information, none of these tell you what is right or wrong, or how to correct it. Thus our first lesson in legacy — no one seems interested in it although it seems to be responsible for a majority of system configuration problems and is the reason so many companies are scrambling to promote new technologies that use Plug and Play methods. Legacy devices could be smarter and could adopt Plug and Play methods — but there are so *many* of them out there, and no way to redesign them in place.

How Windows 95, 98, and NT Provide Device Naming

Earlier I mentioned that it would be nice if we could simply tell a program to "send my report to the Printer in Jack's Office," and off it would go. Indeed, Windows 95, 98, and Windows NT let us do essentially that, by hiding the printer address, port, and even printer type information behind fancy screen names and selection dialog boxes. These aliases or shortcuts are merely another layer of icing on a rather bulky and complex cake. In actual use, Windows does not know if what we called the "Printer in Jack's Office" is really in Jack's office or if it's a FAX modem in the janitor's closet — it's just a name someone called something that shows up in the printer list. If the printer really is in Jack's office, when Jack quits and Sally moves in, someone has to rename it to be the "Printer in Sally's Office."

In some ways Windows 95/98/NT can actually complicate things, at least during setup, because the naming can mean anything or nothing. The item that is actually being named is a reference to a specific printer device driver, perhaps a Hewlett-Packard LaserJet 4P that is connected to the LPT1: port (which could be addressed as either 378h or 278h) on some computer on some network that provides sharing of that device so others can connect to it and use it.

The good news is that once you get beyond the complicated setup process, and if Jack stays there and keeps using that office and computer and printer, printing to the "Printer in Jack's Office" is really a lot easier. Otherwise, at the lowest system level, you would have to remember that you're sending HPPCL code from Microsoft Word running on your computer, which is networked and addressed as 10.1.1.1 through TCP/IP on an NE2000 network card, to a suitable H-P printer on that other machine, whose NE2000 card is IP numbered 10.1.1.2 and its port 378h address. Thus, in Windows 95/98 we not only have physical and logical devices, but we have device drivers and device names to contend with.

The nomenclature you see when creating a network or shared printer presence under Windows NT is a representation of the Universal Naming Convention, adopted from UNIX and other operating systems. This naming convention, or *UNC*, provides for including the name of the networked machine or device that is providing the shared printer services, and the name of the device as known to that machine. Thus, the "printer in Jack's office" might have an actual network name or UNC of \\jack\office-hp (where \\jack represents the server or machine name of Jack's system, and \office-hp represents the name of the device shared for others to use) if Jack is running an NT workstation or server. Thus, another level of potential confusion enters into the overall configuration picture, but it has little to do with the actual hardware configuration problems we may encounter. A similar naming situation happens with shared resources between Windows 95/98 machines in the same workgroup or Windows NT domain. You can give a shared device almost any name you want, regardless of the device's make, model, or connection ports.

Still another or similar level of device naming comes in the form of the friendly name that Windows allows vendors to give devices. We saw a bit of this with Windows 3.*x* in being able to see the vendor's name and model information in a few device driver listings, such as Diamond Stealth (the friendly name of a video adapter card), or

USRobotics V.Everything. This is much more prevalent in Windows 95/98/NT. You don't have to know anything about the device's ports to use it — instead you tell an application program to use a device by its name. Unfortunately, for that device to work properly, it still has to be configured with a proper address and IRQ, especially in the case of modems, which actually serve as COM ports.

A little less specific than friendly names are designations like Dial Up Adapter under Network Neighborhood properties — which refers not so much to a specific device as to a layer of application and network programming code that may be related to one or the other friendly named modems. Similarly, we have *MAPI* (Messaging Applications Programming Interface) for e-mail message application access to network resources, and *TAPI* (Telephone Applications Programming Interface), providing application-to-hardware features using modems and perhaps even sound cards for PC-based voicemail and dialing functions. We also have *ATAPI* (AT-Applications Programming Interface) as a code layer, commonly between CD-ROM or other non-legacy storage devices that connect to common disk drive adapters — but these devices are given logical disk drive letters.

Are you confused yet? Not to worry. Before you get too wrapped up in what Windows names things, you have to get them properly configured first, and that may be the easy part after all!

Logical Disk Drives

Where disk drives are concerned — since there can be diskette as well as AT-, IDE-, or SCSI-interfaced drives in a system — further device numbering is used inside the BIOS to identify these and assign logical drive letters. Drive letters A: and B: are always reserved for diskette drives. They are given BIOS- and DOS-level drive device numbers 0 and 1. Without hard drives, third and fourth diskette drives would be given drive device numbers 2 and 3, and logical designations C: and D:. With a properly configured hard drive present, the first hard drive is given logical drive letter C:.

The first hard disk drive media found is given device number 80h. Second and subsequent drives found are numbered from 81h on. If a Device 80h exists on your system, and is partitioned and formatted to boot into DOS, it will be assigned logical drive letter C:, and so on for subsequent devices. Fortunately, unless you are writing low-level disk drive utility software in Assembly language, you probably won't see or hear much about drive device numbers again.

Logical drive letters are assigned first in the order of devices found, then in the order of DOS partitions found. If you have two hard drives, and the first hard drive has two partitions on it and the second hard drive has only one partition:

- The first partition on the first hard drive is called Drive C:

- The first partition on the second hard drive becomes Drive D:

- The second partition on the first hard drive becomes Drive E:

While you do not have much control over drive letter assignments for hard disk drives, you can influence the letter assignments for CD-ROM, cartridge, tape, and network drives. In the end, these pretty much take care of themselves. Windows NT does allow you to change drive letter assignments with its Disk Administrator tool, but this is something I leave up to special cases.

Note

If you use MSCDEX to gain access to a CD-ROM drive, you could simply allow the drive letter to fall in immediately behind the hard drive letters, typically Drive D:, or force the drive letter to be anything in between the last hard drive letter through Z:. In a multiple partition (and logical drive) system, if you force the CD-ROM to become drive D:, then subsequent hard disk partitions become drives E: and F: and so on. Windows 95/98, because they provide the equivalent MSCDEX functions, also allow you to set the drive letter for CD-ROM and other drive types.

Tip

You could also "lose" one of the hard drive assignments, and fail to have access to that drive if you use a LASTDRIVE= parameter in CONFIG.SYS that is set for fewer drive letter assignments than you actually have or need. There is actually little or no need for a LASTDRIVE statement (such as LAST-DRIVE=N) in CONFIG.SYS, unless you have a specific network requirement (for Novell Netware, Artisoft Lantastic, or other). In those cases, your network administrator will specify what this should be.

What Has to Be Configured?

We usually can't, and probably wouldn't want to, alter the extremely low-level internal configurations of our PC system boards (memory DMA channels, clock interrupts, and so on), but there are numerous devices with configurations that we can and often must deal with throughout the life of any PC system.

Among the frequently added, changed, or removed devices anticipated in the original IBM PC, and subsequently the PC/AT, we typically encounter configuration issues with:

- Serial I/O ports, including internal modems (COM)
- Parallel I/O ports (LPT)
- Video display adapters (MDA, CGA, EGA, PGA, VGA)
- Disk drive interfaces (AT, IDE, SCSI)
- Network interface cards

Developments after the first PC and AT systems provided us with a few new device types to find resources for:

- Pointing device interfaces — bus mouse and PS/2
- SCSI host adapters
- Multimedia/sound cards, with and without CD-ROM interfaces
- Video capture boards

- 3D video accelerators
- Custom document scanner interfaces
- Internal ISDN adapters
- Add-in or built-in infrared I/O ports

All of the devices in our systems require system resources. We can usually take for granted that each device consumes power, creates heat, and must be cooled by one or two meager fans. In addition, all devices in our PC system consume computer-specific resources in addition to power and space.

The system resources of concern here may not at first appear to be resources. But I/O addresses, IRQ settings, and DMA channel assignments are indeed computer system resources. They are limited to what is available with your system type, and cannot be expanded by adding more of them. The only upgrade step for these resources would be to change from an 8-bit (PC- or XT-class) system to a 16-bit (AT- and higher-class) system, or to go from an ISA (8- or 16-bit) system to one with ISA and PCI interfaces, in order to gain access to more, or free-up a few, IRQ and DMA assignments. The Universal Serial Bus, or USB, is showing great promise in providing some resource relief.

Of the configuration resources, IRQ, DMA, and I/O lines, none of them were really designed to be shared.

- IRQ lines can be "shared," but the devices cannot be active at the same time — unless the PC system chips, BIOS, operating system, and applications all support discriminating between different devices when more than one of them simultaneously activate an IRQ line. IRQ signals are short-lived; they don't keep their hands raised until called on by the CPU, and the chips used in the early PCs also did not provide a way to latch onto an IRQ event. However, Windows 95/98 quickly indicate "shared" IRQ conflicts for devices in the Device Manager listings, though they may or may not allow simultaneous operation of them. Best to keep IRQs unique and discrete to each device that uses one.

- I/O addresses cannot be shared unless both the devices and applications support unique ways of addressing different target devices in the same address space — this was never on the minds of the PC designers and would have involved a lot of performance robbing software work. Because data has to pass into these addresses, a piece of data for one device could be interpreted as a command by another device at the same address — not a good condition.

- DMA lines must also be unique because they are used for traffic control of device-to-memory transfers of data. If these lines are shared, the devices sharing them can become confused about which is supposed to accept or send data between it and memory, costing us data loss and precious CPU processing time.

Because of the way legacy devices and the PC design handle these resources, they require the most user or technician attention or intervention during both hardware and software setup processes. In all PC systems, there are a finite number of each of these resources with which we must try to support myriad system options.

If all of the possible combinations of IRQ and DMA signals and I/O addresses could be used in any way we wanted them to be, we would have approximately 2,000 possible configurations to deal with.

As we will see in the sections and chapters ahead, the number of possibilities is significantly reduced by design industry-accepted standards. The most limiting factor is, of course, the least available resource — the number of IRQ signals available to us. This limits us to having only 6–8 I/O devices (see following list) active at any one time (in addition to built-in system board functions), even though we may have 10 or 12 devices in our system. But more about this later.

The typical devices we can have active simultaneously, not counting the internal system board resources, are as follows:

- Mouse (IRQ 12)
- COM1 (IRQ 4)

- COM2 (IRQ 3)
- LPT1, 2, and/or 3 (usually NOT using IRQ 5 or 7)
- Hard drives (IRQ 14, 15)
- Diskette drive (IRQ 6, DMA 2)
- Sound card (IRQ 5 and/or 7, and DMA 1, 3 or 5)
- CD-ROM (w/disk drives, sound, or SCSI - IRQ 11, DMA 1 or 3)
- Network interface (likely IRQ 5, 7, or 10)

This list makes for a pretty full and typical system nowadays, though I know folks who try to add scanner interfaces, infrared I/O ports, extra COM ports, and so on, failing to realize that something must be sacrificed to gain any satisfaction with any one or more of these.

The installation of any new device, or any changes to a device, must be done with the limited availability of these resources in mind, and a knowledge of which resources are being used by other devices.

Addresses Are Expressed in Hexadecimal Numbers

Before we tackle the details of IRQ, DMA, and I/O, a few words about the numbers and letters used in computer memory addresses are in order. You will often see the notation and numbering for I/O and memory addresses expressed in hexadecimal notation, (base 16 numbering). The design and organization of computers, in 8-, 16-, and 32-bit (and larger) increments, dictates the use of a nondecimal numbering system. Because computer information is represented in bits and bytes (8-bits) as 1s and 0s, the numbering used more easily accommodates this. Using a hexadecimal numbering scheme also saves space in memory and on disks.

Using this numbering scheme throughout also saves us from having to convert between systems. Comparing the numbering systems simply gives us an idea of scale. Table 1-2 provides some quick decimal to hexadecimal conversions. Hexadecimal numbers range from 0 (zero) to F, for a total of 16 numerals (0–9, followed by A–F). *F* represents the quantity that's expressed as 15 in the decimal, or base 10, numbering that we're accustomed to using in everyday life; in hexadecimal, if you have *F* of something, you have 15 of them. If you have 10h of something in hexadecimal, you have 16 of them in decimal.

Table 1-2 *Decimal to Hexadecimal Conversions*

Decimal Number	Hexadecimal Number
0	0h
1	1h
2	2h
3	3h
4	4h
5	5h
6	6h
7	7h
8	8h
9	9h
10	Ah
11	Bh
12	Ch
13	Dh
14	Eh
15	Fh
16	10h
17	11h
18	12h
19	13h
20	14h

Continued

Table 1-2 *Continued*

Decimal Number	Hexadecimal Number
21	15h
22	16h
23	17h
24	18h
25	19h
26	1Ah
27	1Bh
28	1Ch
29	1Dh
30	1Eh
31	1Fh
32	20h

Hex numbers may be indicated by a lowercase letter *h* following simple numbers, or by *0x* preceding more complex numbers, as in 0x3FCD, or rarely, a redundant mix of the two as in 0x3FCDh. If you see a reference to IRQ 14, it's a decimal number and is equal to IRQ Eh. All tables and charts pertaining to IRQ, DMA, and I/O addresses will be in, or can be translated to, hexadecimal. Hexadecimal numbers also take up less space (fewer byte locations) in memory than their decimal equivalents.

I/O Addresses

Every hardware device plugged into the I/O slot connectors inside our PCs requires a unique hardware address. During program execution, data and commands are written to or read from these locations.

A PC or XT system affords up to 1 million locations of 8-bit-wide (one-byte) data storage. This one megabyte of space is shared by BIOS and DOS information, hardware I/O addresses, DOS itself, your programs, and data. AT systems by original specification provide up to 16 million 16-bit-wide (one-word) locations. Current systems can provide up to 256 million or more such locations. Not all of these locations are available for hardware devices. In most systems, fewer than 800 address locations are available for I/O devices.

IBM originally determined that specific devices occupy very specific addresses. Some of these devices are internal to the system board or specific to IBM products and uses. Among these, some addresses are reserved, or are to be avoided, because of other system- or IBM-specific uses, leaving approximately 25 possible addresses for all of the possible devices, features, and options we may want to put into our PCs — this is a situation where some devices require 4, 8, or even 32 locations each.

The addresses that are defined but not specifically reserved are used for the common I/O devices that IBM planned for and anticipated in its original system developments. These are the devices we are most familiar with — COM ports, disk drives, and so on. In the progression from the original PC to the PC AT, a few new devices were added, or the primary address of a major functional device (the hard drive adapter, for example) was changed to accommodate the growth from 8-bit to 16-bit systems and more options.

Tables 1-3 and 1-4 list the specific I/O addressing for PC-, PC/XT-, and AT-class systems. Many of the technical terms in the tables are beyond our need to define and understand in the context of configuration management, but we do need to know that something is assigned at a given address. This list is compiled from the dozens of I/O devices, specifications, and commonly available PC reference material.

Table 1-3 *The Original IBM PC and PC/XT Device Addresses*

I/O Address	System Use or Device
000-01Fh	DMA Controller – Channels 0–3
020h, 021h	Interrupt Controllers
040-043h	System Timers
060h	Keyboard, Aux.

Continued

Table 1-3 *Continued*

I/O Address	System Use or Device
070h, 071h	Real Time Clock/CMOS, NMI Mask
081-083h and 087h	DMA Page Register (0–3)
0F0-0FFh	Math Coprocessor
108-12Fh	Not Assigned; Reserved by/for IBM use
130-13Fh	Not Assigned
140-14Fh	Not Assigned
150-1Efh	Not Assigned; Reserved by/for IBM use
200-207h	Game Port
208-20Bh	Not Assigned
20C-20Dh	Reserved
20E-21Eh	Not Assigned
21Fh	Reserved
220-22xh	Not Assigned
230-23xh	Not Assigned
240-247h	Not Assigned
250-277h	Not Assigned
278-27Fh	LPT 2 or LPT 3 – 3rd Parallel I/O Port
280-2Afh	Not Assigned
2B0-2DFh	Alternative EGA Port
2E1h	GPIB 0
2E2h, 2E3h	Data Acq 0
2E4-2E7h	Not Assigned
2E8-2Efh	COM 4 – 4th Serial I/O Port
2F8-2FFh	COM 2 – 2rd Serial I/O Port
300-31Fh	IBM Prototype Card
320-323h	Primary PC/XT Hard Disk Adapter
324-327h	Secondary PC/XT Hard Disk Adapter
328-32Fh	Not Assigned
330-33Fh	Not Assigned
340-34Fh	Not Assigned

I/O Address	System Use or Device
350-35Fh	Not Assigned
360-363h	PC Network Card – low I/O port
364-367h	Reserved
368-36Ah	PC Network Card – high I/O port
36C-36Fh	Reserved
370-377h	Secondary Diskette Drive Adapter
378-37Fh	LPT 2 or LPT 1 – 1st or 2nd Parallel I/O Port
380-389h	Not Assigned
380-38Ch	BISYNC_1 or SDLC_2
390-393h	Cluster Adapter\
394-3A9h	Not Assigned
3A0-3ACh	BISYNC_2 or SDLC_1
3B0-3BFh	Monochrome Video Adapter
3BC-3BFh	1st Parallel I/O Port – part of monochrome video card
3C0-3CFh	EGA Video
3D0-3DFh	CGA Video
3E0-3E7h	Not Assigned
3E8-3EFh	COM3 – 3rd Serial I/O Port
3F0-3F7h	Primary Diskette Drive Adapter
3F8-3FFh	COM 1 – 1st Serial I/O Port

Table 1-4 *The Original IBM PC/AT Device Addresses*

I/O Address	System Use or Device
000-01Fh	DMA Controller – Channels 0-3
020h, 021h	Interrupt Controllers
040-043h	System Timers
060h	Keyboard, Aux.
070h, 071h	Real Time Clock/CMOS, NMI Mask
081h, 082h, 083h, and 087h	DMA Page Register (0-3)

Continued

Table 1-4 *Continued*

I/O Address	System Use or Device
089h, 08Ah, 08Bh, and 08Fh	DMA Page Register (4–7)
0A0-0A1h	Interrupt Controller 2
0C0-0DEh	DMA Controller Chs. 4–7
0F0-0FFh	Math Coprocessor
108-12Fh	Not Assigned or Reserved
130-13Fh	Not Assigned
140-14Fh	Not Assigned
150-1EFh	Not Assigned or Reserved
170-177h	Secondary PC/AT+ Hard Disk Adapter
1F0-1F7h	Primary PC/AT+ Hard Disk Adapter
200-207h	Game Port
208-20Bh	Not Assigned
20C-20Dh	Reserved
20E-21Eh	Not Assigned
21Fh	Reserved
220-2FFh	Not Assigned
230-23Fh	Not Assigned
240-247h	Not Assigned
250-277h	Not Assigned
278-27Fh	LPT 2 or LPT 3 – 3rd Parallel I/O Port
280-2AFh	Not Assigned
2B0-2DFh	Alt. EGA
2E1h	GPIB 0
2E2h & 2E3h	Data Acq 0
2E4-2E7h	Not Assigned
2E8-2EFh	COM 4 – 4th Serial I/O Port
2F8-2FFh	COM 2 – 2nd Serial I/O Port
300-31Fh	IBM Prototype Card

I/O Address	System Use or Device
320-323h	Not Assigned
324-327h	Not Assigned
I328-32Fh	Not Assigned
330-33Fh	Not Assigned
340-34Fh	Not Assigned
350-35Fh	Not Assigned
360-363h	PC Network Card – low I/O Port
364-367h	Reserved
368-36Ah	PC Network Card – high I/O port
36C-36Fh	Reserved
370-377h	Secondary Diskette Drive Adapter
378-37Fh	LPT 2 or LPT 1 – 1st or 2nd Parallel I/O Port
380-389h	Not Assigned
380-38Ch	BISYNC_1 or SDLC_2
390-393h	Cluster Adapter
394-3A9h	Not Assigned
3A0-3ACh	BISYNC_2 or SDLC_1
3B0-3BFh	Monochrome Video Adapter
3BC-3BFh	1st Parallel I/O Port – part of monochrome video card
3C0-3CFh	EGA Video
3D0-3DFh	CGA Video
3E0-3E7h	Not Assigned
3E8-3EFh	COM3 – 3rd Serial I/O Port
3F0-3F7h	Primary Diskette Drive Adapter
3F8-3FFh	COM 1 – 1st Serial I/O Port

When IBM invented its PS/2-series of PC systems, it added a number of internal devices and control ports, which are shown in Table 1-5 for reference only.

Table 1-5 *PS/2-Specific I/O Addresses*

I/O Address	System Use or Device
061-06F	System Control Port B (PS/2)
090	Central Arbitration Control Port (PS/2)
091	Card Select Feedback (PS/2)
092	System Control Port A (PS/2)
094	System Board Enable/Setup Register (PS/2)
096	Adapter Enable/Setup Register
100-107	PS/2 Programmable Option Select
3220-3227	COM 2 – 3rd MicroChannel Serial Port (1)
3228-322F	COM 3 – 4th MicroChannel Serial Port (1)
4220-3227	COM 4 – 5th MicroChannel Serial Port (1)
4228-322F	COM 5 – 6th MicroChannel Serial Port (1)
5220-3227	COM 6 – 7th MicroChannel Serial Port (1)
5228-322F	COM 7 – 8th MicroChannel Serial Port (1)

MicroChannel systems provide an additional I/O data-bus addressing scheme that is separate from the ISA I/O bus and addressing. The last six addresses in the table do not apply or compare to non-MicroChannel systems. See Chapter 3 for more about both MicroChannel and ISA.

The addresses that were not planned for or assigned by IBM make up the only address locations available to new devices. IBM did not and could not anticipate the existence of these devices before they existed. New devices not defined by IBM had to squeeze into the few address spaces left. The addresses shown in Table 1-6 are typical of non-IBM add-on devices.

Table 1-6 *Common Aftermarket or Non-IBM Devices Listed by Addresses Used*

I/O Address	System Use or Device
130-14F	SCSI Host Adapter
140-15F	SCSI Host Adapter (as may be found on a sound card)
220-22E	SoundBlaster (SB), SoundBlaster emulation
-or-	

I/O Address	System Use or Device
220-23F	SCSI Host Adapter
-or-	
228, 289	AdLib enable/disable decode (port is active if Sound Blaster emulation is available and active)
238, 239	AdLib enable/disable decode (port is active if Sound Blaster emulation is available and active)
240-24E	SoundBlaster; sound cards emulating SoundBlaster
280-283	Network Interface Card
-or-	
280-288	Aria Synthesizer
-or-	
280-2FF	NE1000/NE2000 network adapter
290-298	Aria Synthesizer
2A0-2A8	Aria Synthesizer
2B0-2B8	Aria Synthesizer
300-303	Network Interface Card
-or-	
300-31F	NE1000/NE2000 network adapter
320-321	MIDI Port
-or-	
320-33F	NE1000/NE2000 network adapter
330-331	MIDI Port
-or-	
330-34F	SCSI Host Adapter
340-35F	SCSI Host Adapter
-or-	
340-35F	NE1000/NE2000 network adapter
360-363	Network Interface Card (non-NE-type)
-or-	
360-37F	NE1000/NE2000 network adapter
388, 389	AdLib sound device (if no SoundBlaster emulation active)

The addresses listed above may or may not be available on all particular I/O devices of the types listed. For example, not all SCSI host adapters give you the option of selecting either 130h, 140h, 220h, 230h, or 330h. Similarly, these adapters do not use all of these addresses but may offer them as alternatives.

You'll also want to be able to look up the addresses used by specific types of devices as you add the devices in. Table 1-7 organizes the information by device type.

Table 1-7 *Aftermarket Devices by Type*

I/O Devices	Possible I/O Addresses Used
SCSI Host Adapters	130-14F 140-15F 220-23F 330-34F 340-35F
Sound Cards	220-22E 240-24E
Aria Synthesizers	280-288 290-298 2A0-2A8 2B0-2B8
AdLib sound device	228, 289 238, 239 388, 389
MIDI Ports	320-321 330-331
Network Interface Cards	280-283 or 280-2FF 2A0-2A3 or 2A0-2BF 300-303 or 300-31F 320-323 or 320-33F 340-343 or 340-35F 360-363 or 360-37F

Novell/Eagle (NE) -1000 and -2000-compatible cards consume 20h addresses, which can easily use up or possibly overlap other resources.

As you can see, there are at least six aftermarket device types (I/O devices) we will frequently encounter. To accommodate these, there are 14 address locations (possible addresses) available (14 is the number of unique addresses in the table, once repetition is accounted for and eliminated). Since all devices cannot be configured to work in just any or all of the 14 available addresses, there may still be overlap and conflicts despite the fact that there are more addresses than there are device types. Industry acceptance has limited the addresses that certain devices may use to only a few addresses per device type — such as four predetermined COM port addresses, three predetermined LPT port addresses, and so on. Thus, our configuration issues begin.

Why Not Use Any Old Available Address?

So far we've indicated I/O addressing by either IBM standards, or those accepted for use by later developments, and have not considered that perhaps we should be able to use any available address for any device we want. Yes, we could address a SCSI host adapter using an unused COM4 address, for example, but this might confuse the BIOS or lock up the system as the POST tries to check that address for a serial port. The SCSI adapter may not understand the serial port checks, or will accept some data erroneously and respond in some unpredictable manner. Since we have no control over the BIOS and boot-up processes, we're risking myriad unpredictable problems by using just any I/O address.

Conversely, if a SCSI-specific program went snooping around to see if a SCSI adapter is at the COM4 address, and a real serial port was there instead, we could encounter the same risks of locking up our system.

Similarly, as we get to Plug and Play (and specifically PCI and PCMCIA/PC Card devices), to maintain overall compatibility and avoid conflicts and confusion between devices, some of these new devices will also use older legacy-style device addresses.

Finding Out Who Is Where

As we discuss devices and ports, and when we discuss system information-gathering software, you may wonder why no one makes a program that simply goes through and checks all port addresses and detects what things are connected there, rather than following these pre-assigned address rules. Actually such software has been tried with varying degrees of success, but no one has been able to do it reliably or safely enough to avoid the kinds of lockups that inevitably occur when you send the wrong kinds of commands or data to the wrong device. The result here is that we do not usually have visibility into all of the address ports or what they are used for. For some devices that appear at a single address but use two, four, or even eight addresses, you have to look up the specific technical documentation for that type of device to know what resources it may be using and why. Instead, as we'll see with Plug and Play, PCI, and PCMCIA/PC Card devices, better ways have been established to ask devices what exists where in the system.

At least PCI devices are provided with their own address and data bus separate from the ISA bus lines used for legacy devices, providing many more I/O address options, which are negotiated with Plug and Play routines. PCI hardware interrupts are typically combined onto one special interrupt line and handled by a special chip arrangement, avoiding legacy/ISA IRQs. However, many of these devices must still use the legacy resources for common functions in order to maintain backward compatibility with our old hardware, operating systems, and programs. A PCI network card may use PCI addresses DF00–DF3Fh for data and commands, but can also consume a legacy/ISA IRQ of 10. A PCI video card must still be addressable as an ISA device on 3B0–3BBh and 3C0–3DFh and allow data to pass through memory locations A000-BFFFh for non-PCI aware DOS programs, and may also consume a legacy/ISA IRQ line.

Upper Memory Information

Not only do we have to consider the few specific low-memory locations available for any and all hardware devices, but some features and devices require portions of the 384K of memory address space that is the upper-memory area between the DOS 640K limit and the beginning of extended memory at the 1MB address location. This area provides space for the video BIOS, access to video memory, hard disk BIOS, and system BIOS. Not all of this 384K is used by every system configuration. The upper-memory assignments used in the original IBM PC, XT, and AT are listed in Table 1-8.

Table 1-8 *Upper-Memory Locations for Video, Disk, and System BIOS*

Memory Range	System Use or Device
A000-AFFF	Graphics Video Memory (64K)
B000-B7FF	Monochrome and Text Video Memory (32K)
B800-BFFF	Not Assigned *
C000-C7FF	VGA Video BIOS Location (32K)
C800-CFFF	Hard Disk Controller BIOS Location (32K) *
C800-CFFF	Not Assigned *
D000-D7FF	Not Assigned *
D800-DFFF	Not Assigned *
E000-EFFF	IBM ROM BASIC (IBM systems only) *
F000-FFFF	System BIOS (64K)

*Those areas not occupied by a device and not assigned for working video memory (indicated by *) are often configurable for use as upper-memory blocks (UMBs) by using memory manager software such as Microsoft's EMM386 or Quarterdeck's QEMM. The use of these memory areas can provide up to 128K of RAM for the loading of device drivers and memory-resident programs (such as MSCDEX, DOSKEY, and SMARTDRV), instead of consuming precious lower or DOS RAM. If this memory is not otherwise configured or excluded from use by specifically configuring the memory management software or Windows, Windows will also try to use any free memory it can find during its operation.*

Tip

Letting Windows (and in this case I mean all versions – 3.*x*, 95, and 98, but not NT) have free reign of your system's memory is not always a great idea. Often as not, as with the PCI video card mentioned above, the memory range of B800–BFFF is used by many newer video cards and their device drivers for enhanced features of the video card. This is usually undocumented or not obvious when you set up your system, and may not be discovered until later. You won't know you have a problem until the system locks up, and you try various attempts at reconfiguration to reveal the need to specifically exclude this address range from access by Windows. The symptoms of a problem here appear as lock-ups or improper video displays in Windows programs or attempting to load game software. The cure, as confirmed by both the many systems I've tried it on, and many e-mail exchanges, is to add a specific Exclude command to your memory manager. For EMM386, which is loaded in CONFIG.SYS, the additional parameter must be applied to the command-line (minus other commands you may also have there) so it reads:

```
device=c:\windows\emm386.exe X=B000-BFFF
```

Part of the system boot-up process is to search upper memory for add-in device BIOS code (the addresses in Table 1-9). Any BIOS code found and executed then becomes part of the normal system operation. Video adapter, hard-drive, and SCSI adapter cards are the most common devices with their own BIOS on-board, which complements or replaces the functions that would otherwise come only from the system BIOS. Table 1-9 lists the commonly available upper-memory locations and the types of devices you can or may find configured to use them.

Table 1-9 *Upper-Memory Locations that May Be Used by the BIOS in Common I/O and Add-In Devices*

BIOS Address	Use
C000-C7FF	Color video adapters (32K)
C800-CFFF	Hard disk controller or SCSI (32K)
C800-CFFF	SCSI Host Adapter BIOS (32K)
D000-D7FF	SCSI Host Adapter BIOS (32K)
D800-DFFF	SCSI Host Adapter BIOS (32K)
E000-E7FF	SCSI Host Adapter BIOS (32K)
E800-EFFF	SCSI Host Adapter BIOS (32K)
E000-EFFF	LIMS EMS Memory Page Frame (64K)

Note

The PC system BIOS expects any hard disk controller BIOS (for ST506/412-MFM, RLL, ESDI, or IDE-type disk drive adapters) to be at C800h. IDE and SCSI interfaces cannot occupy the same location. If you have both IDE (Integrated Drive Electronics) and SCSI (Small Computer System Interface) interfaces in your system, the IDE interface will be fixed at C800h as its default address, and it will always be the primary interface for the hard drives and boot drive (while the SCSI interface will supply only additional hard drives, CD-ROM drives, and so on). Since SCSI host adapters usually have the flexibility to be configured for any one of six upper memory locations, the addressing shouldn't be a problem. If SCSI is the only interface in the system, it can be assigned to any of the even 32K-increment address ranges from C800h to E800h. In later systems with built-in IDE interfaces, the IDE drive BIOS routines are included as part of the system BIOS, and do not create this conflict.

Caching and Shadowing

Many times the system BIOS offers the feature to cache or shadow certain upper memory BIOS addresses into a 384K section of memory reserved in Extended Memory for this purpose. What this does is copy and redirect the program code from a device's BIOS ROM chip into faster RAM chips, which makes using any special BIOS code for these devices run faster. This is typically acceptable for video and system BIOS ROM chips, but many SCSI adapters will not function properly, or your system will crash when a SCSI device is used, if you allow the SCSI adapter BIOS to be cached or shadowed.

Given the option, or if you find the symptom of unusual problems with SCSI devices, go to your system CMOS setup program and be sure that the memory range for your SCSI host adapter BIOS is not cached or shadowed.

Also, do not cache or shadow any of the memory ranges that are not assigned to or used by a device's ROM BIOS. Attempting to cache or shadow the video memory ranges from A000–BFFFh, or the EMS page frame range (typically E000–EFFFh), can cause unpredictable results.

Some memory managers offer the feature of automatically optimizing upper memory configuration and the process of selecting drivers and resident programs to squeeze into upper memory blocks. For EMM386, this feature is invoked by a program called MEMMAKER. For QEMM, it's the OPTIMIZE feature.

These are amazingly powerful utilities that try to detect upper memory uses and conflicts, and can provide you with a little more free DOS RAM when they are all done with their automatic processes. Unfortunately, they leave a cryptic trail of configuration parameters in the command lines for each driver or program you load, and if you change your configuration you have to rerun the automatic processes to be sure things are set up right again. You cannot manually change these cryptic parameters unless you become an expert in memory management, which doesn't sound like a lot of fun.

The automated processes may not consider all of the programs or hardware device features that may be encountered during games or

Windows use, and you can end up with many more conflicts and problems than you started with. Instead of using the automated processes, consider using different configuration menus or fewer devices and resident programs if you really need more free DOS RAM.

My advice here—keep it simple! If you tangle with your CONFIG.SYS and AUTOEXEC.BAT files, and try to tweak how drivers use memory, be careful. Simply use the DEVICEHIGH, LOADHIGH, LOADHI.SYS, and LOADHI commands manually and sparingly. Configure your system to load the largest drivers and resident programs first, then load the smaller ones later, as a manually operated best-fit technique. Do not try to force a driver or program into the smallest possible spaces, because you can't always account for extra memory needs for data, or the elusive special features of Windows or game software that may crash the system later on. Generally, Windows 95/98 perform better with no device drivers in CONFIG.SYS, but sometimes you need one or the other, such as a CD-ROM driver, to jump-start getting a device to be recognized by Windows.

IRQ

IRQ (Interrupt Request) lines are used by hardware devices to signal the CPU that they need immediate attention and software handling from the CPU. Not all of the devices in your system require an IRQ line, which is good news, because we have only 16 of them in an AT- or higher-class system. Of those 16, three are dedicated to internal system board functions (the system timer, the keyboard, and a memory parity error signal). The use of the other signals depends on the devices installed in your system and how they should be or are configured.

For ISA or non-EISA and non-Micro Channel systems, it is the general rule that IRQ lines cannot be shared by multiple devices, though with some care and well-written software, they can be shared. But since there is no easy way to know which devices and software can share IRQ lines with other devices, this is something we will avoid doing. Table 1-10 shows the predefined interrupts that the PC needs.

Table 1-10 *IRQ Assignments*

IRQ	PC, PC/XT	AT, 386, 486, Pentium
0	System Timer	System Timer
1	Keyboard Controller	Keyboard Controller
2	Not Assigned	Tied to IRQs 8–15
3	COM2: 2F8h–2FFh	COM2: 2F8h-2FFh
4	COM1: 3F8h–3FFh	COM1: 3F8h–3FFh
5	XT HD Controller	LPT2: 378h or 278h
6	Diskette Controller	Diskette Controller
7	LPT1: 3BCh or 378h	LPT1: 3BCh or 378h
8	Not Available on PC or XT	Real Time Clock
9	Not Available on PC or XT	Cascades to and substitutes for IRQ 2
10	Not Available on PC or XT	Not Assigned
11	Not Available on PC or XT	Not Assigned
12	Not Available on PC or XT	PS/2 Mouse port
13	Not Available on PC or XT	NPU (numerical processing unit)
14	Not Available on PC or XT	Hard Disk
15	Not Available on PC or XT	2nd Hard Disk Adapter (later systems)

Add-in devices usually provide a number of options for IRQ assignments to avoid conflicting with other devices when installing and configuring them. Some typical IRQ assignment options for add-in devices are shown in Table 1-11.

Table 1-11 *Add-In Device IRQ Options*

Add-In Device Type	IRQ Choices
SCSI Host Adapter	10, 11, 14, or 15
Sound Cards	5, 7, 10, or 11
Network Card	2, 3, 4, 5, 7, 9, 10, 11, or 12

DMA

DMA (Direct Memory Access) enables a program or device to initiate data transfers between two devices, or between a device and memory, without the intervention of the entire CPU system. DMA operations are typically used for high-speed disk operations, multimedia applications, diskette, and tape drives attached to a diskette adapter.

DMA provides for faster data transfers, because transferring data with the CPU and program code involved takes more time. However, while DMA operations are being performed, CPU operations are put on hold for a short while until the DMA operation completes. Being a faster transfer method, DMA consumes less processor time than using program code to do the same job, so the CPU is off line for less time. (A properly designed DMA application will allow the CPU's operations to execute periodically so that the entire system is not dead or at the sole discretion of the DMA process.)

The defined DMA channel assignments are shown in Table 1-12.

Table 1-12 *PC, PC/XT, and AT DMA Channel Assignments*

DMA Channel	PC and PC/XT Use	AT, 386, 486, Pentium Use
0	DRAM Refresh	DRAM Refresh
1	Available/Not Assigned	Available/Not Assigned
2	Diskette Controller	Diskette Controller
3	PC/XT HD Controller	Available/Not Assigned
4	Not Available on PC or XT5-7	Used Internally to link DMA to first DMA controller
5	Not Available on PC or XT	Available/Not Assigned
6	Not Available on PC or XT	Available/Not Assigned
7	Not Available on PC or XT	Available/Not Assigned

There are four DMA channels on PC and XT systems and eight DMA channels on AT- and higher-class systems. Of these, one channel, DMA 0, is dedicated to memory refresh operations on all systems. DMA 2 is dedicated to the diskette drive system if one is present, but this line is usually not available for connections on non-diskette I/O cards. For systems with built-in disk drive ports, the DMA 2 line may not even be connected to the ISA bus sockets.

Note

The fact that DMA Channel 1 is the only DMA line available on PC or XT systems explains why most sound cards use this channel as their initial default setting.

Once again, we see that PC and PC/XT systems provide little room for expansion. The AT and higher systems provide five DMA channels for expansion use, and in a full system with SCSI and multi-timedia operations, most of these are needed.

The typical DMA channel assignments for add-in devices are shown in Table 1-13.

Table 1-13 *Add-In Device DMA Options*

Add-In Device Types	DMA Choices
SCSI	3 or 5
Sound Card	1, 5, or 7
Network Cards	1, 3, 5, or 7

Plug and Play Implications

Having gotten to this point, you may be ready to jump in to say, first, that "Plug and Play is supposed to handle all of this and make it better . . . ." But you may just as easily add, "but, but, but . . . Plug and Play doesn't set my devices the way your book indicates things should be set . . . ." BINGO!

I won't delve too far into Plug and Play just yet, but this observation is certainly true, and equally or more troublesome if you're trying to maintain a stable configuration. When we cover Plug and Play and how it works, or sometimes seems not to, we'll also cover how to trick PnP into working the way we want it to so we can establish a by-the-book configuration. I'll leave it stated that you must endeavor to get all of your legacy devices into a proper IBM-standard configuration, including all of the subsequent after-market items such as SCSI, sound, and network cards, before considering Plug and Play issues. This approach will reduce the variables you'll have to deal with, and make the entire configuration process easier.

Summary

In this chapter we illustrated the basic principles of some common system configuration items. These are addressed again as we discuss more devices, configurations, and conflicts.

Some of the strongest tools we have to learn from and base solutions on are found in examples of what is, what works, and what doesn't. We began our foundation here by outlining the rules of the original PC designs and BIOS. In the next chapter, we discuss subsequent innovations toward better performance and configurability. Once our foundation is established, we look at a variety of typical system configurations. These configurations must work with and around the original PC designs, the new architectures, and the issues of physical and logical devices.

Chapter 2

Progressions from Then to Now

IN THIS CHAPTER:

- IBM's MicroChannel
- Enhanced Industry Standard Architecture
- Personal Computer Memory Card Industry Association/PC Card
- Video Electronics Standards Association's Local Bus and Video BIOS extensions
- Generic no-standards, no-jumpers, software-configured devices
- Automatic and S.M.A.R.T. hard drive detection and support
- Intel's Peripheral Component Interconnect
- Intel's Advanced Graphics Port
- Universal Serial Bus
- FireWire/IEEE-1394
- Intelligent I/O

As the PC has grown up over time, so have many of its capabilities and complexities. The popularity of PC, XT, and AT systems revealed to the PC industry that higher performance and easier configurability were needed to accommodate the ever-increasing number of users, the resource demands of new applications, and the amount of data being used and generated.

A number of design enhancements have come along to increase performance, configurability, and expandability. I discuss these items in terms of their contribution toward configuration management and conflict resolution, and in reference to Plug and Play as our current hope for no-hassle configurations.

IBM's MicroChannel, COMPAQ and Hewlett-Packard's EISA, PC Card, VESA's Local Bus, Intel's PCI, AGP, USB, and FireWire are all more or less successful attempts at making PCs more manageable for the average user, and to some extent, less expensive for manufacturers and support people. Each attempt to refine or replace the PC's bus and configuration technology, for better performance or ease of use, brings on more complexity at some point.

In the course of working with PCs, PC users, and PC technical people, I have not run across very many who can say they were pleased with the outcome of MicroChannel, EISA, the DOS-based PC Card (PCMCIA), or the VESA Local Bus. MicroChannel meant new and more expensive cards and slightly more involved configuration times. EISA was faster but time consuming and perhaps a bit daunting in using its configuration utilities. PCMCIA (under DOS) was a nightmare of driver and memory incompatibilities. At least the VESA Local Bus didn't involve new configuration worries, and it did deliver faster video and disk interfaces.

Even though they are not PC bus standards, I've tossed in a few tidbits about soft-configured I/O cards, and the addition of secondary hard drive interfaces because they don't really have an identifiable home anywhere else in this book's context.

The talk of the town was and may still be PCI. The speed of the PCI bus and peripherals, combined with a fast Pentium system board, a Plug and Play BIOS and operating system, and little or no configuration worries—what more could you ask for? Oh, yes, doing away with legacy/ISA conflict issues. Well, three out of four isn't all bad, is it?

Many of our configuration worries may disappear fairly soon thanks to the Universal Serial Bus, as we'll also see in Chapter 7. Along the way we'll of course have to touch on FireWire or IEEE 1394 as a new super-fast serial I/O system, and a bit on the Advanced Graphics Port.

First, a brief look at a few interim PC standards. Then we'll uncover a few things about local buses and PCI specifically.

MicroChannel: System Board and Add-Ins

When IBM introduced their new MicroChannel bus and add-in card design with their PS/2-series systems, they hoped to improve and reshape the way developers and users dealt with add-in devices. The system board, add-in devices, and methods of configuration changed to a completely different style and format from ISA (Industry Standard Architecture) systems. Because of the changes in the physical connections and slots that made up MicroChannel, add-in devices designed for PC and AT systems do not fit into MicroChannel systems, and MicroChannel devices cannot be used in ISA systems.

In some ways, this change provides some configuration and performance benefits. In late-model MicroChannel systems, the data or I/O bus expanded from 8 or 16 bits wide to 32 bits wide and operated at faster speeds. The devices contain information within them that can be queried by special configuration software. System configuration can still involve the setting of some jumpers and switches, but it is otherwise aided (or limited) through the use of a system-specific reference disk. This includes a special setup program and resource files that describe the devices in the system.

IBM also required that developers would license or register their new designs with them for inclusion on IBM's reference diskettes. This proved to impede development cycles and gave the impression that IBM wanted to control the market for these systems.

Seeing that this was not a way to gain popularity in the market, IBM removed many of these restrictions from the development of MicroChannel add-in devices. However, this bus architecture did not become very popular or competitive against EISA or the later developments of Local Bus and PCI systems.

Because there aren't any non-MicroChannel devices in the system, the configuration program doesn't need to work around the limitations of such devices. It simply finds and guides you to configure MicroChannel devices into a set of configuration rules for the available system resources. The configuration software provides the user with "pictures" of the devices it knows about and shows the preferred locations for any jumpers and switches on both the installed devices and those to be added. This technology was ingenious and somewhat self-helping, but still it was too expensive and restrictive at the time.

Although the configuration and conflict issues of IRQ, DMA, and I/O addressing still exist, the configuration software does point these conflicts out and indicates the proper, expected settings for certain devices. The configuration or reference disk software is very helpful in some ways, but the methods are limited to MicroChannel systems only. It did begin to set a target for future configurations and designs.

Enhanced Industry Standard Architecture: System Board and Add-Ins

EISA is the result of cooperative design efforts between Hewlett-Packard, COMPAQ, and other system manufacturers. (Noted for its absence from this venture is IBM.) The cooperating vendors recognized the need to make configuration simpler and to provide higher-performance systems.

Higher performance is provided in EISA, with a full 32-bit data bus and higher bus speeds. EISA devices extend the number and type of bus connections specific to EISA system boards — they will not plug into ISA systems. To our benefit, though, EISA does provide compatibility with ISA add-in cards in the same board and socket layout as the new EISA design.

EISA provides several configuration benefits and greater resources through a redesign of how IRQ signals are treated, and by providing extended addressing for add-in devices. These features remove some of the restrictions on the sharing of a small number of IRQ lines and fitting devices into a limited range of I/O addresses. But configuring an EISA system may still require handling jumpers and switches on both EISA and ISA devices installed in the system.

EISA systems use a system-specific EISA Configuration Utility (ECU) program. This program works with special device-specific information files provided by device manufacturers. When you use the configuration program, you can view clunky line drawing "pictures" of add-in devices that show you how to set the jumpers and switches.

Once you've gone through the configuration process, the information is saved to the system's internal memory and on disk. When you start up the system, the configuration of your system is rechecked against the prior setup, and you are alerted to any changes detected. If you must reconfigure your system, the ECU program only enables you to select available resources, thus avoiding a potential conflict between devices.

Though a slow and tedious process requiring special disks, a lot of device configuration files, and navigation of a complex set of menus, EISA configuration is tremendously powerful. It is not automatic, and it does not in itself solve the classic configuration problems we encounter.

PC Cards/Personal Computer Memory Card Industry Association: An Additional Data Bus for Portables

The Personal Computer Memory Card Industry Association (PCMCIA) provides an additional data-bus scheme for any of the existing data buses we may encounter. It is designed to provide quick, temporary, interchangeable expansion for portable PC systems. Desktop systems may also use PCMCIA devices by installing a PCMCIA adapter. PCMCIA, or more simply, PC Card devices, may be hot-plugged or hot-swapped (able to be inserted or removed with the power left on!) and automatically detected as they are introduced into or removed from the system. PCMCIA consists of one or more credit-card-sized external data bus sockets for the interconnection of additional memory, software program cartridges, modems, network adapters, and ultra-small hard disk drives.

For DOS and Windows 3.x use, access to PCMCIA devices first requires the use of device drivers that establish the presence of the PCMCIA data bus and sockets to the PC system and, subsequently, device drivers for the device connected to the PCMCIA socket.

Using PCMCIA and changing devices can require you to reboot your system between uses. It can also require making device choices so that the proper driver software is loaded and does not conflict with other device drivers.

As implemented in most portable systems, PCMCIA should not present any configuration problems to the user—unless two of these devices conflict. A device conflict should be rare, however, because the designers of PCMCIA devices work closely together to establish and follow specific configuration rules. There are no hardware switches or jumpers to be set, only device driver software options to set at the time of installation. The device driver software for different PCMCIA devices can conflict with each other, but this is usually resolved by changing the order in which these drivers are specified in the CONFIG.SYS file, which determines in what order the drivers take effect at bootup.

Windows 95 and 98 have PC Card support built in as part of Plug and Play, and do not require a system restart for a newly inserted device to be immediately functional. Windows 95 and 98 may require installation of additional drivers to support a particular PC Card device, and these drivers may still impose conflicts within the operating system. These occurrences are rare compared to stumbling through jumper settings, editing CONFIG.SYS files, and rebooting to avoid hardware conflicts. If you have a current model laptop with PC Card sockets and have ever swapped cards in and out of the slots, you've seen Windows 95 or 98 in action supporting these devices. Unfortunately, this technology is not as easily implemented for plug-in cards within the main chassis of desktop and tower systems. There is too much risk of damaging I/O cards or the system board as boards are plugged in and removed.

 Caution

My advice for non–hot-swappable devices is to always turn off the power to your system (I/O switch to the 0 mode!) before adding or removing these devices (ISA, EISA, Local Bus, PCI, or similar bus cards).

Video Electronics Standards Association's Local Bus: Video I/O Performance

Seeking to expand the display capabilities of PC systems, the Video Electronics Standards Association (VESA) defined several enhanced video display modes as extensions to the existing VGA display modes. In defining these new modes, which include better color definition and higher screen resolutions, it was obvious that systems would have to transfer more display information from programs to the display adapter.

PC system performance had to improve, at least the CPU-to-video display portions of the system. As fast and capable as EISA is, it did not catch on as a bus suitable for video display adapters. Out of this need came the VESA Local Bus design, providing a 32-bit-wide data path directly from the CPU to I/O devices, and at (then) CPU data speeds; hence the name local bus. This new data bus serves to enhance video display speeds as well as provide a faster interface for other devices, most commonly disk drive adapters. (PCI cards are also local bus cards, but do not use VESA Local Bus style hardware or configuration methods.)

The existence of the VESA Local Bus itself is somewhat invisible to the user as far as device configuration is concerned; the interface chip between the CPU and the bus sockets is aware of whether or not a device occupies a socket, and it handles data and addressing internally. There are typically one to three Local Bus sockets in a Local Bus system. Although Local Bus devices require some interconnection to the ISA bus to gain access to some signals, they do not work when plugged into ISA-only sockets.

The Local Bus itself does not involve any new (or solve any old) configuration issues. A Local Bus video card or disk adapter must still present itself to the ISA bus for proper recognition and access, using the same I/O address and IRQ and DMA lines as an ISA device. When the high-speed Local Bus data transfer features are used, the transfer is done on the Local Bus to improve performance. The system BIOS and Local Bus controller automatically recognize and handle the shifting of data I/O from the ISA bus to the Local Bus.

Generic No Standards, No-Jumpers, Software-Configured Devices: Mostly Modem, Sound, and Network Cards

In trying to eliminate the hassles of switches and jumpers from I/O cards, thus eliminating the need to open up the system box to reconfigure a device, many manufacturers believed they could cheat the PC system configuration and develop hardware configurable with a software program. While this may begin to sound like Plug and Play, and some of these devices may use all sorts of similar phrasing ("easy plug and play ready," "just plug in and play," and so on), it's not. A manufacturer might try to exploit by chance some unused or reserved I/O address as the access point into their particular piece of hardware and its configuration circuits. Through this hidden address port, their specific software program would tell the device what I/O address, IRQ, and DMA lines to use.

This technique has been applied primarily to some advanced internal modems, many network interface cards, and some sound and scanner interface cards. Intel provides devices in each category. National Semiconductor and various offshore, white box, or no-name manufacturers have all provided software-configurable network interface cards at some time or another.

As a typical example, card maker Not Quite Acme, Ltd. produces a fax/modem I/O card that it wants to market as a Plug-and-Play-type device with easy no-jumpers software configuration. The engineers poke around at a few PCs and decide that address 110h might be a good place to put its configuration circuits, and proceed to build in secret stuff that only their software program can find and use. As a safeguard just in case, they also let the card's secret stuff detect if address 110h is already used by something else (a competitor's secret stuff) and allows the card to automatically select address 120h as an alternative place to live. So far this sounds pretty cool. No other standard device uses 110h or 120h normally, so who cares? (OK, the competitor might, if they knew about it, or they might if they knew about the competitor . . . but neither does. . . .)

Let's spice this up a bit and make the competitor's (Sunny Flowers, Ltd.) device not really a competing product, but a very different one, a special caching hard disk controller with secret programmable stuff of its own inside so the user can select cache parameters and maybe even a few disk format and partitioning utilities using a special diskette they provide.

Not Quite and Sunny test their products, demo them at a Fall COMDEX in Las Vegas, get a warm reception and lots of interest, and decide to build and ship 10,000 units each to your local computer retailers. You have no idea who or where Not Quite and Sunny are, but the idea of a no-jumpers 56K fax/modem for $19 and a new fast caching super-duper hard disk adapter for $49 is too much to resist. Off the shelf, into the basket, through the register, and on toward home to upgrade your PC go these two marvelous advances in technology.

Overcome with joy and promise of a system that retrieves e-mail even faster now, you've torn open the boxes, tossed aside all but the setup diskettes and the I/O cards, ripped open the computer case, extracted the old modem and disk adapter cards, inserted the new ones and turned on the power. Perhaps the third or fourth screen message you're greeted with after the memory test and setup prompt indicates that you have the new whiz-bang drive adapter installed but it needs to be set up. You grab the setup disk, press Ctrl+S to load the setup program off the diskette, go through a few barely understandable menu selections, and finally get a screen that says "ready to reboot your system now, press Enter. . . ." (No, we didn't trash your hard drive.)

After rebooting, a few screen messages, and a nice greeting from Sunny, the system starts to boot up. Good news and congratulations! Getting a DOS prompt and then loading Windows 3.*x* takes 10–15 seconds less than it did before you went to the computer store because of the new disk adapter. Now, it's time to try the new modem.

When you start ProComm or your favorite fax program, it says it can't open a COM port or find a fax modem. Oh yeah, probably have to set that up too.

Pop the modem setup diskette into drive A:, go to the menu bar, select File ➪ Run ➪ A:\Setup <Enter>, click, whir, flash, system locked up — YIKES! Gee, probably not a Windows program, sure hope nothing's damaged, take the diskette out of the drive. . . .

Ctrl+Alt+Delete, boot up messages, greeting from Sunny (the disk adapter), and stop at the DOS prompt. Type **A:\SETUP** <Enter> . . . click, whir, screen flash, new message: "Welcome to Not Quite's Modem Setup Program . . . press Enter to automatically detect and configure your new plug-play device . . ." <Enter> . . . click, whir, diskette and hard drive lights come on . . . "Unable to detect modem. Possible conflict device or no modem present. Remove disk and press any key to reboot." <Enter>

Screen flash, video then system BIOS messages, greeting from Sunny, greeting from DOS: "No boot device available." System is locked up.

Nuts! Power off, power on . . . screen flash, video, and then system BIOS messages, greeting from Sunny, greeting from DOS: "No boot device available." System is locked up.

Now your hard drive is trashed. What happened here? Let's examine it.

Not Quite, not knowing about Sunny, their addresses, or their command structure, executed its innocent little detection program just fine. The problem is that the secret stuff that Not Quite used to find and communicate with its modem card, and the code that Sunny used to start a data-destroying destructive hard drive format routine are "by accident" the same code.

If only Sunny and Not Quite had communicated with each other, or even considered that someone else might be just about as innovative as they were, they might have avoided designing similar non-standard hardware or allowing or writing possibly destructive utilities. Of course, you have no idea how to get in touch with either of these companies to discuss the matter. You might take one or more products back to the store — likely the hard disk adapter — complain and not know that the store folks have no idea who these two companies are. They just return the goods to the distributor (or worse, repackage the stuff and put it back on the shelf to sell again).

Thus, a hard lesson could be learned if anyone was paying attention. Simply put: If you've never heard of them, if it doesn't claim a real traceable standard, and especially if you don't have a backup — don't play with it!

This is a harsh lesson some may actually have learned. Similar things have happened even between vendors complying with one standard or another. A lot of "secret stuff" is still going around, and sometimes folks just outsmart themselves, or us, by being too tricky. Outsmart them by using recognizable and properly labeled products from reputable firms.

That's enough bad news for now. Fortunately, many reputable firms have been careful, checked themselves many times and many ways, and brought us successful, new, and yet non-standard products.

So far, the Intel products have successfully provided compatibility with prior devices and techniques, and the setup software automatically checks the existing system resources and configuration before indicating possible configuration options for the new device you're installing. This software applies only to the specific device of interest, not to any other device in the system. Plugging in the new card and running the software leaves you with a clear set of safe options for the configuration of that device.

If you want to use a specific configuration, you may have to manually change other parts of your system until the resources you want to use for this new device are available. While this is no help to the rest of your system, it is a very good way to handle the installation of a new device, because it does detect the available resources it can use and helps you set up for this.

Experience with some of the products available from National Semiconductor and a few from 3Com indicate a similar regard for the existing configuration before allowing configuration for the new device.

Some no-name products work in a similarly friendly and successful fashion, while others seem to be designed and implemented without any regard for other possibilities or the existing configuration. The resulting problem can be that they will allow you to create a device conflict during setup without telling you. There is also the potential for these devices to mistakenly reconfigure themselves internally because of poor design, or to get in the way of other device detection schemes, as we saw earlier. These problems can result in system lock-ups or the device becoming configured to some unknown address or IRQ. Thus, it will not be available for use as previously expected.

All in all, the basic ISA configuration concerns remain the same whether or not it's done by software configuration, automatically, or manually. You have to be aware of what resources are in use and which can be used in your system for various devices.

Hard Drive Detection and Support

As systems have progressed, so have hard drives, both in performance and complexity. Most of today's systems also include one or

two IDE drive interfaces on the system board. With two IDE interface connections, the system can support more than two physical
drives attached to the system; these drives may be a mix of hard
drives and CD-ROM drives.

To provide these two disk drive interfaces requires two sets of hard
drive addresses, the primary (1F0h) and secondary (170h) AT hard
disk interface addresses, and two IRQ lines—IRQ 14 for the primary and IRQ 15 for the secondary. These are fixed resources that
usually cannot be altered in system setup, BIOS, or Windows 95/98
or NT. This means that IRQ 15 is usually not an option for use by
add-in devices or within Plug and Play's automatic configurations.

Additionally, while not an address, IRQ, I/O bus, or Plug and
Play issue, new system BIOS is now able to automatically detect and
configure hard drive type parameters in system setup. This feature
better accommodates large hard drives or those with more than
512MB of space. Hard drives were previously limited to this 512MB
restriction because BIOS and DOS together could not address more
than 1024 physical cylinders, 63 physical sectors per track, or 16
physical heads. By supporting Logical Block Addressing, or LBA
mode, the BIOS removes the physical numbering restrictions from
drive configurations, allowing DOS and Windows 95/98 to actually
handle their current limit of single drive volumes up to 2GB in size,
and Windows 95 OSR2 and Windows 98 to handle drive partitions
as large as 2GB on drives as large as 8GB.

However, because they still use a 16-bit File Allocation Table
(FAT-16), DOS and Windows 95 still maintain a 2GB per partition/volume limit, requiring you to configure multiple partitions
(with FDISK or similar partitioning software) if your disk drive is
larger than 2,048MB. Microsoft released a special OEM version of
Windows 95 (for system manufacturers only to distribute) that uses
a 32-bit File Allocation Table numbering scheme, increasing the
single-volume partition size limit to 2TB (terabytes) in size, using
smaller data cluster sizes of 4K. Since FAT32 is not compatible with
many disk utilities and is not supported by Windows NT, you may
not see it or want it in use on your system until there is much more
support for it.

You can tell if your system has or supports multiple IDE drive interfaces by getting into its CMOS setup program and looking at the main/basic setup screen where disk drive types are listed. If the listing indicates space for details for more than two hard drives, it's likely that somewhere in the advanced parts of your system setup are configuration details to enable or configure the second(ary) IDE interface and drives. Also within the main/basic setup screen or where you configure hard drives for each interface, one of your options may allow you to select Auto or Auto-Config for the drive type, indicating that the bootup portion of the system BIOS is able to detect and configure hard drives automatically.

The configuration details screen for the drive interfaces or the PCI configuration screen may also let you change the address and/or IRQ for these interfaces, but these should be left at 1F0h and IRQ14 for the only/first or primary interface, and 170h and IRQ15 for the second interface, to maintain a standard configuration.

Intel's Peripheral Component Interconnect: I/O Performance and Plug and Play

In yet another effort to provide higher I/O performance in PC systems, and to match it closely with the original CPU designs, Intel and others designed the Peripheral Component Interconnect (PCI) bus. PCI exists essentially for the same reasons and performs much the same service as VESA Local Bus and then some. It performs much the same service as Local Bus, though it uses different techniques. Video display, disk drive, and network interface adapters are the most common items to benefit from PCI's high performance.

These techniques are such that they can be and have been applied to non-Intel, non-PC systems, such as the Power PC. PCI is completely different from VESA Local Bus in connections and configuration. PCI devices physically appear to be backwards from ISA devices, and they use a smaller socket that fits between and apart from

ISA sockets. Typically, there are three or four PCI sockets on a PCI system board, along with three or four other ISA bus connections.

PCI devices maintain compatibility with their ISA counterparts as standard devices as well as being PCI devices — a PCI video card functions just like an ISA video card, only faster. The addressing and IRQ issues do not equate to most of the ISA concerns we have here, because the I/O bus and IRQ lines are routed and handled quite a bit differently.

Interesting Facts About PCI

To appreciate PCI and why it may be the closest thing in hardware we can come up with to preclude having device conflicts, we have to look inside it a bit. Reading about ISA, MicroChannel, EISA, and Local Bus is a bit boring, and I found nothing impressive or worthwhile to include or update about them in this book. PCMCIA comes close to interesting, but not in the context of common PC conflicts. If it were economical, fast, and easily applicable to today's desktop and server PC problems, it would be so noted.

A study of PCI reveals not only examples about and solutions for our need for speed, but also the limitations all PC designs have left us with to date — device identification, configuration, upgrades, more add-ins, and so on. PCI was and is a big technical issue to fund, design, implement, and manage, but we don't have to do much but buy it, plug it in, and enjoy it — really! Couple PCI with Plug and Play, and we've really got something — not everything yet — but something significant.

Local Bus

While the first impression here is that this may have something to do with the VESA Local Bus, we're close, but only in terms of name and theoretical application. I didn't really define this before in this chapter because VESA Local Bus is all but a legacy technology in itself. It seems more important to cover it here because we are trying to configure our systems for optimal performance, and the best way to get that performance at this time is with the kind of technical benefits PCI gives us.

A local bus is a generic term referring to the data and address lines connected directly to the CPU, and typically to memory. The local bus operates at nearly CPU operating speeds — 33 to 66MHz, depending on the vintage of system board and chip set. It's an excellent place to get at raw data fast. Normal I/O bus devices, those legacy/ISA things we're really worried about, do not connect directly to the CPU bus. They connect instead through a set of buffering and interface chips that slow the CPU data down to something more suitable for the older devices we have, and the way they are connected to the system board.

By the original IBM PC/AT-standards, the speed for legacy/ISA bus slots and devices is a mere 8MHz, translating to 8MB/second data transfer rates, even though many systems do run faster (12 or 16MHz). Since we wouldn't gain much benefit out of serial, parallel, or game ports running any faster than they do already, it's okay to leave these devices working at legacy speeds. It's when we begin to run video and audio conferencing, network servers, or otherwise need to move lots of data very fast that a faster local bus really helps us out.

It may be easy to be fooled into thinking that any device built onto the system board — a serial port, network, disk or SCSI adapter — is using a local bus connection. In fact, most systems offering these built-in features are not using a local bus for I/O, except for the specific VESA Local Bus or PCI slots on the board. You may notice that some built-in IDE interface plugs indicate "IDE Interface" and "PCI Interface" separately. Indeed the PCI-labeled plug is a PCI/local bus interface, and can be faster, while the other is using a separate legacy interface scheme and will be slower. It is also possible to have both IDE interfaces connected to the PCI system. The system setup program should also indicate a distinction between the two interfaces.

Speed

There are two important reasons for the flexibility and success of PCI. First, the bus can be very fast. Because of its method of processing data signals on the bus wires, PCI can achieve a maximum data throughput of 528MB per second (64-bit data transfers on a 66MHz PCI bus).

Second, the bus can be as slow as it needs to be—down to 0MHz, or turned off if need be. This allows PCI to serve us for a longer useful life, because initially our PCI add-in devices may be slower than the maximum performance, yet we may want to use much faster devices as we upgrade our systems. Typically, we may experience 132MB per second transfers, which is just about fast enough to keep pace with high speed networking, an application program or two, and maintaining a full-motion video conference. We really are speed demons when it comes to computing these days!

Addressing

The PCI bus, being separate from the ISA I/O bus, does not present us with typical addressing conflicts. PCI addresses are simply not shared with the legacy devices. Since PCI is a standard and all PCI manufacturers must adhere to the standard (we'll see if this holds true for our friends Not Quite and Sunny), addressing ranges are worked out ahead of time before a product is released. The PCI standards organization keeps track of and openly shares information about all developers' devices.

To maintain compatibility with legacy BIOS and operating systems, the PCI chip system reserves and simulates the same device address presence that would be used by legacy/ISA devices. Thus, a PCI VGA video adapter still uses and presents a video adapter address presence at 3B0 and 3C0h, reserves data transfer areas at A000–BFFFh, and uses the video BIOS range of C000–C7FFh. Fortunately these ranges, as well as those for many network cards and disk adapters, are at lower risk for conflicts than serial, parallel, sound, and other legacy adapters.

Interrupts and DMA

Unlike PCI's addressing, IRQs are not handled entirely differently from legacy/ISA IRQs. On Intel-based CPUs, there is only one processor interrupt line. This line must be used by all hardware interrupt drive devices. Thus, the PCI interrupts must pass through the same circuitry as the legacy/ISA interrupt signals. Using a special PCI chipset and interrupt routing scheme, having a higher priority status on the legacy/ISA interrupt chips than legacy/ISA devices, and running off the local bus at higher speeds, PCI presents little interrupt overhead or performance problems compared to our issues with legacy devices. Those devices must be carefully configured for their priority and conflict avoidance.

Using an EISA-like interrupt signal detection system and the PCI interrupt routing scheme, three interrupt lines are actually shared between all (up to 32) physical PCI cards or connections. Each PCI card or connection may contain multiple devices, allowing up to 256 total PCI interfaced items in one system. Sounds like plenty of room for expansion!

Nevertheless, the PCI interrupts will never collide with legacy interrupts, unless you can and do change this configuration in your system setup program to assign a legacy/ISA IRQ line to a PCI device. Not all systems allow you to do this, so you're again protected from the misconfiguration gremlins.

Universal Device Drivers: Fcode

Complex devices such as video and disk drive adapters usually have their own ROM BIOS code that loads at bootup to provide enhanced features beyond the simpler ones in the system BIOS. Since PCI devices can be applied equally well to PowerPC and other PCI-equipped platforms, this ROM BIOS code must be useable by all system types encountered. Just any program code cannot simply run on Intel-based, PowerPC, RISC, and Sun systems — there must either be a common language, or different machine-specific versions of code, to accommodate all platform types.

Rather than stuff a card with all sorts of different CPU program code types, having to figure out what processor the system is running, and having to allow for new CPU types later on, the PCI folks decided to provide code in a relatively little-known, small, fast language known as Forth. In turn, each PCI-based computer system must be able to process Forth code in real time. So, while you might have thought that all low-level hardware code is done in a CPU's native machine code, assembler code, or derived from C, we now have another control language with which to consider opportunities.

This Forth or Fcode is only run at system bootup, as devices are detected, identified, and configured for operation. If the card is designed to accommodate it, a card vendor can supply you with BIOS updates to load into the card, and if you look at those updates closely, you might actually be able to make out snippets of the Forth language as it's stored in the card's memory.

Since there is special Forth code for every PCI device, there must also be special PCI BIOS accommodations made in the system board or chipset to run and use this code. PCI system BIOS handles this and lets us gather and control a lot of information and configuration elements for PCI devices. Each PCI device is uniquely identified by its type, vendor, model, and version, which can be read out of the system with PCI-aware diagnostic or information tools. This information is very important for auditing systems and knowing what's inside.

All of this is not a major configuration issue for us in the legacy world, but it does illustrate how far we've come toward solving some of the problems of the PC world. With that, we begin to see how PCI works so well with Plug and Play.

Plug and Play

PCI devices are by their nature designed to be Plug and Play compatible. PCI device configuration is handled internally through the system BIOS and setup, where addressing and interrupts are assigned by physical socket position. The BIOS does not allow you to configure the system with conflicts at the PCI level. It intervenes and precludes an improper selection if another device or socket already uses the parameters you try to set manually.

PCI's Advantages in Configuration Management

Because the PCI bus is separate from the legacy I/O bus system, there are no addressing conflicts to be concerned with. The interrupts from all PCI card slots are merged into a special interrupt-handling circuit, that also merges in the ISA IRQ lines. While IRQ sharing is not typically allowed or necessary because of how the PCI chipset can handle interrupts, and because there are fewer PCI devices in a system than we might encounter of legacy devices, the chipset could sort out shared interrupts if it had to. DMA channels are of no concern, because a PCI chipset is faster and tied directly into the processor and memory functions. PCI does not use DMA channels per se, so it does not consume legacy resources.

If it seemed truly advantageous in the current scheme of things, many more I/O devices could be removed from the ISA bus and replaced with PCI connected ports, but this would also require a different scheme of things as far as software applications, such as those that are still designed to use legacy devices such as modems, complete with IRQ and addressing weaknesses. Designers are typically not interested in redesigning popular slower older devices (modems and mice, for example) with new technology; instead, they create new devices and device drivers that really can and need to take advantage of higher bus speeds — video, disk I/O, and networking.

Advanced Graphics Port: Even Faster Video

The Advanced Graphics Port (AGP) is one of Intel's latest efforts at satisfying our need for graphics speed. Because so many games and other multimedia applications supposedly need to dump so much graphics information to our screens, while at the same time our systems have so much disk activity going on, someone decided once again that graphics needed their own I/O bus.

AGP is derived from the 66MHz PCI architecture, and it provides additional performance features to enhance 3D graphics applications and display. Of these, delays in processing memory I/O are nearly invisible, addressing and data transfers are handled more efficiently, and bus timings of 133MHz provide for up to 500MB/second data transfers. Considering that a 1024 × 768 pixel screen of 24-bit color information could amount to 18MB of data, and moving that amount of data at a full-motion video rate of 30 frames (screens) per second requires the transfer of 566MB of data per second, you have to wonder if 500MB/second data transfers are fast enough. Because all of the displayed data (image) does not usually change all at once with each frame change, perhaps this bus speed will satisfy us for a little while.

AGP provides no configuration advantages or disadvantages different from PCI. They essentially share a similar chipset access to the CPU system, and if IRQs are involved, they are merged into the processor's interrupt circuits similarly to PCI. AGP essentially taps off of the PCI architecture in such a way that is advantageous to the special demands of 3D video output.

Universal Serial Bus (USB): More and More Devices

I think this is, or is going to be, one of my favorite things about PCs — once some of the bugs are worked out between vendors (not just the vendors of finished goods, but those of the chips and signal handling circuits that go into making USB useful).

As to the basics, USB provides for automatically identified and configured devices, all external to the main system case, that can run at either 1.5Mb per second (low-speed) or 12Mb per second (high-speed). This is not as fast as the internal PCI or AGP data bus, but it is right up there with T-1 and Ethernet data circuits, without the overhead of networking protocols, numbering schemes, and so on.

USB was under development when I was working on the second edition of this book, but it did not merit mention because no one had a USB I/O interface or device available for sale on the open market. We also did not have an operating system or even patches or drivers to support it. That situation has changed considerably. While USB is not available in *every* new PC you can buy, it is appearing in many systems, and will appear more in the next few months. I will be very surprised if you cannot find USB in every *new* PC before the year 2000.

Today, USB is showing itself in many of the devices it was intended to—low to medium speed devices such as keyboards, pointing devices, document scanners, digital cameras, digital speakers, external storage medium, and various I/O expansion devices. USB is quite impressive for its few modest qualities:

- No legacy configuration issues—zip, nada, none at all, period.

- Simplified cabling—power and data are carried in a single four-wire cable for many devices.

- (Almost) truly Plug and Play—certainly so in standards, a little less than ideally so by recent experience and circumstances.

- A capacity to handle 127 connected devices, of any type—and we'll be hard pressed to find 127 *different* PC-related devices to hook up to it. But perhaps some household appliances will employ USB for some purpose.

- Hubs—can be used to create extended device interfaces, and in doing so, can spread out power distribution, as well as more or less guarantee data signal integrity.

While the devices just mentioned are typical of the USB product offerings, we can add to the list a variety of communications devices and applications—such as serial and parallel I/O port expansion units and network adapters. Even the popular LapLink PC-to-PC data transfer utility software comes in a USB-capable version. This provides a significant enhancement to its prior serial and parallel transfer features, without having to fool with complicated network adapters and protocols to achieve network speeds for sharing files between PCs.

Within and between USB devices and the actual bus itself is a sophisticated layer of program code that signals and negotiates device presence, identification, and configuration. There are no more messy jumpers, switches, configuration programs, resource settings tabs, and menus for each device. Provided your operating system supports or is at least aware of USB, and if it has or you install appropriate device drivers (because the operating system didn't come with them), USB can be truly Plug and Play compatible and as easy to use as we expect it to be. If USB is built into your system, or if it is provided as an add-in card, it will consume only one set of address and IRQ resources — and those are typically self-configured and on the PCI bus rather than the ISA bus.

As wonderful as the configuration issues sound, and they really are, we do have to be more concerned with aspects of hardware interaction that we hadn't really considered before — device power consumption and signal compatibility. The power issue can be somewhat confusing or impossible to deal with. USB devices will be either bus-powered (that is to say they get their power from the USB hub via the USB cable), or they will be self-powered (obtaining power from a power supply that connects to the device). Hubs are required to supply power, but how much is not specified.

Power draw from any single hub port is supposed to be no more than 25 watts (VA) — which is a whopping 5 amperes at the 5 volts supplied in the USB cabling, though a hub might have lower over-current protection limits. Power from one hub or port is not carried on from the prior hubs, so you cannot accumulate power capacity as you go. The commonly available hubs, with four or eight device ports, are not capable of delivering that type of power to connected devices. If hubs could supply this much power, their power supplies would be about the size of the supplies used in the PC itself. The power supply for one hub tested here is only capable of delivering 12 watts, and some of that is consumed by the internal hub circuits. This tells us that at best I can have one 10 watt device, or four 2.5 watt devices connected to it. The most common devices such as cameras and mice do not draw significant power, so you're generally fine with a few of these connected to your system or a hub. Larger and faster devices such as document scanners and speakers will typically have their own power source.

The compatibility of digital signals between USB ports, hubs, and devices is not supposed to be an issue, but some early generation internal chips and products can have a little trouble communicating properly. The most common incompatibility symptom is that the operating system may be told by a port or hub that a new device has been connected, but the device and the operating system fail to communicate to identify and activate the device. Plug the device into another port or hub and all may be well — but the device drivers for the device must come with or be installed into the operating system first. Again, there should be no legacy configuration concerns with either USB ports, hubs, or devices. For more specific information on USB devices and specifications, visit www.usb.org.

FireWire / IEEE-1394: More and More Fast Devices

If I was big into high-end video camera equipment, and I had systems that could make the most of truly high-speed I/O devices, FireWire could ring my bell loud and clear. My problem with FireWire is that few if any devices we mere mortals would typically have in our homes or computer rooms are affordable or available yet.

FireWire is yet another high-speed serial I/O scheme, for both internal and external devices, capable of 150MB/second transfer rates. We are rapidly approaching the time when disk drive I/O performance, and the need for it, will exceed the limits of the existing SCSI and IDE drive interfaces. With the ever-increasing need for instant access to huge volumes of data, FireWire is an ideal medium to move that data around — inside our PCs as well as to and from various external devices.

I can think of nothing except my video card that can or needs to have data fed to it this fast. Perhaps that it why most of the

FireWire capable devices I researched are high-end video cameras, playback, and recording equipment. While many of us have camcorders, I don't think many of us need to get a self-made 3-hour docudrama loaded onto our PCs, or have the hard drive storage capacity to hold it even if we had made one. But, if I had a FireWire interfaced disk drive, I know I could get that video data onto it quite fast as well.

If you follow the news and know features and differences concerning various operating system software and processing hardware, you may realize that as wonderful as a 450MHz or more impressive 1000MHz processing systems are and will be, many of the things we normally use, and the operating systems we interact with, are either not capable of or do not require operations of such blinding speeds. We can only type 10–60 words per minute. Typical human reaction times for interactive multimedia, such as games with joysticks, or steering wheels and pedals, are no different than those of your average freeway driving experience — and are measured in large fractions of seconds. A video game can feed us more content to absorb than we've ever had to or should deal with on a regular basis, and we humans are not getting faster about comprehending all of this at the same rate the information processing is coming at us.

Even if we humans could deal with information and react to it faster, the average computer system and operating software has been inadequate to the task of such high speed transfers. Microsoft Windows 95 and 98 cannot take full advantage of the fastest UltraDMA-33 hard drive capabilities, much less those of UltraWide SCSI-3 devices, so FireWire could be a tremendous disappointment in the average PC. FireWire will however begin to benefit those high-end appliance users and server systems, those items that must deal with instant transaction processes and real-time data handling. Our increasing tendencies for instant gratification do have some payoff in technology.

In the next year or so we will begin to see more FireWire devices in the average PC and typical consumer markets. Devices that will benefit us most with FireWire will be video cameras and such devices with a lot of data needing an efficient way to get it some-place. Just when we managed to get a personal Web page together, we'll now have to know how to edit our own home movies.

Fortunately, in terms of PC system configuration, FireWire is implemented as a single interface, similar in this way to SCSI and USB. Each single interface to the PC can accommodate many internal and external devices, so each new device on this "bus" does not consume more system resources, beyond those required for the single interface. For more information on this technology, visit the FireWire Web site at www.firewire.org.

Intelligent I/O: Getting I/O Out of the Way of the CPU

Intelligent I/O is one of those things we probably thought we had already, what with Plug and Play, device BIOS code, and all. However, except in the case of certain DMA operations, the devices we have are not capable of communicating with each other without calling upon the CPU for help.

Intelligent I/O, abbreviated I_2O, is an initiative sponsored by Intel, Adaptec, Hewlett-Packard, Microsoft, Novell, and several other notable technology firms to create yet another new I/O archi-tecture. This architecture is to be used primarily between network and storage devices that can communicate among themselves and handle transfers of large amounts of data without operating system and thus CPU intervention.

Because the operating system and CPU of a server is primarily needed and used to provide authenticated access to network based data, there is nothing that says that once authenticated, the data should not be able to move about on its own. If the I/O devices involved are made smart enough to accept access control from a server's operating system and then negotiate source and destination information, the operating system can go back to do other things.

Thus I_2O is about making I/O devices, or at least their interfaces, a lot smarter, more aware of, and cooperative with each other. In essence, this group is creating a multiple-CPU interoperating system, separate from but accessible to the CPU and operating systems, to handle I/O operations. Perhaps this is what we've expected or anticipated of I/O devices — but is significantly more than having a graphics processor embedded in a video card. I_2O does not yet enter into the realm of PC system configuration for the masses, but we'll keep an eye out for it in the future.

Summary

This overview of enhancements to the original PC designs should indicate to you how much things have changed in a few short years, and how much they can and will change toward making PC systems easier for us to set up and use.

Now that we have an initial set of legacy rules to go by — and this overview of more recent advances — we can proceed to create our own "plug and play" PC systems. Armed with our new skills and all of this information, we are better able to deal with conflict resolution. This, in turn, allows for easier system upgrades as well.

Chapter 3

Rules to Configure By

If you've rushed right into this chapter from the front cover, you may find it more beneficial to take the time to at least look over Chapters 1 and 2. These two chapters provide a lot of helpful introduction, background, and reference information that lead up to the direct conflict resolution we'll encounter here. If you've gone through all the chapters, you'll recognize many of these items from the in-depth coverage already given them, but they're worth highlighting here because they are frequently encountered conflict problems.

This chapter is about working with legacy systems. I feel it's important to cover legacy issues as soon as possible, because everything going forward is built on the legacy foundation. Without a firm grasp on the legacy issues, moving up to a new system board, Plug and Play devices, or a new operating system can be a very frustrating experience.

The information in this chapter applies before performing any upgrade, including:

- Adding or replacing hardware, either legacy or Plug and Play
- Changing from IDE (Integrated Drive Electronics) to SCSI (Small Computer System Interface) hard disks, or mixing both hard disk types
- Changing from DOS or Windows 3.*x* to Windows 95, 98, or NT

Somewhere in one of these upgrade processes, a device might conflict with another device; a port might be improperly addressed; or a logical device might not be available or it will not function as you expect it to. If you're lucky, the installation program for your new sound or network card will help you through the configuration details. Operating system upgrades are considerably more complex, because they must work with all devices in your system.

If you're not so lucky, you may be able to get through an upgrade process, but having finished the installation, suddenly nothing works. You encounter a system error message and the system is frozen. Either that or you're clicking around in a fresh installation of Windows 95 trying to find your system settings, and you decide to add a new network protocol in the Add New Hardware Wizard. In checking your hardware, the Help dialog box displays the following message: "Device conflicts with another in your system . . ." What will you do?

You could fight these problems for an hour or so and then call another expert or call technical support. Worse yet, you might simply back out of the process, uninstall the upgrade, try it again, or give up and keep using DOS and Windows "the old-fashioned way." Instead of the frustration and within a few minutes — perhaps 30 at the most — you could determine your configuration, correct any problems, and begin enjoying the new upgrade. Without further delay . . .

Working with the Rules

In Chapters 1 and 2, we discussed the hardware, BIOS, and DOS design rules for PCs. The rules or design of PC systems could not and did not anticipate the number, variety, and complexity of the devices that have been invented to plug into a PC, even though this may seem a bit odd for a system that was designed by and for engineers. It took many other engineers only a few years to work around the existing rules to fit new devices into the holes and gaps left available in the IRQ, DMA, and I/O design.

The challenges were significant. Engineers designing new hardware had to hope that IBM would not overshadow any new work and try to force major new devices into the existing PC standard. Fortunately for us and several hundred hardware and software companies, IBM — perhaps not knowing what to do with the PC after it was introduced — decided to let the market and new designs flourish on their own (for the most part).

Since the release of the IBM PC to the marketplace, we have seen dozens of innovations that have allowed us to be more productive and comfortable with the PC, and we have been able to enjoy it a lot more. Some of these innovations have come from IBM, and many have come from third-party or aftermarket sources. Not all of them were introduced for the PC initially, but made their way to the PC market as users and investors saw their potential. These innovations and their originators are listed below:

- Monochrome graphics (Hercules)
- Color graphics (IBM)
- Enhanced color graphics (IBM)
- 16-bit data and processing in the i80286 CPU (Intel)
- 32-bit data and processing in the i80386, i80486, and Pentium CPUs (Intel)
- High-resolution color display (VGA)
- Enhanced VGA display (VESA)
- Networking (Novell and others)

- Memory expansions and enhancements (Lotus, Intel, Microsoft, and others)
- SCSI (an ANSI standard)
- Pointing devices (Xerox)
- Graphical user interfaces (Xerox)
- High-speed modems (Hayes, USRobotics, Ven-Tel, and others)
- High-capacity/high-performance disk drives (Shugart, Seagate)
- CD-ROM drives (Sony)
- Sound and music interfaces (Creative Labs)
- High-performance I/O interfaces (COMPAQ, Hewlett-Packard, IBM, Intel, and others)
- EISA (COMPAQ, Hewlett-Packard)
- VESA Local Bus (Video Electronics Standards Association)
- PCI (Intel)
- Real-time video capture and playback (various)
- High-performance and multiple-processor systems (systems using Intel's Pentium-series processors)

Fitting all of this into a system with relatively few expansion options (considering the original PC design) is indeed amazing. Yet we are here, doing it and enjoying it. Combining and progressing through these features over the years has been tremendously exciting for millions of people. It has caused a great many of us to learn new things and provided untold opportunities for users, designers, programmers, content providers, and the like.

The existing rules have added to the original rules, and just when we think we've run out of room, ideas, and resources, something else comes along to extend the life of what began as essentially a smart data terminal.

In the process of upgrading our system's hardware and software, we are going to work with all of the rules and enhancements that IBM and others have provided for us. We will see some limitations

Divide and Conquer

As we go along, it should not come as too much of a surprise that it may be more efficient to invest in a second PC system, dividing the type of work to be done between systems configured specifically for one type of application and hardware or the other. For instance, one system may be set up with several modems or a mix of modems and network cards to handle telecommunications, while another system could be set up for multimedia production work with scanners, CD-ROM drives, and printers. You would share data between the two systems as a small peer-to-peer network.

If an application works best under one operating system or the other, but this differs from the other applications to be used, configuring the ability to switch operating systems at bootup may also be considered. If information needs to be shared among systems, networking and the attendant configuration issues with that upgrade is another consideration. This is part of the planning and configuration management process, as well: evaluating the type of work you do, what you do it with, and what system configuration will get it done best.

and make some judgment calls based on available resources, the hardware we have at hand, the hardware we want to add, and our overall needs. We will also expand on I/O addressing as it relates to the memory types in your system.

General Configuration Considerations

Most of the precautions in this book apply to all system configurations, but some have special significance for new operating systems and most hardware upgrades. When setting up your system, either to establish an initial configuration or to change devices with an upgrade or replacement, there are any number of known and often unknown limitations we could face, including the obvious limitations imposed by an add-in device or its software.

Add-in devices don't always allow complete freedom of choice for their configuration options. Some devices provide a list of fixed options, locking certain addresses, IRQs, and DMAs together without any flexibility. You might find this circumstance with cards that provide only a few jumpers or switches to set only a few predetermined options.

Similarly, not all software allows complete and flexible configuration of the ports, IRQs, and DMA channels it will support. Investigate carefully how configurable a software package is before buying. Many stores will let you view the software on a demo system, allowing you to check out the setup and other features of the package.

Generally speaking, operating system upgrades and use are quite possible and successful. Large companies (Microsoft and IBM) have invested a great deal of time and money in making their products succeed. To do so, the products have to be readily installable.

If you can reconfigure other devices in your system around any limitations your new hardware may present, you'll be OK. If not, consider buying a more flexible add-in device — one that lets you set any configurable item independent of the others.

Note

In more than one case, accepting a common default network card I/O address of 300h has been known to cause problems with installations of, or changes to, OS/2 and Windows 95. This address is specified by IBM to be for a "prototype card." Even though the address range at 300h has a full 20h locations (300–31Fh) mapped out for it, OS/2 and Windows 95 don't always like this location in some systems. The best solution appears to be to set the network card for an adequate and clear address range, such as 280h, 2A0h, 320h, or 340h. The default IRQ for many network cards is IRQ3, which obviously conflicts with COM ports 2 and 4; thus, a reconfiguration of at least the IRQ is required.

Information, Please

I hope this is the only place I suggest that you may want to skip ahead briefly to Chapter 8 and the appendixes to become familiar with system information gathering software tools. I suggest this for two reasons. First, you'll want to know what your current configuration is anyway. Second, you may get more out of the rest of this chapter if you have some real-world examples with which to follow along.

Pop the CD-ROM that accompanies this book in your CD drive, and navigate to and copy the entire PCDR directory to a similar directory on your main hard drive, or to a diskette. Restart your system into DOS or command-prompt mode. Then, go to the location or diskette where you copied PCDR and run PCDR.EXE. Run through the system information screens and save the results to a file or print them out. This will give you a set of baseline legacy data with which to work.

Having acquired the information from your system, you've just completed one of the first steps of configuration management — knowing what it is you have to manage. Feel free to restart and continue with what you were doing on your PC before.

Memory Types and Address Ranges

Addressing and memory present certain connotations and expectations in terms of your system configuration. There are several significant address ranges, regions, areas, or types of memory in your PC system. By "type," we are not referring to the electronic or technical details of the components involved (such as RAM, ROM, CMOS, FLASH, dynamic, or static), but instead to the typical contents and uses for the memory and its addressing in our systems relative to devices and their configuration.

Discussion of these areas and their differences is also important for operating system setup, memory management, and their use as system resources for some devices and all application programs.

The areas of memory you will encounter with your system configuration are:

- Base or DOS memory, including lower memory (Type=RAM)
- Upper memory, including Upper Memory Blocks (UMB), expanded (LIMS-EMS) memory, and BIOS addresses (Type=RAM and ROM)

- Extended memory, including high memory (HMA, Type=RAM)
- Virtual memory, swap space, or swap file (Type=Disk file)

Memory areas can be represented or expressed without a comprehensive study of computer memory, but those that are pertinent in the context of this book are shown in Table 3-1, and somewhat graphically in Table 3-2.

Of these memory types, in the context of hardware configuration management and conflict resolution, only the base memory and upper memory areas are of concern and discussed in depth here. For specifics about your system memory or memory management software, consult the documentation for your system, operating system, and software.

Table 3-1 *Memory Addressing Areas*

Memory Area	Address Range	Amount
Base or DOS memory	0:0000-9:FFFFh	640K
Lower memory	0:000-0:A00h	64K (within base memory)
System Internal I/O	0:000-0:100h	256 bytes (within lower memory)
Hardware I/O	0:100-0:3FFh	767 bytes (within lower memory)
BIOS data area	0:400-0:4FFh	256 bytes (within lower memory)
DOS data area	0:500-0:5FFh	256 bytes (within lower memory)
DOS	0:600-0:A00h	1024 bytes (within lower memory)
Program and data area	0:A00-9:FFFFh	576K
Upper memory	A:0000F:FFFFh	384K
Graphics memory	A:0000-A:FFFFh	64K (within upper memory)
Text display memory	B:0000-B:FFFFh	64K (within upper memory)
Video BIOS	C:0000-C:7FFFh	32K (within upper memory)
Hard drive BIOS	C:8000-C:FFFFh	32K (within upper memory)
LIMS-EMS expanded memory	E:0000-E:FFFFh	64K (within upper memory; see text under "Upper Memory")
System BIOS	F:0000-F:FFFFh	64K (within upper memory)

Memory Area	Address Range	Amount
Extended memory	from 10:0000h	Above 1MB. Could be up to 256mᴅ or more in some systems. Up to 4GB by specification.
High memory	10:0000-10:FFFFh	64K (within extended memory)
Virtual memory/ swap space	Depends on configuration	Limited to available free disk space

What's Your Address?

The variety of memory addresses shown in the tables in this chapter are expressed in what is called *segment/offset notation*. This notation makes expressing and calculating a wide range of addresses much easier to organize for programmers and hardware designers, and, to some extent, easier for us as well: The numbers aren't as "big" or as hard to perform arithmetic on.

Each address includes two numeric ranges; the first is the hexadecimal number for the segment, representing a 64K block of memory. The second is the hexadecimal number for the offset, the location within – and relative to the start of – the specified segment. Thus, address 0:0h is the first byte in the first 64K of memory, and C:8000h is 8000h bytes from the bottom of the 64K segment twelfth (0Ch equaling 12 in the decimal system).

Since hexadecimal numbering starts with 0, 0Ch is the thirteenth segment and it starts at 768K (12 times 64K) from the first byte of memory. By convention, because the addresses for I/O devices are in the lowest or 0 segment, the segment notation is left off of these in most places, so the abbreviated 378h is really 0:0378h in segment/offset notation.

Similarly, when we are dealing within the same area of memory, such as upper memory, it has been common to combine the segment and the offset together for brevity. Thus, where you may see C800-CFFFh, the segment/offset notation is really C:8000-C:FFFFh. The abbreviated notation is how these addresses typically appear in the documentation for various devices. It is not necessarily incorrect, just seemingly less complicated.

Table 3-2 *Memory Mapping from the Bottom Up*

Memory Region Name	Memory Region Location
Extended Memory	Begins at 1MB
	Could be up to 256MB or more in some systems. Up to 4GB by specification.
XMS Extended Memory	Begins at 1MB + 64K
	Up to 256MB or more
XMS High Memory Area	Begins at 1MB
	64K in size
System BIOS	Begins at F:0000
	64K in size to F:FFFF
LIMS-EMS Memory	Typically begins at E:0000
	Access window is 64K in size.
	May be 64K of Upper Memory, or IBM ROM-BASIC
Upper Memory	Begins at D:0000
	64K in size to D:FFFF
	(This is the EMS access window if IBM ROM-BASIC is above)
Hard Drive BIOS	Begins at C:8000
	32K in size to C:FFFF
Video BIOS	Begins at C:0000
	32K in size to C:7FFF
Unused or special video card memory access	Begins at B:8000
	32K to B:FFFF
Text display memory	Begins at B:0000
	32K to B:7FFF
Graphics memory	Begins at A:0000
	64K in Size to A:FFFF
Program and data area	576K
DOS	64K
DOS data area	256K
BIOS data area	256 bytes
System Internal I/O	256 bytes

RAM

RAM, or Random Access Memory, is the memory you usually think about when you buy or consider how good a system is. In the PC, XT, AT, and early 386 days, we bought discrete chips in 16, 64, 256, or 1,024K increments, 9 or more at a time, to fill rows of sockets on the system board or a memory add-in card. In later-386, certainly 486, and early-Pentium days, we bought RAM in SIMMs or Single Inline Memory Modules, usually 30-pin circuit-board style devices with 9 discrete RAM chips on them. For later-486 and still early-Pentium systems, we bought, and still can buy, 72-pin SIMMs, and have three choices as to the type of RAM we're getting (at least Fast Page Mode, EDO, and now SRAM). Many current Pentium systems and likely all future ones will only use DIMM or Dual Inline Memory Modules, packing still more memory onto a small plug-in circuit board.

RAM is used for native or hardware memory covering Base or DOS RAM (0-640K) and any Extended Memory (above 1MB) in our system. Upper Memory Blocks, High Memory, and LIMS-EMS memory are special segments of RAM memory created and managed through memory management software, such as EMM386 or Quarterdeck's QEMM product.

RAM is considered pretty fast, and it gets incrementally faster as we have progressed from older RAM chips, through SIMMs, to Fast Page Mode operation, to EDO (Extended Data Output) RAM, and recently to SRAM or SDRAM (Synchronous DRAM). All this refers to the electronic technology used inside the chips and how data is addressed and kept fresh inside the system. Normal RAM loses its contents when we shut our systems down, which is one of its drawbacks. CMOS RAM, the kind that holds your system setup parameters and date/time settings, is a special lower power consumption RAM chip that sustains its contents with a small battery, but is much slower than normal RAM.

ROM

ROM, or Read-Only Memory, is a special memory component that has data written into it with a special device, but it allows the contents to be read by the system and software we use. A PC uses ROM to contain the special bootup code and parameters for many SCSI disk drive and video adapters not supported by the BIOS and DOS programs. A special type of ROM (Flash ROM) can be written to in-place in the system by special software. It is quite popular in new designs instead of older-style ROM chips because it allows users to download and upgrade system and adapter's BIOS code without having to open the box to replace chips. ROMs hold their contents nearly forever without batteries or constant updates to keep the contents fresh.

Virtual Memory

Virtual memory is an allocated file space on the disk drive that is used for temporary storage of the contents of semiconductor or chip memory. It is used when the operating system or a program determines that another program or data set needs more RAM (chip-memory) to work with; then the contents of the RAM is stored to the disk space for later use. This process is called *swapping*.

All multitasking operating systems use some form of virtual memory as part of their normal operations. This is more evident in Windows 95, NT, and OS/2 because we seem a little more sensitive to the performance of our systems and all the noise our disk drives make as swapping occurs. Operating systems and applications depend less upon swapping when there is more actual RAM with which to work—though it seems like Windows slows down and swaps more if you have more RAM, because it makes a bigger swap file and tries to use it.

In its actual implementation, virtual memory is nothing more than a single large disk file managed by the operating system that has to keep track of the swap file's various contents and how much of the swap file the contents occupy. Because it is used as memory, many system crashes and faults are caused by disk errors or confusion in the swap file manager, as much as they are caused by bad programming practices or flaws in the operating system itself.

An Address Assignment Can Consume Multiple Memory Locations

As you refer to the PC, XT, and AT device-addressing tables shown here and in Chapter 2, you might notice that some devices use a range of addresses starting at a given single location. I/O ports, using the serial port address for COM1: as an example, are typically known by a single address. In the case of COM1:, it would be 3F8h. This is called the base I/O address, but the port really uses a range of addresses from 3F8h to 3FFh, or eight memory locations. Each memory location represents a different portion or function of the serial port—one for data sent to the port, one for control information, and so on. This is typical of many I/O devices.

This issue also pertains to the BIOS addresses for many I/O devices, because the BIOS occupies a wider range of address space and can usually be configured for a variety of different locations within upper memory, as I'll discuss later.

Using More Space Than Expected

One of the most common and little-known cases of potential addressing overlap can occur with a common network interface card; the NE1000- and NE2000-compatible cards. These cards use more than the standard four addresses mapped out for the IBM PC network card (360 to 363h), actually mapping out 20h, or 32 full memory locations, from 360 to 37Fh for data and control information.

You'll see that placing an NE1000- or NE2000-type network card at address 360h will cause the network interface card to overlap the default address for an LPT port at 378h. If you have trouble staying logged on to your network while printing, or you have trouble printing while connected to your network, this is a good place to start looking. Change the network card's address to something else (280h, 2A0h, 320h, or 340h are generally good alternatives).

For most add-in devices and all standard devices such as COM ports, we know by design and published standards which addresses and how much address space is mapped out for a given device. You will see very few cases in hardware I/O address tables where a standard I/O device is designed to allow addressing overlap, but this does happen.

Lower Memory

We have primarily been concerned with I/O device addressing in what is called the lower memory region of the PC system. This region is a 64K section of the greater region of memory called the system base memory or DOS memory, which itself encompasses 640K of memory addresses. Within lower memory are stored a variety of system parameters and some parts of the BIOS enhancements and the operating system that are placed there during the system bootup process.

System information software may look at the BIOS and DOS data areas to report on certain logical devices, the state of the keyboard, types of disk drives, and other tidbits critical to the system BIOS and DOS. What we do as part of system configuration affects the information that ends up in these areas.

Hardware I/O Area

In terms of system hardware addressing, we are concerned with a very small range of addresses: the hardware I/O range from 100h to 3FFh. Within this area, based on design and current uses, we have approximately 20 usable hardware addresses within which we can configure our I/O devices. This area and its addresses are handled separately from system RAM. You may see several similarities between the hardware address range and the same addresses in memory, but they are indeed separate address spaces.

Anytime there is activity between the CPU and I/O devices, some portion of this address space is accessed in order to gain access to the hardware, control it, and exchange data with it.

Upper Memory

Upper memory occupies 384K of memory range between the base or lower memory area ending at 640K and 1024K (1MB). There is, by design, no actual system or accessible RAM memory in this area. In terms of total system memory (base or DOS RAM plus extended memory), this area is skipped over and not used or filled in with RAM. Any system memory greater than 640K begins at 1024K. Except in some very rare and unusual cases which 99.9 percent of us will never encounter, I/O devices are not assigned addresses here either (but any BIOS ROMs they have might be). Within this area are specific blocks for specific system functions — the video display BIOS and data paths, the system BIOS, or the BIOS for some of the I/O devices.

This region has been exploited by more than a few system features. Among these are:

■ Shadowing, or backfilling part of this area with RAM from the Extended memory region, in which system, video, and device ROM code can be placed so it runs faster.

■ Upper Memory Blocks, or filling this region with RAM from the Extended memory region to place some program code or data in the RAM to relieve base memory use.

Shadowing is a feature that is either built into some systems' BIOS programs, or it is provided by memory management software programs. Without going into a lot of technical details, the components that store the system BIOS and any hardware BIOS are many times slower than system memory. By copying or shadowing the contents of the BIOS chips into faster system memory chips, many system functions work more quickly. Shadowing is implemented by some system BIOS programs and may be controlled in the system setup screens. This technique may also be complemented by BIOS caching so that the ROM's data is available to the system even faster. In addition to or instead of shadowing, memory management software such as DOS's EMM386 and Quarterdeck's QEMM perform these enhancements with software loaded when you start your system.

Upper memory block (UMB) assignments in this memory region are only provided by memory management software such as EMM386 or QEMM. These software programs may make it possible to use some portions of upper memory for storing and running device drivers and other resident software, including parts of DOS. This is a feature known as loading programs high (placing them into UMBs). The drivers and other resident programs you can load high would otherwise consume base memory, leaving less memory for application programs and their data. By loading programs into upper memory blocks, and in some cases also redirecting some of the extended memory into empty upper memory space, EMM386 and QEMM make more base memory available. This leaves more of the full 640K of DOS memory for use by applications software.

Expanded Memory

Within upper memory, there may be a 64K segment configured as the access to expanded memory—memory conforming to the Lotus/Intel/Microsoft–Expanded Memory Specification (LIMS-EMS). LIMS-EMS is a special type of memory conceived and designed to provide additional memory for a variety of applications on older PC and XT systems that did not have the capability for more than 640K of memory. EMS or expanded memory requires special device-driver software (EMM386, QEMM, and the like) and, prior to the i80386 systems, also required special add-in memory cards.

This memory area was intended for the data created and used by large applications, such as the spreadsheet program Lotus 1-2-3.

This memory type, and how it is handled, also provided more manageable and useful memory than the extended memory that became available with AT systems (IBM called this *expansion memory*). Later versions of LIMS-EMS also made the first implementations of multitasking and program swapping possible, before the i80386 systems became available. Today, EMS is still useful and available for data storage, disk caching, and loading programs high. It does not bear any special system configuration.

BIOS Addresses

The BIOS for most devices requires 32K or 64K of upper memory. The beginning address for the device BIOS must typically start on a 16K, 32K, or 64K address increment, although some devices may allow the beginning of the BIOS address to be set in increments as fine as 4K or 8K. A listing of typical and recommended BIOS addresses for certain devices is given in Table 3-3.

Table 3-3 *Expected and Optional BIOS Addresses*

Device	Expected BIOS Address	Optional BIOS Addresses
Video Card BIOS	C:0000–C:7FFFh	None
XT and AT Hard Disk BIOS	C:8000–C:FFFFh	None (unless SCSI)
SCSI Host Adapter	None	C:8000–C:FFFFh; D:0000–D:7FFFh; D:8000–D:FFFFh; E:0000–E:7FFFh
Network Adapter Boot ROM	None	C:8000–C:FFFFh; D:0000–D:7FFFh; D:8000–D:FFFFh; E:0000–E:7FFFh
LIMS-EMS Memory Page	None	D:0000–D:FFFFh; E:0000–E:FFFFh; (see Note that follows)
Plug and Play ESCD storage area	E:8000–E:FFFFh	None
IBM ROM-BASIC	E:0000–E:FFFFh	None
System BIOS	F:0000–F:FFFFh	None

Note

If you use the enhanced features of memory management products such as Quarterdeck's QEMM program, the 64K LIMS-EMS memory page frame may occupy any available and continuous 64K address range in upper memory. This is due to special memory handling techniques unique to these products, the discussion of which is handled extremely well in their respective documentation.

The issue of address overlap can be a problem with the BIOS for certain I/O devices, just as it can be with certain hardware I/O addresses. As with hardware I/O addresses, to avoid conflicts you should find documentation pertaining to the amount of BIOS address space the device may need. Some devices may require only 32K for the actual BIOS program, but in fact occupy a full 64K of address space. This is a critical consideration if you have multiple devices that require BIOS address space. You must be able to configure all of the devices' BIOS to fit into the limited number of address segments without having their total required space overlap. You'll find more on this problem in the section on address decoding later in this chapter.

Extended Memory

Extended memory became available with the introduction of the 16-bit PC/AT system and its additional addressing capabilities. AT-class systems based on the 80286 CPU could address up to 16M of RAM. Although Windows NT can address up to 4GB of RAM, most PC chipsets are limited to addressing only 128 or 256MB of RAM. If you're building a large server system, select your system board chipset carefully and expect to pay a lot of money for the board or a dedicated server.

With the first megabyte of RAM occupied by the 640K of DOS or conventional memory and the 384K of upper memory, 15MB of RAM was left for programs to store the data they worked with. This memory area can also be used for creating virtual disk drives or RAM disks, being assigned a logical disk drive designation, and able to "fool" DOS and other programs into using RAM as a very fast disk drive. Extended memory is also a common place to reserve memory for use in disk caching (storing frequently used data as it passes between the system and a disk drive) or printer caching (holding data on its way to the printer) to improve system performance.

Until MS DOS 5.0 was released, use of extended memory was limited, because neither DOS nor other programs had a cooperative way to manage the use of extended memory. DOS 5.0 provided the HIMEM.SYS device driver to be loaded at system startup through the CONFIG.SYS file, which provided extended memory with better control via an enhancement called XMS, the Extended Memory Specification. With XMS, program developers could reliably use extended memory and thus began to enhance their programs to use XMS instead of EMS (expanded memory). Since extended memory exists as part of the system hardware, rather than being created and managed by a device driver (as when EMM386 creates expanded memory), it can be accessed faster and provides higher performance than EMS.

High Memory

High memory is a 64K portion of extended memory, just above the upper memory area, into which DOS can load one program or set of data, instead of placing that program or data into the lower or base memory. This area is created and controlled by the HIMEM.SYS device driver or a similar memory management program. Typically, it is occupied by a portion of DOS itself, when you use the DOS=HIGH command line entry in the CONFIG.SYS file.

Address Decoding

While known to be an issue as technology progressed from the 286 days to the 386 and beyond, Plug and Play now pays a lot more attention to the issue of a device's address decoding capabilities.

In the good old days of PC and XT systems, with an addressing capability of only 1MB using 20 bits of address lines, no one cared to facilitate the use of more address bits to fully and properly qualify a device, BIOS ROM, or memory address. (Remember, a PC or XT used 8 bits for data, but still had to be capable of addressing the entire 1MB address range, doing so separately from the data lines.)

I/O devices typically use 12 address bits, covering a total range of 4K, more than adequate for the I/O range of lower/base memory (100–3FFh). I/O devices with a BIOS ROM might properly use the entire 20 bits of addressing lines, or they cheat by using only the higher 8 or 12 bits of the 20 address bits.

Ignoring full addresses by not using all of the bits is incomplete information. It is like telling someone that you live in the 300-block of some street, instead of specifically at 312. On most streets, the person trying to go to your house could end up at any of twenty or so houses. They have a 1 in 20 chance to get to the right house. Picking just any house number from 300–399 isn't close enough. In a computer, ignoring the last 4K of possible addressing could cause a program to try to read or write data to or from a hardware device, instead of the section of upper memory expected.

Also, if the hardware or device driver software does manage to locate a device on the proper address boundary, they may scrimp on using the logic fully by referring only to a relative or an offset address rather than the full address. They could allow the program or operating system to lose track of the device's full address, causing serious faults in the system's operation.

Computers can deal with the full precision of their given resources. A hardware or software designer who fails to take advantage of this (in order to save money by eliminating a few logic devices on the hardware) is cheating all of us out of what we need and expect, leaving our systems open to failure.

Incomplete Information

Some devices specify that their BIOS code occupies only 32K of space (say from D:0000–D:7FFFh), but they don't tell you that the actual ROM that contains this code is a 64K device—thus there is something (albeit useless) in the address space of D:8000–D:FFFFh.

This can occur in any size BIOS or ROM situation, be it 8K of code in a 16K device, 16K of code in a 32K device, or 64K of code in a 128K device. This is an obvious waste of limited resources, somewhat the inverse of inadequate decoding logic on the device. Ignoring this possibility—or a vendor not telling its users about it—can cause a lot of grief if the memory manager or your configuration program can't detect the existence of this ROM device. This despite the actual, lesser length of the code in the ROM. Quarterdeck's QEMM program, and to some extent, Microsoft's EMM386 program using the HIGHSCAN option, can avoid excess ROM collisions when trying to allocate Upper Memory Blocks into the upper memory region.

Determining if a Device Uses Addressing Improperly

Unfortunately, without getting into all of the details, perhaps even into the schematic diagram with the complete parts listings for a particular piece of hardware, you won't know exactly what resources the device occupies (as opposed to those it actually uses). The device documentation or packaging may yield some clues, but as yet, truth and complete and proper disclosure in advertising in this highly technical marketplace does not seem to have caught on. If hardware designers flooded their boxes with all of this technical data, it might seem a little too daunting although I contend we all have some responsibility to provide and comprehend a considerable amount of technical information. It's either that, or we pay someone else to know and deal with this stuff.

Along with the items discussed thus far, this chapter covers common conflicts and their solutions. In Chapter 8, I cover software tools that give us a lot of information about what areas of memory are occupied by detectable devices.

Please Excuse the Interruption

The PC accommodates only one hardware interrupt input to let it know that something needs its attention. Because of this, the IRQ signals from I/O devices are sent first to a component on the system board known as the *interrupt controller*. This component handles up to eight possible interrupt signals, providing for IRQ 0 through 7. It also assigns a priority to the interrupt signals it receives. Priority is given to the lower-numbered IRQs. The system clock is given the highest priority, using IRQ 0, to keep the computer's "pulse" going, and the keyboard is given the second-highest priority, using IRQ 1, so you can get the computer's attention.

Only one interrupt controller is present on the 8-bit IBM PC- and XT-compatible systems. It's responsible for sending all hardware interrupt information it receives to the CPU. It also sends, when the CPU "asks" for it, the identification of which IRQ line generated the interrupt activity.

AT-compatible (16- and 32-bit) systems contain two interrupt controllers, with the second one handling IRQs 8–15. Because the CPU provides only one connection for one interrupt controller to signal the CPU, the interrupt signal from the second component is connected to the IRQ 2 input of the first interrupt controller. Because IRQ 2 receives the next highest priority after the clock and keyboard, and it gets input from the second component's IRQs 8–15, these higher-numbered IRQs actually receive higher priority than the lower-numbered IRQs 3–7.

Add to this a PCI bus and controller with only three interrupts and feed the PCI interrupt into the second interrupt controller circuit, and you have to wonder how it can all work strung together like this. Amazingly, it all does, and though it's probably still not an ideal system, it's all we have.

Making the Best Use of IRQ Selections

High-speed communications programs, working with modems making connections between two PC systems, will perform better if they are on COM2: using IRQ 3 (or on COM4: using IRQ 3, but not at the same time that COM2: is being used) because IRQ 3 gets a relatively high priority. This is either by design or luck as far as the PC and XT systems are concerned; hard drive use (IRQ 5), printing (IRQ 5 or 7), and diskette use (IRQ 6) are not as interrupt-intense. This practice seems to fall apart when we get to higher speed AT-class systems, except that they are faster, and the devices that use higher priority interrupts 9–15 are also not as interrupt-intense.

At connection speeds of 9600 bps or higher it is recommended that you give high-speed communications the highest priority and CPU time you can. This will avoid loss of data as it is transmitted, received, and handled by your communications software.

Caution

COM ports are logical devices, pre-assigned by the system BIOS to physical serial ports and IRQs. Because of this, you should not try to change the IRQ settings of COM ports to an available higher-priority IRQ line (9 to 15) unless you can and want to reconfigure your software for this type of configuration. Windows and Plug and Play do allow for this reconfiguration, but it is unusual and often overlooked, and it could make support difficult later on. (See Chapter 1 for an explanation of logical devices and how they're assigned.)

Note

Also in the realm of high-speed communications and IRQ priorities, configuring 16-bit network cards for either IRQ 9 or 10 will ensure efficient network communications since networks operate much faster than serial ports. Similarly, if you are doing high-quality/high-speed multimedia work, you may wish to configure your sound or video capture card for a higher priority IRQ (9–15) if the card and its software provide for this configuration.

Top Ten Conflict Areas and How to Deal with Them

In this section, I discuss some of the most common questions and conflicts encountered with PC system configurations and provide solutions. Some of the items are straightforward: If this, some of the items are a little more anecdotal.

Number 1: IRQ Signals

Taking each IRQ line one at a time in a summary format, I break them down into the devices that might be configured on them, where the most conflicts seem to be, and what seems to work best in most cases.

Tip

The most common IRQ conflicts I hear about are between the two COM ports that are used for a mouse and a modem. A typical symptom is that an online session with the modem crashes whenever the mouse is moved, or the mouse fails to work whenever an online connection or fax call is made. If both the mouse and the modem are connected to COM1 (IRQ4), this problem is usually avoided by reassigning the modem to use COM2 or COM4 (IRQ3). If you have two modems, you might want to assign them to COM2 and COM4, suffering an apparent conflict between them at IRQ 3, but simply don't use both modems at the same time! Otherwise, a couple of my more unusual alternate IRQ assignments for a COM port (5 or 7) might be better for your situation.

IRQ 0: Assigned to and used internally for system timing. The IRQ 0 signal line is never available to add-in cards; it is connected only to the internal system board circuits. If a conflict appears to arise with this IRQ , as indicated by system information software, the chances are that your system board is bad. A diagnostic program may help determine if this is the case.

IRQ 1: Assigned to and used internally for the keyboard. The IRQ 1 signal line is never available to add-in cards; it is connected only to the internal system board circuits. If a conflict appears to arise with this IRQ as indicated by system information software, the chances are that your system board is bad. A diagnostic program may help determine if this is the case.

IRQ 2: Assigned for older EGA video adapt
line is typically available unless one of your app
grams needs this line connected on your video ᵣor
backward compatibility with the older EGA video functions.
With most of us having VGA video adapters and displays,
this IRQ typically has no primary, useful assignment and can
be used for other devices. If another device needs or uses IRQ
2, make sure that the jumper or switch for this IRQ is disabled on your video card. This is a good alternative IRQ
option setting for sound or network card use. Because IRQ 9
uses IRQ 2 to communicate with the CPU, you should be
aware that a device using IRQ 2 may conflict with any device
on IRQs 8–15, and especially IRQ 9, if your software for
either of the devices using IRQ 2 or IRQ 9 can't determine
which device caused the IRQ activity. Fortunately, most can.

IRQ 3: Primarily assigned to COM2: (at 2F8h) and COM4:
(at 2E8h). Unless your system is misconfigured and you've got
crossed port address assignments with COM1: or COM3:, or
you are trying to use devices on COM2: and COM4: at the
same time, there are few conflicts if this IRQ is used for
COM2: and COM4: only. Sound cards, serial I/O (COM)
ports, modems, network cards, and possibly other devices
offer this IRQ configuration option. Many network cards
come preset to use IRQ 3 when you buy them. Avoid IRQ 3
for the network card if you use serial port COM2: or COM4:.

IRQ 4: Primarily assigned to COM1: (at 3F8h) and COM3:
(at 3E8h). Unless your system is misconfigured and you've got
crossed port address assignments with COM2: or COM4:, or
you are trying to use devices on COM1: and COM3: at the
same time, there are few conflicts if this IRQ is used for
COM1: and COM3: only. Sound cards, serial I/O (COM)
ports, modems, network cards, and possibly other devices offer
this IRQ configuration option and should not be put here.

IRQ 5: Primarily assigned to the second parallel port (at address 278h). Sound cards, serial I/O (COM) ports, modems, network cards, and possibly other devices offer this IRQ configuration option. Normally, you would reserve this IRQ for LPT2: use, unless you need to use it for another device and you are aware that you may have to give up any interrupt-driven printing operations for a second LPT port.

IRQ 6: Assigned to the diskette drive system and is available to add-in cards through the add-in card slots. If you have diskette drives in your system, do not set any other devices for IRQ 6. Few if any I/O cards let you assign anything here anyway, so there should be no conflicts.

IRQ 7: Usually assigned to the first parallel port (at address 3BCh or 378h). Sound cards, serial I/O (COM) ports, modems, network cards, and possibly other devices offer this IRQ configuration option, which is okay if you don't need the IRQ for printing. Normally you would reserve this IRQ for LPT1: use, unless you need to use it for another device and you are aware that you may have to give up any interrupt-driven printing operations for the first LPT port. If you need two printer ports, don't set them for 3BCh and 378h. Leave the first one at address 378h (proper for LPT1: in a color system), and configure the second printer for address 278h and IRQ 5.

IRQ 8: Reserved for the internal real-time clock for AT- and higher-class systems. The IRQ 8 signal line is never available to add-in cards; it is connected only to the internal system board circuits. If a conflict with this IRQ appears in one of the system information programs, the chances are that your system board is bad.

IRQ 9: Another common IRQ option for 16-bit network cards. If you have a sound card and can't set it to IRQ 9, put the network card here. Remember, this IRQ also equates to IRQ 2, so it will get a high priority during use. If high-speed network performance is your priority, set the network for this IRQ and use another IRQ for less critical devices.

IRQ 10: A common IRQ option for 16-bit network cards. This is a safe bet unless you have other devices set for this IRQ. Check the IRQ setting of your sound card if you suspect conflicts here.

IRQ 11: A common IRQ option for many SCSI host adapters and 16-bit sound cards. Few if any conflicts exist using this option unless you have multiple SCSI host adapters, multiple network cards, a sound card, a mix of SCSI, network and sound cards, or some other device(s) set for IRQ 11. If you already have a SCSI host adapter set for IRQ 11, try using IRQ 10 for the network card.

IRQ 12: Used for the PS/2-style mouse port (also known as the internal, or on-board, mouse port) included on many system boards. If the PS/2 mouse port is enabled in your system's Setup program, and you are using a PS/2-style mouse plugged into this port on the system board, don't set any other adapters or devices for IRQ 12. IRQ 12 is commonly one of the IRQ setting options for SCSI host adapters and sound cards, which you can't use if you're using the on-board PS/2-style mouse port on IRQ 12.

IRQ 13: Reserved for the NPU (a.k.a. math chip, numeric coprocessor, or floating-point processor). The IRQ 13 signal line is never available to add-in cards. It is connected only to an NPU or CPU socket. If a conflict with this IRQ appears in one of the system information programs, chances are your system board is bad.

IRQ 14: Assigned to hard drive adapter/controllers for AT systems, and a common optional IRQ setting for some SCSI host adapters. If you are using the hard drive interface built into your system board, or if you have an add-in card disk drive adapter, and you have or are adding a SCSI host adapter or any other add-in device, do not set the SCSI host adapter or any other add-in devices for IRQ 14.

IRQ 15: Assigned to secondary hard drive interfaces, and a common IRQ option for many SCSI host adapters—few if any conflicts will exist with other devices. If you have multiple disk or SCSI host adapters, they cannot be set for the same IRQ, so IRQs 9, 10, and 11 would be likely next choices.

Note

Remember that Plug and Play can and will make its own decisions about many IRQ assignments. Under Windows 95, the only place to make PnP resource assignment changes may be under the specific device's Resource tab within the Device Manager under Control Panel ⇨ System, or use the SETUP program that came with the device.

Number 2: DMA Channels

As with the IRQ signals above, we'll be looking at each DMA line one at a time, in a summary format. We'll break them down into the devices that might be configured on them, where the most conflicts seem to be, and what seems to work best in most cases. Remember that DMA lines may be separated on your add-in cards into DRQ (DMA request) and DACK (DMA acknowledgment) signals, both of which must be configured to the same-numbered channel for the add-in device to work correctly.

Only in the case of a self-proprietary software-configured sound card have I ever had an obvious DMA conflict between two devices. More commonly, the device and its DOS-level driver or Windows 95/98 Device Manager are not configured to the same parameters, and the sound card may lose the ability to transfer data properly for recording or playing back sounds. If it's not a conflict, it may be simply misconfigured!

DMA 0: Assigned internally to the system board for memory refresh. You shouldn't be able to even get at it.

DMA 1: Has no predetermined assignment. It's a common choice for sound cards and SCSI host adapters.

DMA 2: Assigned to the diskette subsystem. If you have no diskette drives, you may configure anything that offers this line as an option here, but there are several others from which to choose.

DMA 3: Has no predetermined assignment. It's a common choice for sound cards, network interface, or SCSI host adapter cards.

DMA 4: Has no predetermined assignment. It's available for various uses.

DMA 5: Has no predetermined assignment. It's a common choice for sound cards and SCSI host adapters.

DMA 6: Has no predetermined assignment. It's available for various uses.

DMA 7: Has no predetermined assignment. It's a common choice for sound card use.

Note

Remember that Plug and Play can and will make its own decisions about many DMA assignments. Under Windows 95 or 98, the only place to make PnP resource assignment changes may be under the specific device's Resource tab within the Device Manager under Control Panel ➪ System.

Number 3: I/O Addresses

You've heard about a couple of my pet peeves more than once prior to this chapter — and they would be?

- The LPT1: port at 378h and an NE1000 or NE2000 network interface card at 360h. An overlap/conflict — good example! Next?

- Network interface cards at address 300h. Excellent — where the system or operating system gets confused about what kind of device is at 300h, the original prototype card address assignment.

Surely there are others: SCSI adapters and sound cards that can be assigned to the same address, such as 130h, 220h, 330h, and so on. Beware!

Also becoming more and more common are addressing (and IRQ) conflicts with sound cards that have built-in IDE interfaces to support CD-ROM add-ins/upgrades. These will conflict with the built-in IDE interfaces on system boards. Ditch the sound card IDE interface and use the one on your system board!

130h: A common alternative for SCSI host adapters.

140h: A common alternative for SCSI host adapters.

170h: The address for the second AT-type hard drive interface, or what we know today as the Secondary IDE Interface. Beware, the IDE interface on your sound card may want to be here too. That's if you don't have the secondary interface on your system board enabled.

1F0h: The address for the first AT-type hard drive interface, or what we know today as the Primary IDE Interface. Beware, the IDE interface on your sound card may want to be here too — a no-no!

220h: Typically used for Sound Blaster or Sound Blaster emulations (WAV files) on sound cards.

240h: An alternative selection for Sound Blaster or Sound Blaster emulations on sound cards.

278h: Assigned to LPT2: or LPT3: and goes with IRQ 5.

280h: One of the typical choices for your network card, or the rarer Aria Synthesizer.

2A0h: Another common choice for your network card or Aria Synthesizer.

2E8h: Assigned to COM4: and goes with IRQ 3.

2F8h: Assigned to COM2: and goes with IRQ 3.

300h: A common but not ideal choice for a network card. Avoid it for OS/2 and Windows 95/98/NT.

320h: A good place for a network card if you don't have a SCSI or MIDI adapter at 330h.

330h: A common place for many SCSI host adapters.

340h: A common alternative for many SCSI host adapters, or a good place for your network card if you don't have a SCSI host adapter here.

360h: If you need to put your network card here, be careful. You might want to put LPT1: at 3BCh, not 378h, or the network card may conflict with the LPT port at 378h.

378h: The assignment for LPT1: in color systems; goes with IRQ 7. Beware of an IRQ conflict if you have an LPT port at 3BCh.

3BCh: LPT1: in monochrome systems; goes with IRQ 7. Beware of an IRQ conflict if you have an LPT port at 378h. Be aware that Windows 95 and 98 do not know what LPT number to assign to a port at this address, because 3BCh is the LPT port for older monochrome systems, which the Windows folks have never heard of.

3E8h: Assigned to COM3:, which goes with IRQ 4.

3F8h: Assigned to COM1:, the first or only COM port you may have. It goes with IRQ 4.

Number 4: OS/2 Warp or Windows 95 Won't Complete Installation or Run with a Network

In OS/2, networking features are an option that has to be added to an existing OS/2 installation, even if your system was networked before you installed OS/2. The installation of networking is not a complex process, and typically it proceeds rather smoothly. Networking is not available until after the installation of the add-in software and device drivers, and a shutdown and restart of the operating system. It's during the restart of the operating system that you may encounter a system error message such as SINGLE01 or

SYS3175, which will be your first indication of a possible configuration conflict between your network card and OS/2.

For Windows 95 and 98, the installation and configuration of networking are automatic aspects of the installation process when a network interface card is detected. Although the process may detect the network hardware and appear to configure Windows 95 or 98 correctly, you might discover that networking simply does not work after installation. This may be indicated by the lack of a Network Neighborhood icon on the Windows 95/98 desktop or network configuration problems, which you may see in Windows Device Manager if the card was even recognized, if the card is not present in Device Manager Windows, or if the device driver failed to recognize the card.

If you encounter network problems such as these, check the hardware address for your network interface card. If the card is set up at address 300h, change the address to 280h or 340h. To avoid conflicts with any present or future SCSI host adapter cards at 330h, do not use address 320h; to avoid conflicts with a present or future parallel port card at 378h, do not use address 360h.

For those upgrading from prior network situations, reconfiguration of a network card may also require editing any and all of the NET.CFG files that are part of your particular network configuration. Normally the NET.CFG file may be found in the root directory of your boot drive. For Windows 95 and 98, you must also change the resources configuration under the Windows 95 or 98 Network or System icons within the Control Panel to reflect the new network card address.

Number 5: Coincident Printer Port and Network Problems

If you're experiencing problems staying connected or logged in to your network server when you print a document on a local printer, or if you're having problems printing locally while working with files on your network, check the addresses used by your network interface card and your printer port.

If you have an NE1000, NE2000, or compatible . face card that's set up to use address 360h and your loc. is set up at address 378h, you have an overlap of a￢ ￢ space. NE1000, NE2000, and compatible network cards require a full 32 (20h) address locations, including their base address of 360h. Address 378h of the parallel I/O port card falls at the 25th address location required by the network card.

The solution is to change the address assignment of one of these devices. You have three addressing options for the parallel I/O port — 3BCh, 378h, and 278h. Most network interface cards provide at least six addressing options: 280h, 2A0h, 300h, 320h, 340h, and 360h.

Since most of us have color video display systems rather than monochrome graphic adapters that have parallel ports included on them, and the LPT1: port for these systems is generally accepted to use address 378h, it is probably best to reconfigure the network interface card to use another address. The best alternatives are often 280h or 340h, to avoid further conflicts, since 300h may cause problems with OS/2 Warp or Windows 95/98, and 320h will overlap the common SCSI host adapter address of 330h.

For DOS-based network setups, reconfiguration of a network card may also require editing any and all of the NET.CFG files that are part of your particular network configuration. Normally the NET.CFG file may be found in the root directory of your boot drive. For Windows 95/98, you must also change the Resources configuration under the Windows 95/98 Network or System icons within the Control Panel icon to reflect the new network card address.

Number 6: Coincident Network Card and SCSI Host Adapter Problems

If you are experiencing problems with your SCSI-interface CD-ROM or hard disk drive while working with files on your network, or if you're having trouble staying connected or logged on to your network server when you access your disk drives, check the addresses used by your network interface card and your printer port.

If you have an NE1000, NE2000, or compatible network interface card that is set up to use address 320h and your SCSI host adapter is set up at address 330h, you have an overlap of address space. As expressed before, NE1000, NE2000, and compatible network cards require a full 32 (20h) address locations, including their base address. Address 330h of the SCSI host adapter card falls at the 17th address location required by the network card, whose base address in this case is 320h.

The solution is to change the address assignment of one of these devices. Depending on the requirements and design of your SCSI host adapter, you may not have any addressing options other than 330h. Since most network interface cards provide at least six addressing options (280h, 2A0h, 300h, 320h, 340h, and 360h), it's probably best to reconfigure the network interface card to use another address. The best alternatives are often 280h and 340h. They avoid further conflicts, since 300h may cause problems with OS/2 Warp or Windows 95/98, and 360h will overlap the parallel port address of 378h.

For DOS-based network setups, reconfiguration of a network card may also require editing any and all of the NET.CFG files that are part of your particular network configuration. Normally the NET.CFG file may be found in the root directory of your boot drive. For Windows 95 and 98, you must also change the resources configuration under the Windows 95 or 98 Network or System icons within the Control Panel icon to reflect the new network card address.

Number 7: There's No Sound, the Sound Card Output Stutters, or Voices Sound Like Your Computer Took a Deep Breath of Helium

Your sound card requires three distinct, non-conflicting system resources — an IRQ line, a DMA channel (for both DMA Request and DMA Acknowledgment), and a hardware I/O address. A sound card will not function properly if one of the following occurs:

- The physical configuration of your sound card does not match the settings for the card in your Windows SYSTEM.INI file.

- The device driver loaded in CONFIG.SYS, or in the Device Manager under Control Panel ➪ System does not match your device.

- There is an IRQ or DMA conflict with another device in your system.

If you can't correct these symptoms through the methods indicated here, the sound card may be defective.

Most sound cards can be configured without conflicts to use address 220h or 240h, IRQ 5, and DMA channel 1 or 3. Common conflicts may be with a SCSI host adapter that uses address 220h or 240h. Even the SCSI adapter on your sound card may use these addresses as alternates.

Begin solving these symptoms by using a system-information reporting program to determine what resources are used and, indirectly, which resources are available for your sound card configuration. Make any necessary configuration changes to the hardware to suit the available resources, and then use the sound card's installation or Setup program to view the existing sound card configuration to be sure it is correct and works with the program designed for the card. In most cases, the configuration details may also be viewed and edited directly within the Windows SYSTEM.INI file (for Windows 3.*x* users).

Examples of driver configuration entries in the Windows SYSTEM.INI file for five different popular sound cards are provided below. Make sure the entries in your file match the actual physical configuration of your sound card.

Creative Labs Sound Blaster, Old Driver Version

```
[sndblst.drv]
port=220
int=5
dmachannel=1
Palette=
MasterVolume=10, 10
FmVolume=8, 8
CDVolume=8, 8
LineVolume=8, 8
VoiceVolume=8, 8
```

Note: Above, port means the I/O address, and the hex address is implied; int stands for "interrupt," or the hardware IRQ.

Creative Labs Sound Blaster, New Driver Version

```
[sndblst2.drv]
port=220
int=5
dma=1
```

Aria Synthesizer

```
[aria.drv]
dspport=0x2b0
dspirq=12
midiport=0x330
midiirq=9
savemix=1
recsource=1
extmon=0
CDmon=0
extmode=0
CDmode=0
extlevel=1
```

Note: Again, port means the I/O address.

MediaVision ProAudio and ProAudio Spectrum

```
[mvproaud.drv]
dma=1
irq=5
```

Note: The port is not specified here because there may be only one choice for this device, or because the device driver determines the I/O address when it loads or as it is read and assigned by the device driver in the CONFIG.SYS file.

MediaVision Jazz and Jazz16

```
[jazz.drv]
dma=1
irq=5
```

Note: As above, the I/O address is self-determined or assigned in the CONFIG.SYS file.

For Windows 95 and 98 users, you'll be going into the Control Panel ⇨ System icon, then to the Device Manager, to find the sound card interface listing, and to a specific sound card type to get to its Resources tab. By the time you get into the Device Manager, you might see a bright yellow circle with an exclamation point that indicates a device conflict exists. Go to that device's listing and begin to explore what's what. Figure 3-1 shows the typical device address settings for a Sound Blaster sound card, and Figure 3-2 shows the card's IRQ settings.

If your device is a Plug and Play card, you may or may not be able to change the settings in the Resources dialog. If it's not a PnP device, changing settings here will only specify what you want the setting to be, not what the card is actually set for. To change the resources on the actual card you'll need to remove the card from the system, or use the card's proprietary Setup program.

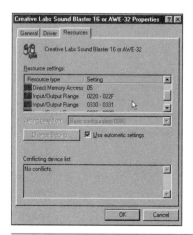

Figure 3-1 *Device Manager showing typical address settings for a Sound Blaster card*

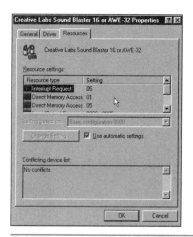

Figure 3-2 *Device Manager showing typical IRQ and DMA settings for a Sound Blaster card*

Number 8: Windows SETUP Indicates Not Enough Memory to Run SETUP

This message reflects less of a conflict than a configuration dilemma, but it can become a common aggravation in the process of cleaning up your system configuration or performing upgrades. This message may be presented during a number of possible upgrade and configuration activities. Among them:

- Using the Windows SETUP program to add or change video cards, driver files, or display resolutions
- Using the Windows SETUP program to add or change network features
- Using the Fonts feature under the Windows Control Panel to add display and printer fonts
- Reinstalling Windows

There are two common causes and related cures for the problem.

Possibility A: The WIN.INI File Is Too Large

The most common cause for the appearance of this error message is that your WIN.INI or SYSTEM.INI file for Windows configuration exceeds 64K. These files often increase in size if you have installed a lot of printer or screen fonts, or application programs that add a lot of parameter lines to these files. The WIN.INI file contains more information and thus grows faster and larger than the SYSTEM.INI file. If Windows finds the critical elements that it needs to load and run in the first 64K or characters of the WIN.INI file, you can prevent the above error message. This can apply to both Windows 3.*x* and Windows 95.

A quick fix is to rearrange the contents of the WIN.INI file. This is done with a text editor (DOS EDIT or Windows' NOTEPAD programs) to move some elements within the file to a different place in the file. You should be familiar with the Cut and Paste features of the editor of your choice.

Following is a listing of the groups of information in the WIN.INI file. (These are not the actual files, as they do not contain the full details that are to be found in the files.) By rearranging the sections of WIN.INI, at least by moving the [sounds] section to the bottom of the file, you can fit the file's critical setup sections within the first 32,768 characters. The [fonts] section should be near the top of the file, because fonts are critical to the appearance of Windows. Since the Windows SETUP program is used to change video configurations and these video configuration changes often affect the [fonts] section, SETUP needs to be able to find it in the file.

Note

When you rearrange the groups of information in the listings, move the detailed information that follows each bracketed group heading (in the actual file, but not shown here) with the heading; the heading will be the first line of the entire group.

Primary Windows Environment Details at the Top

[windows]

[Desktop]

[intl]

[MS User Info]

[colors]

[ports]

Screen and Printer Appearance Items

[FontSubstitutes]

[TrueType]

[fonts]

Printer Specifics Below

[PrinterPorts]

[devices]

[Canon BJ-200ex,LPT1]

[Epson FX-86e,LPT2]

[Generic/Text Only]

[PostScript,LPT1]

[PostScript,LPT3]

[PSCRIPT]

[HP LaserJet Series II,LPT1]

[spooler]

[Network]

[Extensions]

[mci extensions]

Windows Applications–Specific Details

[Compatibility]

[embedding]

[Windows Help]

[Cardfile]

[drawdib]

Application-Specific Details

[CorelGraphics4]

[GenigraphicsDriver]

[Genigraphics GraphicsLink]

[Microsoft Graph 3.0]

[Microsoft Query]

[Microsoft System Info]

[Microsoft Word 2.0]

[MSAPPS]

[MS Proofing Tools]

[MS Setup (ACME) Table Files]

[MS Shareres]

[MSWrite]

[Paintbrush]

[pcdos]

[Visual CD]

[WAOL]

[WinFax]

[WinComm]

[WinZip]

Text and Graphics Conversions (usually large sections)

[MSWord Text Converters]

[MS Graphic Import Filters]

[MS Spreadsheet Converters]

```
[MS Text Converters]
[MS Graphic Export Filters]
```

Sounds at the End

```
[sounds]
```

End of WIN.INI File

If your WIN.INI file is less than 64K, the next possibility is likely the cause of SETUP's error message.

Possibility B: There Are Too Many .INF Files in the WINDOWS\SYSTEM Directory

The second most common cause of the "not enough memory to run Windows SETUP" comes from having too many SETUP*x*.INF, OEMSETUP.INF, or OEM*x*.INF files (where *x* represents numbers to differentiate many separate filenames) in your disk drive's C:\WINDOWS\SYSTEM subdirectory. These files are used by the Windows SETUP program to allow you to select from a variety of hardware options for video display adapters, sound cards, and so on. You can move the files that are named OEMx.INF to a spare or backup subdirectory, or delete them from your disk. If you reinstall a piece of hardware, you'll be prompted for the hardware's disk with these files on it anyway.

Number 9: Games or Windowed DOS Applications Appear Fuzzy, or Colors are Changed Between Windows and Windowed DOS Sessions, or the System Just Plain Locks Up When Changing Programs

Roughly 30 percent of the "help me" e-mail I get concerns the bizarre symptoms that we'll see if we have memory conflicts. While everyone else is scrambling around looking for bad hardware, reinstalling applications, or Windows itself, most folks find a lot of relief in changing or adding a couple of simple lines in their CONFIG.SYS file and restarting the system. This is true for almost any system — Windows 3.*x* or Windows 95 or 98.

If you click the MSDOS icon under Windows, it usually opens a full-screen DOS session within Windows (no frame, dialog boxes, Windows wallpaper, and so on); but you do have the option of running DOS applications in a window instead. This is controlled by a selection for each DOS application by its .PIF file. For Windows 95 and 98, the shortcut icon represents the old PIF or Program Information File and contains many of the same DOS-compatibility details and then some.

Fuzzy-windowed DOS applications and changing colors are caused by the Windows drivers for your video adapter, or how your video adapter uses portions of upper memory, and the possibility that your memory manager or Windows is using a portion of upper memory that the video driver needs to use. This problem may be quite common with games. To solve the problem, one or two memory management changes are necessary.

The first possible solution is to add command-line modifiers to exclude the B000–B7FF or B000–BFFF upper memory range in the configuration of your memory manager (EMM386.EXE, QEMM386.SYS or similar) in the CONFIG.SYS file. These ranges are used for placing DOS text on your video screen, and, in many cases now, for accessing advanced features of the new whiz-bang VGA cards. Usually Windows and memory managers avoid this area because of this, but a Windows device driver for some video cards may conflict with the memory manager and cause display problems for DOS text applications running in Windows. If this region is left available and used by Windows as upper memory for loading programs or data, conflicts can also occur. Using the text editor of your choice, open the CONFIG.SYS file for editing, and if your EMM386 or QEMM command lines look like the first lines in the groups below, change (or add) them to appear as the lines that follow them.

For EMM386, change from:

```
DEVICE=C:\DOS\EMM386.EXE RAM
```

to:

```
DEVICE=C:\DOS\EMM386.EXE RAM X=B000-B7FF
```

or:

```
DEVICE=C:\DOS\EMM386.EXE RAM X=B000-BFFF
```

For QEMM, change from:

```
DEVICE=C:\QEMM\QEMM386.SYS RAM ROM ST:M
```

to:

```
DEVICE=C:\QEMM\QEMM386.SYS RAM ROM ST:M X=B000-B7FF
```

or:

```
DEVICE=C:\QEMM\QEMM386.SYS RAM ROM ST:M X=B000-BFFF
```

Save the CONFIG.SYS file and exit the editor. Reboot your system for these changes to take effect. Then, run Windows, open a DOS Window session, do what you did before to cause the problem to happen, and see if your problem has gone away. If not, try the next step.

Older versions of DOS and Windows 3.x include a file named MONOUMB.386 or MONOUMB2.386. This is a special device driver file to be used within Windows to keep it from conflicting with the video memory range in the upper memory blocks (UMBs). Locate this file on your DOS diskettes or on your hard disk. If it is not in the C:\WINDOWS\SYSTEM subdirectory, copy it from where you find it to that subdirectory. If you find a file named MONOUMB.38_ or MONOUMB2.38_ instead, you will have to be at a DOS prompt and invoke the EXPAND program that comes with Windows to decompress the file. The command line to use for this is:

```
EXPAND MONOUMB.38_ MONOUMB.386[Enter]
```

or

```
EXPAND MONOUMB2.38_ MONOUMB2.386[Enter]
```

When this file is properly in place in your C:\WINDOWS\SYSTEM subdirectory, the SYSTEM.INI file in the C:\WINDOWS subdirectory needs this device added under the [386Enh] section, to appear as follows:

```
[386Enh]
device=monoumb.386
```

or

```
[386Enh]
device=monoumb2.386
```

Save and close the SYSTEM.INI file and restart Windows, repeating the steps that previously caused the display problem. If the problem has not gone away after both of these changes have been made, you should check with your system or video card vendor to obtain technical support or new video driver files. In the meantime, if you want to keep on working but with reduced resolution and colors, you can use the Windows SETUP program to reconfigure Windows to use a plain old VGA video driver. This will avoid the special video drivers entirely until the problem can be fixed properly through contact with vendor technical support or the help of a more experienced user.

Note

Since there are so many new devices being produced very quickly for Windows 95 and 98, it pays to check the Web site, BBS, or online forum of all of your hardware vendors to see if there are updated driver files for one or more devices. You may even find drivers that should have shipped with your device, but did not, that could be crucial to the setup of your video card or system board. This is also a perfect time to check the BugNet database at www.bugnet.com for analysis of commonly reported and verified conflicts between different software and hardware products.

Number 10: But I Really Need to Use More than Two COM Ports at One Time

Using two COM ports at the same time is fairly common, as many systems are configured with a serial port mouse on COM1: and a modem on COM2:, and these two ports do not have the same IRQ assignment. If the use of a third port is required, it would logically have to be COM3:, but this port would normally be assigned to use IRQ 4, which conflicts with COM1:.

Note

The examples in this section may be used as guidelines for editing your SYSTEM.INI file if the options presented in Windows Control Panel/Ports/Settings/Advanced dialog boxes are not sufficient to define your special configuration circumstances. Each of the three examples provides command lines to be entered under the [386Enh] bracketed heading in SYSTEM.INI; there will be lots of other configuration lines starting at the [386Enh] brackets before getting to any COM . . . lines.

If you have a system and add-in card that use the MicroChannel data bus, you can simply add a third COM port and share IRQs between COM ports 1 and 3 or 2 and 4, which must be specified in the Windows SYSTEM.INI file by adding the following line under the [386Enh] section:, as indicated in Example A:

Example A:
```
COMIrqSharing=1
```

This option applies only to MicroChannel and EISA systems. For ISA or non-MicroChannel, non-EISA systems, this line must be left set to 0 (zero) or NO, or it should not be present.

For non-MicroChannel, non-EISA systems, one solution may be to find an unused IRQ line that can also be configured on the COM3: port. Unfortunately, most add-in COM ports were designed with the original PC design and configuration rules in mind and provide switches or jumpers for the conventional IRQ settings for COM ports — IRQ 3 or 4. If your add-in COM port board allows you to assign an IRQ other than 3 or 4 to one of your new COM ports, and one of those IRQs is not in use by another device, do so, and then use Windows Control Panel to indicate the new IRQ for the COM port of interest. If you can assign a unique IRQ to each COM port, you need to tell Windows which IRQ goes with a specific port. (IRQs 5 and 7 are simply examples here.) Example B is representative of this new configuration:

Example B:

```
COM3Irq=7
COM4Irq=5
```

Note

An electronics technician might be able to make an electrical modification to the add-in card IRQ connections to allow you to select IRQs other than 3 or 4.

The remaining option is to seek out and purchase one of many special COM port add-in cards that provide non-standard COM port addressing (COM port addresses other than 3F8h, 2F8h, 3E8h, or 2E8h) and additional IRQ options. These cards are typically used by people who operate dial-up or electronic bulletin board systems (BBSs) under Windows or other operating systems. Inquire of your local computer dealer, a local BBS, or one of the popular on-line service forums (CompuServe, America Online, and so on) for specific information in locating one of these boards.

If you put one of these special-purpose COM port options in your system, you might need to tell Windows exactly where these ports are addressed and which IRQ goes with a specific port. Addresses 130h and 138h and IRQs 5 and 7 in Example C aren't necessarily accurate for any particular card:

Example C:

```
COM3Base=0130
COM3Irq=7
COM4Base=0138
COM4Irq=5
```

Windows 3.*x* Bonus Points

Though not conflict resolutions, two more sets of command lines will be helpful here.

The following four lines really help the performance of communications programs running under Windows 3.*x*. These lines would be added at the end of the [386Enh] section of your SYSTEM.INI file.

- COMBoostTime=100 (This line gives comm programs more of Windows' time for high-speed data transfer.)

- COM2FIFO=1 (Include a line like this for all of the COM ports that have a 16550A UAR/T chip.)

- COM2Buffer=12 (This line augments the "FIFO" specifier for high-speed data transfer.)

- COMIRQSharing= (This will be a 1 or a 0 to indicate that you have (1) or do not allow (0) two COM ports to be active on the system at the same time.)

Add the following lines to [NonWindowsApp], which is below the [386Enh] section:

- CommandEnvSize=1560 (This should match the /E:#### setting in the SHELL= line of CONFIG.SYS. "####" indicates a numeric variable value.)

- FontChangeEnable=1 (This allows you to scale fonts in a Windowed DOS dialog screen.)

- MouseInDOSBox=1 (This requires that a DOS mouse driver is loaded before running Windows, which allows you to use a mouse for DOS programs running under Windows.)

Windows 95 and 98 should not need any of these lines because they already provide support for mouse functionality in DOS sessions, and handle higher speed COM ports (typically to 57,600 or 115,200 bytes per second).

Upgrading a Typical Configuration

Now let's look at two system configurations, covering the most available and obvious aspects of system configuration: one before we add in new features and options, and another that includes everything you might find in a fully equipped, networked, multimedia PC.

Jumping right into a 386, 486, or Pentium configuration does not necessarily ignore the many PC, XT, and AT systems that are still in use. The rules applied to, and primary resources available on a PC (8088-CPU-based system) and an 80486- or Pentium-based system are fundamentally the same, except that a 286, 386, 486, or Pentium system provides more IRQ and DMA channels. Likewise, many of the problems and problem-solving processes are the same for all types of PC systems. However, because the PC and XT systems have limited resources, it's unlikely or often impossible to consider these systems as upgrade candidates for the types of software and hardware we want to run, or which we will encounter problems with today.

For our purposes, we must take for granted in our example many of the built-in items and some unusual low-level system configuration items that are in use and can't be changed. These include the system's keyboard, memory, and clock circuits, and pre-assignments made for diskette IRQ and DMA resources.

When you consider any upgrade project, especially one as significant for you and your system as a new operating system or a major hardware addition, you should make every effort to ensure that your system is configured properly before performing the upgrade. This helps ensure that the upgrade goes smoothly and quickly so you can begin to enjoy it rather than regret it. Of course, this is no different from the advantages of having your system configured properly in the first place, but if you've waited until now to deal with the issue, you may as well deal with it all the way.

As often as it's possible to make just about any combination of PC hardware devices work together, there are cases where two devices are just not compatible in the same system. This is usually because one or both devices lack flexibility in their configuration options, or because the software for one device or the other is equally inflexible or just poorly written.

You will find more compatibility problems with older hardware and software (designed when only the PC, XT, or AT systems existed) than you will with most products designed after i80386 systems came along. The latter are faster and take into account more memory addressing and management considerations. Not only were the electronic components used in I/O devices and system boards prior to the i80386 slower than today's components, but the methods used by some manufacturers to address their I/O devices led to conflicts with 16-bit and 32-bit systems. This consideration—the use of older (and likely slower) I/O devices—applies mainly to moving older COM and LPT ports, memory cards, and non-SCSI or non-IDE disk controllers for older-style disk drives into faster 386, 486, and Pentium systems. Some of these older devices may work, but at the cost of limited performance or possible configuration conflicts.

If you have decided to upgrade several items, you should add or upgrade only one feature or component at a time. This prevents you from creating conflicts, ensures that each new device functions properly with your present system, and avoids any confusion that could be caused by trying to deal with multiple configuration issues at the same time.

You will find it beneficial to test each individual upgrade item separately to be sure each works with your system. Then, add each consecutive item back until all of them are in place and working together.

Save Plug and Play upgrade items for last in a multiple upgrade situation, and again, add only one device at a time. This will allow the PnP items to configure themselves around the non-PnP and other PnP items. This one-at-a-time method also allows you to control some of the variables of the PC and operating system's Plug and Play functions.

Note

This is our first big hint towards preventing ar ing any device conflict, especially those with ____ ᴾlay devices. While conflicts are not typical with ᴾnP devices, how they become configured – to what resources they are assigned – is greatly affected by what device is installed and set up first.

Out of the Box

Most new PC systems sold today come equipped with the basic features and software that we will need to get started in computing. These include display, data storage, some facility for a mouse or pointing device, and access to communications features. These are provided with common I/O ports and default settings that work in almost every system for most of the common applications software. If you buy a complete new system, these features are expected to exist and work properly. A typical configuration you might expect to find is listed in Table 3-4.

Table 3-4 *Resources Used in a Typical Basic System Configuration*

Device	Address	IRQ	DMA	BIOS Location
Serial port/COM1:	3F8h	4		
Serial port/COM2:	2F8h	3		
Parallel port/LPT1:	378h	7		
Diskette drives	3F0h	6	2	
Hard drive (IDE)	1F0h	14		C:8000–C:FFFFh (32K)
PS/2-Mouse port	64h	12		
VGA video	3B0–3BBh, 3C0–3DFh			C:0000–C7FFFh (32K)
Internal use (BIOS)	No hardware address	0, 1	0, 2, 4	F:0000–F:FFFFh (64K)
NPU (Numeric Processing Unit)	No hardware address	13		

Based on the resource allocations listed in Chapter 2, this basic configuration leaves quite a few system resources available for expansion, shown in Table 3-5.

Table 3-5 *Remaining System Resources Available for Expansion Use*

Resource Type	Resource Units
Addresses	130h, 140h, 280h, 2A0h, 300h, 320h, 330h, 340h, 360h
IRQs	2, 5, 9, 10, 11, 12, 15
DMA Channels	1, 3, 5, 6, 7

Note

Table 3-5 was derived by subtracting the already assigned resources in Table 3-4 from the total of all available types of resources. This process of elimination, and tracking what's used and what's not, is key in configuration management. You will probably want to keep a list of these items handy as you work with your PC's configuration, rather than doing the work in your head. Unfortunately, most system information software that you might use to detect resources will indeed only report what is in use most of the time, but not what is left available.

Getting Ready to Upgrade

The lure of virtual travel to exotic places through new e-mail pen pals, the sights and sounds of innovative World Wide Web pages, exciting multimedia CD-ROM offerings, and games can be resisted no longer. We've decided to upgrade, and we're going to do it all at once, since we'll have the covers off and the wires exposed.

Hmm, inside this system doesn't look like it's going to provide us with a scenic coastal drive; it's more like an endless, narrow, twisty mountain road, or some fourteen-car freeway pile-up. Still, we'll drive on and see where this search for adventure takes us.

Let's start with the configuration of some common devices as they are taken out of their boxes. The first step is to list the system resources these devices are set up to use before we fiddle with installation programs, switches, and jumpers. If we upgrade this system by installing as many new devices as we can think of, our initial new configuration might begin to look like Table 3-6 (minus what's already in the system).

Table 3-6 *The Default Resources for Common Upgrade Devices*

Device	Address	IRQ	DMA	BIOS Location
Serial port/COM3:	3E8h	4		
Serial port/COM4:	2E8h	3		
Parallel port/LPT2:	278h	5		
SCSI adapter	330h	11	5	D:8000–D:FFFFh (32K)
Sound card	220h	5	1	
MIDI port	388h			
Network card	300h	3	3	

If we overlay Table 3-6 with the details of the original configuration (Table 3-4), we see some conflicts already, as shown in Table 3-7. Conflicts or duplications are indicated with an asterisk (*).

Table 3-7 *The Upgraded Configuration Before Resolving Conflicts*

Device	Address	IRQ	DMA	BIOS Location
Serial port/COM1:	3F8h	4 *		
Serial port/COM2:	2F8h	3 *		
Serial port/COM3:	3E8h	4 *		
Serial port/COM4:	2E8h	3 *		
Parallel port/LPT1:	378h	7		
Parallel port/LPT2:	278h	5 *		
Diskette drives	3F0h	6	2	
Secondary diskette or tape drive adapters	370h	6	2	
Hard drive (IDE)	1F0h	14		C:8000–C:FFFFh (32K)

Continued

Table 3-7 *Continued*

Device	Address	IRQ	DMA	BIOS Location
PS/2-Mouse port	64h	12		
VGA video				C:000–C:7FFFh (32K)
SCSI adapter	330h	11	5	D:8000–D:FFFFh (32K)
Sound card	220h	5 *	1	
MIDI port	388h			
Network card	300h	3 *	3	
Internal to system		0, 1	0, 2, 4	F:0000–F:FFFFh (64K)
Reserved (NPU)		13		

After a quick review, two conflicts should be quite obvious: The new network card is trying to use IRQ 3 with COM2:/COM4:; and the new sound card is trying to use IRQ 5 which LPT2: is using. Deciding which device gets to keep its assignment and which one must change is first determined by knowing what the rules are. Then, resolving these conflicts is relatively easy.

I've flagged, but do not consider there to be a real conflict (yet), between COM1/COM3 and COM3/COM4, because this is a given according to the rules. As we saw earlier in this chapter, IRQ 3 is designed to be assigned to both COM2: and COM4:. While this can be a conflict in itself, we must first adhere to the original standard. This means that the COM ports retain the IRQ 3 assignment and the network card must be given a new assignment.

Our First Conflict Solved

Which IRQ we assign to the network card depends a great deal on how many different ways we can configure this card. If it is a 16-bit network card that provides the options of using IRQ 2, 3, 4, 5, 7, 9, 10, or 11, we should opt for one of the other available IRQ settings. Obviously it should not be 4, 5, 7, or 11 because the COM ports, LPT ports, sound card, and SCSI host adapter are already using these. The obvious choice for a fully configurable network card seems to be IRQ 10. If the card is an 8-bit card, usually only

IRQs 2, 3, 4, or 5 would be available, so IRQ 2 would be the only choice, so far.

Note

Check the type of network card you have carefully. If it is NE2000-compatible, and Windows 95 or 98 detects it and assigns an NE2000 driver to it, then you can be limited to the resources allowed according to the NE2000 specification. This is not much of a problem if the card comes with its own driver that allows it to use the full range of available addresses and IRQs.

But there is more to consider in this choice. In a 16-bit system, IRQ 2 receives all of the interrupt activity from the second interrupt controller, and it is recommended that a device that would normally use IRQ 2 be moved instead to IRQ 9. Since you can't get access to IRQ 9 with an 8-bit card (the connection is simply not there), IRQ 2 will have to be assigned to and share any use of IRQ 9. This will work only if your applications can properly discriminate between which hardware uses IRQ 2 and which uses IRQ 9. The only way you'll know may be to set up the configuration using both IRQs, use the software for the devices that use IRQs 2 and 9, and see if any problems arise. If either of the applications does not work properly, you will have to reconfigure one of the devices to use a different IRQ. This is one case where some configurations that should be allowed are not adequately supported by application programs. The detection and resolution of such problems is by trial and error. Of course, we're trying to prevent trial-and-error configuration processes, and can very often do so.

Our Second Conflict Solved

Going on, we'll resolve the IRQ 5 issue between the LPT2: port and the sound card. There is a little-known consideration to bring up at this point: Most applications that support LPT port functions (printing) do not have any provision for or ability to use the IRQ. Those that do use IRQs during print operations would be said to provide interrupt-driven printer handling — for example, the remote print server application (RPRINTER) for Novell NetWare and the interrupt-driven printing option for OS/2 Warp. (Unlike earlier versions of OS/2, Warp requires an IRQ for LPT port functions only if you have added the /IRQ option to the DEVICE=PRINT01.SYS line in your OS/2 CONFIG.SYS file.)

Since we are probably not dealing with a NetWare server or print server here, or at least not one with a sound card, and with the rarity of interrupt-driven printing in mind, we could keep the sound card on IRQ 5 and move on. However, there are other uses for the parallel port to consider. Applications such as Traveling Software's LapLink that provide high-speed system-to-system file transfer features can use specific interrupts; and there are parallel-port connected network adapters and external SCSI host adapters we might use sometime. Programs that use the parallel port with these options might need the IRQ signal intended for the parallel (LPT) port. You might also have to assign a DMA channel for some applications that use Enhanced Parallel Port (EPP) functions.

We'd prefer a really "clean" system configuration to avoid problems later on, but we might not always get it. As with the network card example, if the sound card is a 16-bit device, it should allow us access to IRQ lines 2, 9, 10, and 11, and possibly others. Early cards allowed only the choice of 2, 5, or 7. Because IRQs 5 and 7 are assigned to LPT ports, we could use IRQ 2 if it doesn't have to be assigned to the network card. Under the most ideal circumstances, and if the card or the drivers for the operating system allow for it, all these choices would be great. Unfortunately, in one case or another, we may run into limitations outside of our control. While I could probably use IRQ 2 or 9, Creative Labs' Sound Blaster and compatible cards seem to prefer IRQ 5, and many Windows 95/98 drivers for these cards do not allow the use of any other IRQ assignment, so we'll stick with this non-standard convention. This conflict is resolved more by reason and understanding our present needs and applications than by hard-and-fast rules.

Note

If you're lucky enough to be able to use network/server-based printing, perhaps you only need the one LPT port (LPT1: at 378h using IRQ 7) for all your external peripheral needs and the sound card can continue to use IRQ 5, as in our example.

We're already beginning to encounter decisions and trade-offs in what types of things we are currently or might be using our computer for. Weigh the options and consider carefully. We'll leave the sound card at IRQ_5, a typical default, and chance that LPT2 will not use the interrupt. The resulting configuration appears in Table 3-8.

Table 3-8 *The Upgraded Configuration After Resolving Conflicts*

Device	Address	IRQ	DMA	BIOS Location
Serial port/COM1:	3F8h	4		
Serial port/COM2:	2F8h	3		
Serial port/COM3:	3E8h	4		
Serial port/COM4:	2E8h	3		
Parallel port/LPT1:	378h	7		
Parallel port/LPT2:	278h	5		
Diskette drives	3F0h	6	2	
Hard drive (IDE)	1F0h	14		C:8000–C:FFFFh (32K)
PS/2-Mouse port	64h	12		
VGA video				C:0000–C:7FFFh (32K)
SCSI adapter	330h	11	5	D:8000–D:FFFFh (32K)
Sound card	220h	5	1	
MIDI port	388h			
Network card	280h	10		
Internal to system		0, 1	0, 2, 4	F:0000–F:FFFFh (64K)
Reserved (NPU)		13		

Well, this new upgraded configuration looks pretty good. Everything has a workable assignment — or does it? What about the COM ports sharing IRQs 3 and 4? Is there any way to resolve this potential problem?

In most cases, not all of the COM ports are used at the same time. If we have, in the past, used some COM ports at the same time we were using other COM ports, we've probably encountered some lockups, slow performance, scrambled e-mail messages onscreen, or loss of data. Typically, if you have a mouse or other pointing device that uses a serial port, it is connected to COM1:.

Using Multiple COM Ports

You may have a need to use COM3: or COM4: at the same time as COM1: or COM2:. This situation will normally create an IRQ conflict between COM1: and COM3: or between COM2: and COM4:, since they occupy (but do not really share) the same IRQs.

A workaround might be to take advantage of the possibility that the LPT ports might not need to use the IRQs assigned to them. (DOS and Windows don't; OS/2 and a Novell network server provide the option to do so or not.) This would give us IRQs 5 and 7 to work with. This will work only if the software to be used with COM3: and COM4: can be reconfigured to allow the use of IRQs 5 and 7 respectively. As well, the I/O device provides switch or jumper settings so you can set the device for either of these non-standard (for COM ports) IRQs. Many new add-in COM port boards offer more IRQs to choose from — 2, 3, 4, 5, 7, 9, 10, 11, and 12 — so we may not be stuck with compromising on only 5 and 7, especially if IRQ 5 is in use by your sound card, as is quite common.

If you need to use two COM ports, your mouse is on either COM1: or COM2:, and if you have a PS/2-style mouse connection on your system, change your mouse to one with a PS/2-style connection to free up the COM port you are using now. Some pointing devices come with or can use a special adapter cable to convert them from a serial port connection to a PS/2-style connection.

There aren't many easy options for using multiple COM ports no matter how you look at it. Usually something in the configuration has to give, either in hardware or in software.

Plug and Play Enters the Fray

Furthering our quest for more, faster, and better, we've decided to (or had to because of a failure) swap our network card for a newer model, decided to upgrade the old sound card to a fancier version, and add a CD-ROM writer to the system. To make it all even more interesting, our system board is fully Plug and Play compatible, including the built-in hard drive adapter, and everything we're adding or upgrading with is also PnP-compatible. And of course, we're using Windows 95 or 98.

This sounds great, doesn't it? All we have to do is remove the old boards, forget the address, IRQ, and DMA mess, plug in the new devices and off we go.

What happened?

First, let's not toss out everything old and toss in everything new all at once. Following this principle, a good question to ask is "Exactly what do we want to change or add first?" Tough choice, huh?

A tactic that has been successful for me is to consider each device in the order I want resources assigned, or that I will eventually assign them, since Plug and Play will try to fit devices into available resources in somewhat as-available or perhaps even numerical order. This gives us a little more control over Plug and Play's "crap shoot" process. If we can assert and nail down a desirable configuration for each device, one at a time, the variables tend to fall by the wayside.

Upgrading to a PnP Sound Card

In this case, the sound card seems to be the first device we'd want to change. Not only does it use lower-numbered IRQs, it can also use more resources than any other single device, since it probably supports MIDI as well as WAV operations.

Having removed our old sound card before putting in the new, initially PnP may find IRQs 9, 11, 12, and maybe 15 available and try to assign one of these to the card. We may or may not get the IRQ 9 assignment we used before. Fear not; Windows 95 and 98 will let us reconfigure this if we want, and with the other devices coming along, we probably do.

When your system boots up after installing the new sound card, you may or may not see messages appearing onscreen that indicate the presence of the new card, and/or an ESCD update message with some PnP device information listed. Whether this information is displayed or not depends entirely on your system's BIOS. Systems from IBM, COMPAQ, and Hewlett-Packard do not display this information. Generic or clone system BIOS, such as that from Award, often will show the information. For COMPAQ systems, you can access the information in the system's built-in Setup program (later model systems with diagnostic boot sections of the disk anyway). Hewlett-Packard systems usually require that a special Setup program disk be used to work on the system's setup.

Once Windows 95 or 98 starts up, it will probably flash up a dialog box indicating that it has detected new hardware, perhaps is even removing old hardware from the configuration, and may require you to restart the system to enable it. If all goes well, your system will start up properly and you'll have sound still/again. If not (or in any case), we probably want to see what our new configuration is.

To see what's what, we need to get into the Plug and Play Configuration Manager portion of Windows 95/98, otherwise known as the Device Manager. To do this, find the Control Panel, either through the My Computer desktop icon or the Start Menu ⇨ Settings selection, and open it. Once the Control Panel is open, double-click System. You'll see four tabs across the top of the dialog box, one of which is the Device Manager. Click this tab and then you'll see a list of all the devices in your system, from a somewhat high level.

Locate the Sound, video, and game controllers listing and double-click it, or click the + sign next to it. This will reveal the various types of devices contained on your new sound card. Our concern here is for the WAV or perhaps Sound Blaster-compatible device in this sublisting. Double-click it and you'll get a new General

Information dialog box with more tabs at the top. Select the Resources tab.

In this case we got lucky; our sound card ended up configured just the way we wanted it to be, or perhaps, as much as the driver would let it be (address 220h, IRQ 5, DMA 1). Attempts to change any of these values manually (by unchecking the Use automatic settings configuration box and double-clicking the resource name we want to change) results in a message box telling us that these values can't be changed. Plug and Play didn't help us much here. Both the device and the driver limited our ability to work on the configuration.

It's probably a good thing we chose this device first or another device might have taken the only resources that this card could use, although PnP is also supposed to check to see if a device in question can be changed, and if not, move other devices around to accommodate the unchangeable device.

Upgrading to a PnP Network Card

Moving right along, the next existing device we have to upgrade would be the network card. I'd select this device rather than the new CD-ROM device, because we also know that this type of device does work in our system and with what resources.

Beware of a very important factor with this upgrade. If you are changing from a generic/NE2000-style card to something completely different, all of your networking parameters will have to be reentered for the new card (network number, workgroup, IP address, DNS, gateway/router information, and so on). If changing from one style (non-PnP) to a new style (PnP) but not changing the card make/model/type, the new card must be configured to use the same resources as the original; then, usually, the network parameters do not have to change. Still, you should have all of this information written down, copied from the appropriate Network dialog box — usually the one for the TCP/IP protocol, shown in Figure 3-3.

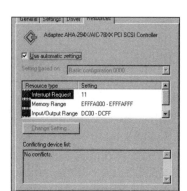

Figure 3-3 *A typical Windows 95/98 TCP/IP Network Configuration dialog box*

Once you've determined and logged the network information you need to retain for possible reentry after the network card upgrade, we can proceed.

Having shut the system down, removed the old card, replaced it with the new card, and begun to restart your system, you might again see PnP and ESCD update information appearing on your screen. Windows 95 or 98 will likely indicate that it has found new hardware, and needs to restart, or not. After this we can go back to the Device Manager, locate the Network card listing and see our results, as shown in Figure 3-4.

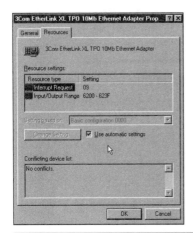

Figure 3-4 *Device Manager showing network adapter resources*

Do you notice anything unusual about this figure? Well, yeah, the IRQ is set to 9, but we'll fix that. How about the I/O address? 6200–623Fh? This one happens to be a PCI network adapter card, and as such it uses a completely different address and data bus than our previous legacy device. We needn't worry about the address, but I really prefer that the network adapter have its own IRQ (10), rather than possibly sharing as IRQ 9 does with IRQ 2. So, can we change this, and if so, how?

In most cases you can uncheck Use automatic settings, select the attribute/resource to be changed, and select Change Setting or double-click the resource to be changed. You are then presented with a dialog box containing the resource and controls to raise or lower the value indicated. If your system, the device driver, or device does not enable the settings to be modified, you will see a message box telling you so. In these cases, you may need to run the configuration utility specific to that device to affect a resource change.

Sometimes you have no choice, and no opportunity to intervene in the Plug and Play process. This can become a real problem if you elect to install a non-PnP device with limited resource configuration ability, or a PnP device that is stubborn about its configuration, once your existing system is all set up and working fine.

The section about Plug and Play losing its mind will give you the good news and the bad news.

Adding a SCSI Host Adapter

Finally, we'll add our SCSI host adapter, as a typical interface for many document scanners and writeable CD-ROM drives. Here again, Plug and Play has established the configuration for us, though we may wish to intervene and set the configuration manually if we have preferences and if the system allows us to do so. Our resulting SCSI configuration as shown in Figure 3-5 cannot be changed, but PnP has found and set nonconflicting resources for us.

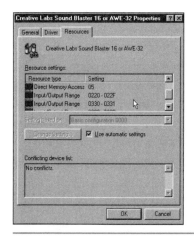

Figure 3-5 *Device Manager showing SCSI host adapter resources*

When Plug and Play Loses Its Mind

If for some reason your system crashes, or you played with some Plug and Play utility, a virus gets you, whatever, and things are really messed up, you may have to drop back a few yards and start your system configuration over again.

This would mean stripping the system of all devices not critical to booting the system up (for example, leaving the video and disk adapters in the system and enabled), then restarting to let the BIOS,

PnP, and Windows 95/98 reset themselves with a basic system configuration. PnP will then forget about the other devices that are no longer there. Windows 95 or 98 will probably complain about one device or the other that it knew it had but can't find anymore, but it should run.

Once this basic configuration is reestablished, you can then begin to reinstall your modem, network, sound card, CD-ROM, scanner, and other adapters, in some order.

The order in which you reinstall devices may be determined by chance, by previously known behavior, or configuration limitation of the device. If you have legacy/ISA devices such as COM ports or modems that ought to be accounted for first, that's probably the place you should start.

If your COM ports are built into the system board and already configured with the new startup, then you would start installing other devices by the order in which you want IRQs assigned to them so that they get proper or desired IRQ priority handling when they run. Ultimately you may reinstall the devices in the order in which you need them to go to the next step. It might make more sense to install a CD-ROM adapter card (or your sound card if it hosts the CD-ROM interface) if you'll need the CD-ROM to be available to reinstall networking or other drivers. Otherwise, you may need to have the network interface available first if you download drivers from a local server or off the World Wide Web through your local area network.

If you're looking for logic and reason from Plug and Play here, you probably won't find any other than that which you impart on the system yourself.

If you are lucky enough to have a system and devices that allow you to use Set Configuration Manually through the Device Manager in Windows 95/98, or another similar function in another operating system, I have a trick for you. My technique for fooling Plug and Play is a little like that kid's game in which you have 15 numbered and moveable square pieces in a frame sized for 4×4 squares. You have to move other pieces to make room for or navigate still more pieces to get the right openings in the right places and the right pieces in the right places. OK, so you may think of this to be a little more like the Rubik's Cube toy; it can be that mind-boggling.

Because I prefer my systems to have a predictable and known assignment for IRQs and such, I have to look into each device's Resources tab under Device Manager ⇨ <device> to see what is where, thus giving me an idea of what resources are unused and available. This way, I can change one or more devices to get the desired affect.

If my network card is currently on IRQ 9 and I want it on IRQ 10, but my video card has IRQ 10, I'd probably look to see if I could move the video card to IRQ 15 (if it's not in use). Then I'd move the network card to IRQ 10. Since IRQ 15 might be used later for the second IDE disk drive interface, I'd probably go back to the video card Resources tab and change the video card to use IRQ 9 instead. Windows 95/98 will update the PnP data and in most cases will let me continue to use the system without a restart.

Thus, I've deliberately affected my configuration to suit what I want it to be, rather than leaving it any more up to chance than necessary.

The successive process of one-device-at-a-time may look a lot like what you'd try to do for resolving conflicts with legacy/ISA devices or basic system troubleshooting. Again, we've come a long way to get to about the same place that we started at.

What to Expect from a New Operating System

Software marketing departments, the press, and users have been anticipating the direction computer owners would turn for a higher-performance operating system and interface environment. The old 8- and 16-bit DOS we've been using since 1981 has been enhanced and stretched to its limits with a variety of utilities and user interfaces.

All of the DOS add-ons to date have had to maintain a firm grasp on compatibility with the DOS file systems and other system- and software-related I/O functions so that the same software and files could be shared with older, slower 8- and 16-bit PCs. This may not be true much longer. Because you can't buy a new 8- or 16-bit PC any more, and we demand higher-speed everything, the only choice is to make a transition into operating systems that make use of the power and speed available in 32-bit PC systems.

For the most part, PC-based operating systems still strive to maintain file-system compatibility with good old DOS, just to keep things simple for the time being. With FAT32 (Microsoft's optional new file system definition to use larger drives more efficiently) and NTFS (Windows NT File System, a completely different and faster disk file tracking system available only with NT), things are sure to change fairly soon.

We have also come to expect that systems be easier to set up, easier to use, and easier to fix or upgrade. As you might expect, "easier" should also apply to our pocketbooks. We should be able to enjoy greater productivity at lower cost, and now our demands are finally being met.

We've had access to the UNIX operating system for years and still will. UNIX is very powerful and works on more types of computers than any other operating system, but it is also very costly and complex to implement and use. There are many attractive and effective graphical user interfaces for UNIX, but they have been costly and complex. Even though UNIX is almost universal across various hardware platforms, it had until now never been designed, packaged, or supported for use by the general public. Yet we've wanted to be able to use something with the high-performance, multitasking, interconnection features of an operating system like UNIX.

You can buy LINUX (a UNIX-clone operating system) with a bunch of great little utilities in one or the other how-to books for about $40 in nearly any bookstore in the country. The LINUX support community at large has been making great strides in producing this "Joe Average"-can-run, setup-and-go version. LINUX may not yet support as much hardware as Windows 95, 98, or NT, nor run as much software as Windows, but LINUX is making UNIX more accessible to the general public.

Yes, I've built a LINUX system and got it running on my network. I hope to do more with it soon. I've used Sun OS, Ultrix, and a smattering of Solaris. But my available learning curve time versus my need to be productive, as well as that of millions of others, keeps many of us bound in Microsoft-land for mainstream operations.

The problems we have with PC configurations are not bound to the operating system. The x86 hardware devices and their problems are here to stay awhile longer. When I can create a Word document on a UNIX-based or like system to share with my PC and Mac friends, the world will truly be a lot better off. Still, an x86-based UNIX or LINUX system requires a proper configuration, just like everything else.

At one time, Microsoft and IBM were codeveloping the operating system that became IBM's release of OS/2. Due to a variety of competitive and business differences, Microsoft left OS/2 for IBM to develop by itself while Microsoft pursued a higher-performance variation of Windows, which became known as NT, for new technology. Thus, the user market already struggling with the differences in system performance, and the tentative shift to using Windows, had to wait a little longer for Windows NT and/or OS/2 to come on the market and be competitive. Unfortunately OS/2 lost its edge in the marketplace with insufficient stability or applications, and NT is still too expensive for most of us to use as an everyday desktop OS. There are also other concerns about backward compatibility with older DOS programs, especially graphical ones like games and scientific/engineering programs.

Windows NT gained popularity and was implemented on a large number of various platforms and user systems in very special, limited environments. Versions of NT were developed for systems other than x86-compatibles — such as the PowerPC — as a power-user's operating system. OS/2 made it to market and stuttered along mostly in IBM-supported corporate environments until version 2.0 was stable enough for power users to buy and try. Even though IBM made it to market first with a 32-bit operating system that users could afford and work with easily (OS/2), the majority of PC users have a significant investment in Windows and have decided to bet on Microsoft.

By the time Microsoft gave us our first glimpses at test versions at what finally became Windows 95, IBM had put enough polish and support behind OS/2 upgrades to release version 3.0 as the first 32-bit operating system for the average user. Many of us have enjoyed full-time use of OS/2 while running side-by-side comparison tests with Windows 95. There are some tremendous similarities in the two systems' improvements in ease of installation, use, and performance versus DOS and Windows 3.*x*. Also, these operating systems share certain system configuration requirements and precautions before they can be beneficial to the general user market.

We still see many places using DOS and Windows 3.*x*. Lingering Windows 3.*x* users may have meager or no networking requirements, or simply do not have a compelling reason or the budget to upgrade their 386 or 486 systems to handle 95, 98, or NT adequately.

Many corporations have not yet upgraded from Windows 95 to 98. Many of them may not. For them the relative improvements in a "point upgrade" (Windows 4.0 to 4.1) are not worth the costs involved to do so. They may also have other time and budget priorities — year 2000 compliance, new business applications systems — or they will now wait until Windows 2000. For a personal user, upgrading an operating system may seem significant in terms of cost or time. In contrast, upgrading an entire corporation worth of PCs, whether it's 100, or 10,000 systems, is *very* costly.

Only recently have we had to factor in the cost of major overhauls of hundreds of desktop computer systems — versus upgrading a mainframe system or two as in the old days. We've now come to expect that a new PC system is satisfactory in performance, capabilities, and features for fewer than 3 years. Five years ago no one had to think of whether or not a DEC VT-100 or IBM 3270 terminal unit had adequate features compared to a new model over a 5–10 year equipment lifespan. There were no new models or features as far as the user's terminal were concerned. The features were dictated by mini- and mainframe computer systems far from the user's desktop. OK, so the features of an old VAX or System 90 still haven't changed much, but now every CxO, VP, director, and manager absolutely *needs* to be able to mix mainframe data with new UNIX or NT based SQL data and have it presented on the corporate Intranet. Every corporate level software vendor seems to require that every user that is the recipient of reported data have a 350MHz Pentium-II with 128MB of RAM and a GB hard drive in order to run their own special data reporting tool. This ought to be hogwash if they'd make tools to produce data reports accessible through Web browsers — but that's another discussion.

The logical corporate upgrade path, for current systems and ever more important security reasons, is to Windows NT. NT may not share the same security confidence as most UNIX systems, but it is a far cry better than Windows 3.*x*, 95, or 98 when it comes to keeping most casual lurkers out of individual workstations. As more attention is drawn to security and privacy issues, NT will be the operating system of choice for many of us in the short to mid-term future. In a year or so, this choice may be inevitable if Microsoft truly does abandon the current Windows 95/98 consumer path. No matter — a system is only as good or stable as the hardware it starts with and the operating system support it has.

IBM's OS/2 Warp

Not to give IBM's impressive new operating system a bad name, but in my experience, OS/2 Warp can be incredibly unforgiving if the system hardware and configuration details are not set up properly. The cryptic, numbered error messages you might receive are unfriendly, poorly documented, and generally not the least bit helpful to you in terms of correcting problems.

Warp comes with a System Information Tool, but this is not normally installed unless you specifically select it at installation time. If you forget to install this tool, when you can't get the new operating system to run, you can't get to the tools that might be able to help you solve the problem.

If you have a problem with Warp, go back to DOS, check your configuration, correct any problems found so that your system has no IRQ , DMA, or address conflicts, and start over. An easy Warp installation can take up to an hour of your time if all goes well. A problem-ridden Warp installation may never succeed, consuming entire evenings or days if you let it.

Windows 95, 98, and NT

Windows 95, 98, and NT are impressive and almost fun to experience, even during the installation process. With over three years of tinkering with and using Windows 95 and, recently, about a year's worth of tinkering with Windows 98, I'm still disappointed in one thing — while you can save many personalized configuration items here, you can't save some other critical system settings. For instance, personal desktop preferences are not stored apart from the entire installation, which might allow Windows 95 to ignore bad system/hardware configuration data and let you do a clean reinstallation if something gets confused.

On most systems the installation is remarkably smooth, trouble-free, and reliable for a long time. On still others, owing either to Plug and Play, system board chip set, memory, or peripheral issues, Windows 95 has been a virtual "dog" to install or maintain. The name brand, cost, or perceived quality of a system does not seem to matter in this regard. I have home-built clones that have been trouble-free and high-end commercial systems that have consumed too many days of my time to get working right. Some say they've had bad experiences upgrading to Windows 98 as well, and I believe this to be for similar reasons that Windows 95 was problematic for some:

- Basic configuration issues (of course I'd say that)
- Lack of support for the operating system by hardware vendors
- Lack of support for various hardware items on the part of Microsoft

How can you tell before you start if you will have installation or maintenance problems with Windows 95 or 98 on your system? From the outside, or looking to the inside, you probably can't tell.

My suggestion is to check out the Web sites and online forums for your system's manufacturer to see what the presence of various FAQ (frequently asked questions) lists, bug fixes, README, and patch files can tell you.

Windows 98 was reputed by reviewers to have had numerous problems with video drivers. I would speculate that this is because Microsoft has encouraged vendors to incorporate the Windows Driver Model, as used in Windows NT, in their Windows 98 device drivers.

The differences between Windows 95, 98, and NT in this and other regards might be obvious, or not. Windows NT was a much further developed 32-bit operating system than Windows 95. Windows 95 and 98 both must use DOS as a starting foundation, maintain full compatibility with most DOS and Windows 3.*x* applications, and support 32-bit applications at the same time, under the same boot and run conditions.

Windows NT is admittedly more complex, and in the current release (4.0) does not fully support Plug and Play. However, this support should appear in Windows 2000. When installed and running, Windows 98 and NT are both quite stable and perform very well.

Note

This all makes for considerable complexity and provides many opportunities for failure, either by hardware or memory conflict. As easy and forgiving as some aspects of Windows 95, 98, and NT are, they too will consume an hour of your time to install, or a day if things don't go well because of a bad system configuration or lack of device support. In any case, be prepared – you have the resources in hand to make it all work.

Summary

This chapter has taken on a lot of diverse topics in an attempt to put the PC configuration rules and upgrade concerns into the integrated perspective of typical upgrades.

What I've discussed should serve as a model for the many considerations that are encountered with most systems. It is unlikely that too many systems will differ from the examples. Many systems will benefit significantly from duplicating the configuration as shown.

With the background information about the design of PC systems, a set of rules and examples, and these quick hints, you should have eliminated the most common system conflicts and have a really clean and functional system configuration with which to go forward.

Chapter 4

Configuration Management: What It Is and How to Do It

IN THIS CHAPTER:

- Why manage your PC's configuration
- Taking inventory
- Gathering system information
- Backing up your configuration
- Making and recording configuration changes

Configuration management is the process of planning, implementing, organizing, and even changing a variety of factors that affect the hardware and software in your system. Simply put, it is keeping track of what is in your system — what changes have been made, and why, so the changes can be undone, if necessary — all while trying to keep your system running smoothly. As we've seen in Chapters 1, 2, and 3, there are a lot of details to be taken care of within a PC.

Establishing your initial system configuration usually occurs at the time your PC is designed and built, by a manufacturer or yourself. Managing the configuration begins with the person who installs the system and sets it up for use. The process involves detailed information about every aspect of your system: the installed hardware, the system setup values (also known as the CMOS setup), disk partitioning and formatting, and the operating system and applications software. Through these steps we can discover, resolve, and prevent system conflicts.

Properly managing your system configuration is done (or is often left undone) every time a change is made to your system setup. This could mean editing the DOS CONFIG.SYS file or AUTOEXEC.BAT file, editing any of your batch, INI, or device parameter files, or modifying the Windows Registry.

If changes are made to your hardware by adding or removing an option card, memory, cache chips, or CPU, or by changing the address on a network or other card, you are dealing with the details of your system configuration. Some of these details will concern the address, IRQ, or DMA assignments for one or more hardware devices. With Plug and Play, the system BIOS and operating system try to help you manage the configuration automatically. This process may or may not work correctly; it varies by system BIOS and device type.

Other details involve device drivers, either generic or vendor-specific, which are somewhat outside the scope of this book. What you do to keep track of these details sets the level of configuration management you practice with your system.

Why Manage Your PC's Configuration

Configuration management is important to anyone using or supporting a PC system. It is critical to all end users who want a reliable, stable, properly functioning PC system — whether you maintain the system yourself or rely on others to do so for you. It is especially critical when more than one PC system or group of support people is involved, as in an office or corporation.

Some of the more significant benefits of configuration management are:

- Reliability
- Easier servicing
- Loss prevention (equipment auditing and tracking)
- Equipment amortization and tax purposes
- Software licensing and copyright compliance

Your goal may be as simple as getting all of the components in your system to operate together correctly with stability and maintainability. Some software installations alter your configuration files or the settings of your modem, video card, or software-configured devices, and this changes the way things worked before. You should also see benefits in ensuring that you can reconstruct your system and get back to work efficiently in case something fails or becomes corrupt. This is known as recoverability.

Stability, maintainability, and recoverability are three important issues for any user. If you share your system with other users, or if someone else is responsible for maintaining your system with or without your presence or immediate awareness, I cannot overemphasize the importance of stability and recoverability.

If you have dozens or hundreds of PCs in a workgroup or corporation, getting and keeping them all the same or similar — and at least properly configured and documented — saves a considerable amount of time and money when you need to repair or upgrade one or more systems.

Most PC systems sold today are preconfigured at the factory, but many of us still buy components and build our own systems. Even after obtaining a factory-built system, we find ourselves replacing, adding to, or upgrading one or more system components with off-the-shelf items purchased from the local computer store or by mail order. Replacement components sent by system manufacturers usually need some additional configuration.

Considering that many users and companies will be upgrading to higher-performance components and operating software at some time, it is important to know if existing PC systems are capable of all the tasks required of them, if software or hardware upgrades are warranted, or if they are even possible. If you don't have a handle on the configurations of all of your PCs, implementing the move or operating system upgrade of these systems will either be impossible, or at the least excessively time consuming, while you custom-tailor each system move or upgrade.

For a small 10–30-system office where only a few systems may be used differently than most (and thus likely configured differently to suit a different set of tasks), keeping track may be fairly simple. Maintaining the configuration of hundreds of systems by more than one or two people is a significant task that requires planning, sound procedures, and discipline. The fewer systems you have that perform different functions, with few or no specialized configurations to suit those functions, the easier it is to maintain them.

Fortunately, configuration management for any number of systems consists conceptually of just a few basic procedures. The user considering IBM's OS/2 or Microsoft's Windows 98 or Windows NT will save a lot of time and frustration knowing what components are in the system, how they are configured, whether the system is properly configured, and how to correct configuration problems. This way, any upgrade work can proceed smoothly and successfully.

You should only trust the operating system and applications software so much, within limits, and be able to determine for yourself if it has misidentified or failed to identify a critical component in your system. Even systems running Windows 3.x or plain old DOS can benefit from a properly configured system. You cannot fix a bad configuration by upgrading a DOS or Windows 3.x system to Windows 95, 98, or NT. Often as not, you will not be able to perform the upgrade if the system is misconfigured.

Both the beauty and the curse of PC-compatible systems is that they are so flexible and easily reconfigured by the user. This provides us many opportunities for interesting and unique working situations, and just as many opportunities for things to go wrong. Managing the configuration by locking the covers on the box and write-protecting critical files is one method that has been used, but it does not do enough, especially if the system is locked down in an improper configuration.

System configuration management begins with the steps you take to ensure the integrity and recoverability of the hardware, software, and configuration file items within your system. This includes system inventories and frequent and regular backups. The original configuration should be recorded and saved for future reference.

Then, as you make changes to the system (such as upgrading or adding components), record these changes. With this information, you can trace the changes and reestablish the original configuration, if need be.

Backing Up Configuration-Critical Files

Before any work is done on your system, you should make backup copies of all files applicable to your system configuration. As changes are made to your system, these files may also be changed, and it's possible that one or more configuration changes will fail. Recovering from such failures is much easier if you can go back to a set of configuration files that allowed the system to work properly. These copies may be kept on the system's hard disk, or on a diskette dedicated specifically to this purpose. If you keep these files on a diskette, you should format the diskette to be a bootable (or system) diskette. This makes it easier to access DOS if you encounter problems with your hard disk during reconfiguration. Ideally, you should maintain complete and current backups of all files on your system's hard drives on tapes or diskettes.

The minimum files for which you should keep backups are:

- **CONFIG.SYS** (found in the Root directory of your C: drive)
- **AUTOEXEC.BAT** (found in the Root directory of your C: drive)
- **WIN.INI** (found in your Windows subdirectory)

- **SYSTEM.INI** (found in your Windows subdirectory)
- **PROGMAN.INI** (found in your Windows subdirectory)
- **CONTROL.INI** (found in your Windows subdirectory)
- **SYSTEM.DAT** (for Win95/98/NT, found in your Windows subdirectory)
- **USER.DAT** (for Win95/98/NT, found in your Windows subdirectory)

Include with the CONFIG.SYS and AUTOEXEC.BAT files any device driver or program files that are necessary to boot up and run your system at least at the DOS level.

You may also wish to keep copies of all of your Windows .INI files (those files with the **INI** extension after their filename) and your Windows Program Group files (those with the **GRP** extension after their filename). The INI files are used by Windows and applications to store a variety of configuration information that defines how Windows or its applications appear on screen and function. The GRP files, functional only in Windows 3.*x* and earlier versions, are important to keep around in case you need to reinstall Windows 95/98 and maintain these old groups. GRP files define each of the major folders on your Windows desktop and contain application and file references.

Note

While GRP and INI files maintain compatibility with some older 16-bit (Windows 3.*x*) applications under Windows 95/98 and NT, you should back them up along with all of the new INI files created by Windows 95/98. Much of this old information is moved to and contained in the Registry (SYSTEM.DAT and USER.DAT) and Shortcut (.LNK) files, but if a system crashes, these older files may help you get your system back together faster.

Note

For Windows NT, two files can be critical to system recovery: The file(s) NTUSER.DAT exist under both the `\WINNT\ Profiles\Administrator`, and the `\WINNT\Profiles\ [user name]` sub-directories. The file USER.DMP is in the `\WINNT` directory. These files contain information about the user and system setup information with which the system was last run.

Tip

If you are in a networked environment that uses DOS-based networking software (typically, Windows 3.*x* environments), you may also wish to keep a copy of your network configuration file (typically, NET.CFG) with your backup files so you can recover network protocol and address information. This information may also be stored in yet another (non-Windows) INI file specific to the network software.

Taking Inventory

The most important step you can take is to inventory your system. This includes both a physical inventory and a configuration inventory, covering these items:

- A list of all your hardware items
- A log of how your hardware is configured
- A list of all your software and configuration files
- All of the manuals for your hardware and software stored together in a convenient place
- Hardware-specific software and data files (on their respective diskettes) gathered together

This inventory allows you to establish a baseline indicating the present condition of your system. In the process, you may discover misconfigured items (according to standards or certain rules that apply to PCs).

In multiple-system situations, the system administrator or computer support department may also take inventory where you work. Some of this information can be retrieved automatically during routine system and network maintenance. It is in everyone's best interests to maintain system inventories, for all the reasons stated earlier as well as for network management.

Physical Inventory

A hands-on, physical inventory of your system and system configuration information should be performed when you first buy, unpack, or build your system. You should have a written or data-file record of all the makes, models, versions, serial numbers, descriptions, and technical support numbers of the components in and around your system. This includes everything from the power supply to the mouse, hard drive adapter to sound to multimedia cards. Take a look at your system. You will see components and cabling similar to the items in Figure 4-1.

For your system board and add-in cards, note the numbers printed on any labels attached to the tops of chips or the boards. These numbers likely reflect revisions of BIOS (Basic Input/Output System) for the system, and for SCSI (Small Computer System Interface) host adapters, video adapters, and sound cards (some of these are visible onscreen during system startup, or appear on a label on the boards themselves).

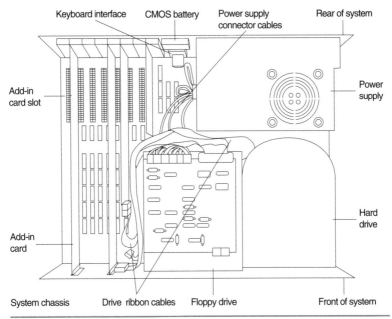

Keyboard interface   CMOS battery   Power supply
                                       connector cables   Rear of system

Add-in
card slot   Power
                                                           supply

Add-in   Hard
card   drive

System chassis   Drive ribbon cables   Floppy drive   Front of system

Figure 4-1 *Your particular system configuration may differ from the AT-style
desktop system shown here, but the general appearance of the
boards, power supply, cables, and disk drives is basically the
same in all systems.*

A typical physical inventory list might look like this:

System Make/Model:	Homemade
System Board:	Clone w/Ali chipset
System BIOS:	AMI for MSI
Power Supply:	250-watt ATX mini-tower style
CPU:	AMD K6-2/350 MHz
RAM:	2 ea. 32M SDRAM DIMMs
Hard Drive Adapter:	On-board IDE disabled, using SCSI
SCSI Adapter:	Adaptec 2940W
Hard Drive:	Quantum Bigfoot 9GB SCSI
CD-ROM:	Pinnacle Micro RCD 4x4 SCSI
Diskette Drives:	Sony 3.5 1.44M
Diskette Controller:	On-board

Video Adapter:	Diamond Viper 550 AGP
Video Monitor:	ADI Microscan 6P USB
Ports:	COM1 (on-board, 2nd port disabled); COM2, (clone add-in w/ 16550 UAR/T)
LPT1 (on-board):	Built-in parallel port
Mouse:	Logitech Trackman Marble PS/2
Network Card:	3Com 3c905 PCI, 10BaseT port
Modem:	USRobotics V.Everything on COM2 Internal Version #: DSP Version #:
Keyboard:	Northgate OmniKey/Plus

 Cross-Reference

You can obtain additional modem-specific information by using software to look inside the modem. A program such as Hank Volpe's Modem Doctor, which is available from many BBSs and online services, or nearly any communications software (or even Windows' HyperTerminal) can be of great help to identify your modem, especially if it is an internal model.

With your communications software offline, running in direct or terminal mode, type the command **AT13[Enter]** and wait for a response, then type **AT17[Enter]**, and the following displays:

```
at13
USRobotics Courier V.Everything
OK
at17
USRobotics Courier V.Everything Configuration Profile...
Product type          US/Canada External
Options               HST,V32bis,Terbo,VFC,V34+,x2,V90
Fax Options           Class 1,Class 2.0
Clock Freq            20.16Mhz
Flash ROM             512k
Ram                   64k
Supervisor date       03/13/98
DSP date              03/13/98
```

```
Supervisor rev        7.3.14
DSP rev               3.0.13
OK
```

The first line after the AT13 command usually returns the modem's model number. The last four lines shown here, not including the OK, are typical pieces of information that the modem manufacturer may ask you for during a support call. Major manufacturers such as Hayes, USRobotics, Supra, Practical Peripherals, Intel, and AT&T provide these internal facilities to help with either manual or automatic identification of modems, which can be very useful during automatic setup of communications and facsimile programs. Clone or no-name white box modems may not be as helpful.

In addition to identifying the various devices in your system, you should also record the settings or positions of the jumpers and switches present on these devices. This is another part of any recovery process you may need to invoke later on if you have to change something to resolve a conflict.

It's also a good idea to clearly label each device and all of its settings. Using a non-conductive, self-adhesive, removable paper label attached directly to the device is an excellent way to keep a convenient and accurate record.

System Information

To properly manage a PC configuration, you need at least three types of information about the devices in your PC. So key are these to configuration management that this book's title is based on them — IRQ, DMA, and I/O.

Let's refresh ourselves with some basic definitions:

- **Interrupt ReQuest (IRQ) assignments**. These are signal lines connected between a variety of devices, both external (through add-in cards) and internal to your system board (containing the central processing unit [CPU] or main computer chip, and the connections for built-in and external devices).

Devices such as the serial (COM) port, keyboard, and hard disk drive, and some internal computer functions use IRQs to signal the computer that an activity on that device needs the CPU's attention to move data or to handle an error situation. Two devices cannot share or use the same IRQ line. Because there is no indication of what device may have generated an IRQ signal, these assignments must be unique, preassigned, and known per device by the operating system and software.

- **Direct Memory Access (DMA) channel assignments**. A DMA channel is a set of two signal lines, one line for DMA request (DRQ) and the other for DMA acknowledgment (DACK). These are assigned in corresponding pairs as simply one DMA assignment to devices that have the ability to exchange data directly with system memory without going through the CPU (many disk drive functions and multimedia cards use DMA to speed data throughput).

  With a DMA channel, a device signals the computer or the CPU signals a device about the need for (or status of) direct access between two devices, one of which is usually system memory. These lines must also be unique and known for each device that uses them.

- **Input/Output (I/0) addresses**. These are numerical representations of actual memory locations. They are used for the data bus (the 8-, 16-, or 32-bit data lines interconnecting devices within the computer) or system RAM memory (from DOS or low memory, through the first 640K of RAM, to the upper memory areas through any and all Extended Memory).

  I/O addresses are used to uniquely identify the places in your system where data and control information can be written to or read from for the interactions between devices, the CPU, and system memory. Each device, such as a serial port or disk drive, is said to occupy a specific address or location in memory. Only data or commands specific to the device that occupies a particular address should be sent to or expected from its location.

You may also need to know the memory location of a particular device's internal BIOS, known as the BIOS address (which may also be referred to as the ROM address or ROM BIOS address). This information is usually standardized, though there can be a lot of variables, typically for SCSI host adapters used to connect disk, tape, scanner, and CD-ROM devices.

If you think technology should take care of itself, that you have no need for the technical details of your system, and that utility tools such as the Norton Utilities are for someone more technical, the time has come to reconsider. Ready or not, you are in the market for some diagnostic or utility software.

Gathering System Information

Gathering the IRQ, DMA, and I/O information you need requires one or more pieces of software for gathering information from your system. It also might entail a closer physical inspection of the hardware to find labels or legend markings, with the manuals for your system and add-in cards as critical references to help you isolate and make note of these items.

Even Microsoft, one of the world's largest software companies, saw the need for a technical information tool to help with software support. In an attempt to fill this need, Microsoft created MSD, the Microsoft Diagnostics. It's intended to be used by any user to give a basic snapshot of generic system hardware by device type (See Figures 4-2 and 4-3). MSD is no longer in wide distribution. Microsoft now relies on the automatic device detection capabilities of Windows 95/98 to figure out what's there, and the Device Manager displays under Control Panel's System applet to tell you what it found.

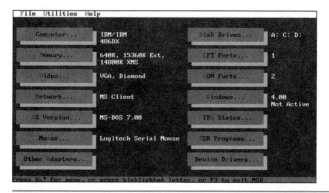

Figure 4-2 *Microsoft's MSD program's basic information screen*

IRQ	Address	Description	Detected	Handled By
0	0B9E:0382	Timer Click	Yes	2PCX.COM
1	0B9E:03DE	Keyboard	Yes	2PCX.COM
2	F000:EF5A	Second 8259A	Yes	BIOS
3	F000:EF5A	COM2: COM4:	COM2:	BIOS
4	F000:EF5A	COM1: COM3:	COM1:	BIOS
5	F000:EF5A	LPT2:	No	BIOS
6	F000:EF57	Floppy Disk	Yes	BIOS
7	0070:0465	LPT1:	Yes	System Area
8	F000:E845	Real-Time Clock	Yes	BIOS
9	F000:E2AD	Redirected IRQ2	Yes	BIOS
10	F000:EF5A	(Reserved)		BIOS
11	F000:EF5A	(Reserved)		BIOS
12	035D:3E8E	(Reserved)		SCSIMGR$
13	F000:FEA8	Math Coprocessor	Yes	BIOS
14	F000:E95C	Fixed Disk	Yes	BIOS
15	F000:EF5A	(Reserved)		BIOS

Figure 4-3 *Microsoft's MSD program's IRQ information screen*

Cross-Reference

MSD is available with many Microsoft product packages, or from online services such as CompuServe and America Online. Microsoft wants you to have this program to make its own technical support life easier. That a software company found itself needing hardware information to support software packages should tell us something about the tremendous universal need for technical information about our PC systems. Unfortunately, as you may discover, MSD is not complete nor entirely accurate in its detection and reporting of system details.

A preconfigured PC system may come with some form of diagnostic, information, or support software. Well-defined hardware add-in kits, such as multimedia adapters and network adapters, embed system information utilities such as these into their installation programs.

Cross-Reference

If your system did not come with diagnostic or utility software, after-market programs such as Symantec/Norton's NDIAGS is available as part of the Norton Utilities. Still others may be found in online system libraries as public domain software or shareware by searching for the terms such as *sysinfo*. These all provide basic configuration information. (See Figure 4-4.)

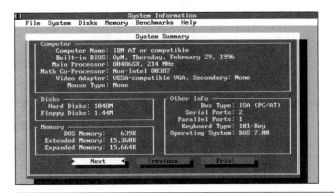

Figure 4-4 *The Norton Utilities system information screen from NDIAGS.EXE*

The complexity of systems and the variety of add-in devices available causes many of the commonly available utilities to miss or simply not provide important details, or they give erroneous or assumed information. You might have to use more than one of these programs to ensure that most or all of the devices in your system are properly detected, and to confirm any possible irregularities.

For a more accurate and complete identification of system hardware and resource usage than many other programs provide, an evaluation copy of Watergate Software's PC-Doctor program for DOS and an IRQ and DMA specific utility (RCR) by Doren Rosenthal are included with this book.

Tip

PC-Doctor is developed and frequently updated in close cooperation with many PC device and system manufacturers, often at their request, for their own uses. This program, accompanied by the specific details in your add-in device manuals and a physical inspection of the hardware, will give you a complete picture of the existing system, and of changes as they are made. (See Figures 4-5 through 4-8.)

```
 Diagnostics    Interactive Tests    Hardware Info    Utility    Quit    F1=Help
╒════════════════════════════╣System Configuration╠════════════════════════════╕
║SYSTEM CONFIGURATION                                                            ║
║                                                                                ║
║    Operating System - DOS 7.0                                                  ║
║             CPU Type - 12 MHz Cyrix 6x86 2X Clock (in Virtual86 mode)          ║
║                CPUID - N/A                                                      ║
║     Coprocessor Type - Cyrix 686 Compatible                                    ║
║    Expansion Bus Type - ISA, PCI                                               ║
║        ROM BIOS Date - 02/29/96                                                ║
║   ROM BIOS Copyright - Copyright (c) 1996                                      ║
║        Additional ROM - C800[32kB] C800[10kB]                                  ║
║         Base Memory - 640 kB                                                   ║
║     Expanded Memory - 15664 kB (Driver Version 4.0)                            ║
║     Extended Memory - 15360 kB (CMOS Configuration)                            ║
║          XMS Memory - 14800 kB (XMS 3.00, Driver 3.5F) A20=ON                  ║
║         Serial Ports - 2 - COM1:3F8 COM2:2F8                                   ║
║       Parallel Ports - 1 - LPT1:378                                            ║
║        Video Adapter - VGA: S3 Incorporated. 86C325                            ║
║    Fixed Disk Drives - 1072 MB                                                 ▼
╘════════════════════════════════════════════════════════════════════════════════╛
 Use ↑ ↓ to move screen. F2 to print. F3 to save to a file. ESC to exit.
```

Figure 4-5 *Watergate Software's PC-Doctor program – the first system information screen*

```
 Diagnostics    Interactive Tests    Hardware Info    Utility    Quit    F1=Help
╒════════════════════════════╣System Configuration╠════════════════════════════╕
║         Serial Ports - 2 - COM1:3F8 COM2:2F8                                   ▲
║       Parallel Ports - 1 - LPT1:378                                            ║
║        Video Adapter - VGA: S3 Incorporated. 86C325                            ║
║    Fixed Disk Drives - 1072 MB                                                 ║
║    Floppy Disk Drives - 1 - 1=3½"/1.44M                                        ║
║             Mouse - No Mouse                                                   ║
║           Joysticks - None                                                     ║
║          Sound Card - N/A                                                      ║
║   CAS Fax/Modem Card - N/A                                                     ║
║     Disk Compression - N/A                                                     ║
║             CD-ROM - MSCDEX V2.25, Drive: D:                                   ║
║           Disk Cache - N/A                                                     ║
║          IDE Drive 0 - (unable to obtain data)                                 ║
║          IDE Drive 1 - (unable to obtain data)                                 ║
║              SCSI - ASPI, Host Adapter: ADAPTEC AIC-7870                       ║
║             Network - N/A                                                      ║
║    Power Management - Not available, or APM driver not loaded                  ║
║                                                                                ▼
╘════════════════════════════════════════════════════════════════════════════════╛
 Use ↑ ↓ to move screen. F2 to print. F3 to save to a file. ESC to exit.
```

Figure 4-6 *Watergate Software's PC-Doctor program – the second system information screen*

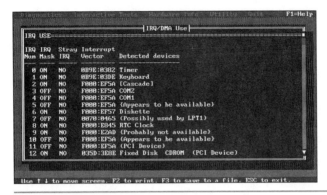

Figure 4-7 *Watergate Software's PC-Doctor program – the first IRQ information screen*

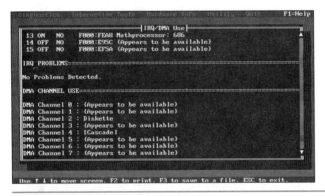

Figure 4-8 *Watergate Software's PC-Doctor program – the second IRQ and DMA information screen*

Any utility or system information program can only report on the presence and configuration of the devices that they are designed to identify (by extensive research). This occurs only if they are functional enough to be identified by any program as existing in your system. You will get a report of the functioning devices that exist and the resources they use. Software cannot report on devices that physically exist but are defective or functionally inactive. Nor can they report conclusively on whether or not a resource is available, unused, or otherwise unoccupied.

Only by process of review and elimination will you be able to summarize the resources (I/O addresses and IRQ and DMA assignments) that remain available to you, but we'll be helping with that process as we go along.

People who support multiple systems will likely use network management-specific tools to perform many of these inventory and tracking functions, but if you are supporting only one system, you can get by with PC-Doctor.

Using at least one of these programs, you should gather and record all of the information you can get about your system. Most programs such as these provide the ability to print the information or store the information in text files on disk. Keep this information with your physical inventory and settings records.

Compare the information you collect with the "rules" and information provided in this book. From this comparison, you will have the information you need to assess your present configuration and correct it if necessary. You will also (by process of elimination) have information about the resources available for any changes you want to make to your system by adding a new hardware feature or converting your system to use Windows 95/98 or OS/2.

Tip

You can gather some information about your system from the initial boot-up screen that appears when your system starts, and from the system's CMOS setup program. During bootup you can press the Pause key to read the screens as they come up. Pressing any key will resume the bootup process. Entering your CMOS setup program varies between systems. Sometimes you are prompted during bootup to press the Del key to enter setup; for other systems you might have to press the F1, F2, F10, or Esc key at just the right time in the bootup process. For still others, you might have to use either a combination of keys such as Ctrl+Alt+S, Ctrl+Alt+Esc, or a special program sent with your system after the system has booted up into DOS.

Caution

The CMOS setup program screens for many systems may contain and allow you to change some very tricky technical settings that are not applicable to the configuration of IRQ, DMA, or I/O addresses for your hardware. Be wary of what you might change, and avoid changing anything until you have analyzed and determined that you need to make configuration changes. Then, do so only for specific I/O devices, as needed.

Recording Changes to Configuration Files

Adding remark or comment lines within the configuration files to highlight and explain the changes is a positive and highly recommended step of configuration management. You will find that many programs that make modifications to your setup files also add their own unique comments for your possible inspection.

Since all of these files are ASCII text files, you can use any basic text editor (one that reads, creates, and saves files in plain ASCII text, without regard for type style or size, justification, and so on) to create, edit, and add comments to them. Under DOS (from version 5.0 on), you can use the DOS EDIT.COM program. Under Windows, you can use the Notepad program, usually found in the Accessories program group.

Caution

Unless you are familiar with them, do not attempt to use programs or tools, or to change files or commands – especially without a backup of a working file. You should be familiar with (or refer to DOS- and Windows-specific documentation) the finer points of text editors, DOS commands, batch files, and command-line structures that are illustrated in this section.

Don't be concerned right now about how the specific command lines used in this section would affect your configuration, they're only examples used to illustrate the process of commenting on changes. Make new backup copies of at least the setup and configuration files on your system, if not your entire hard drive system, before making changes.

Tip

To make a backup of your CONFIG.SYS file, for example, use the DOS COPY command to copy your working CONFIG.SYS file to a similar filename. Pick a filename that is easy to remember, and one that would likely not be overwritten, deleted, or used for another purpose. Using the original filename and a unique extension, such as your initials, usually suffices. For this example, you must be in the root directory (the highest level directory) of your boot drive, assuming that your boot drive is C:. If in doubt, at the DOS prompt type **C: [Enter]**, then type **CD \[Enter]**, and then type **COPY CONFIG.SYS CONFIG.JA [Enter]**, where **.JA** are your initials.

The method for adding comments to your configuration files is very simple. You must provide some form of mark or delimiter at the start of each comment line so that the program reading these files does not confuse comments with actual commands. Typically, this is a REM phrase for CONFIG.SYS and AUTOEXEC.BAT files and a semi-colon (;) for INI files.

Note

You will see that we have used lower case characters to set off the remarks and comments from the typically upper case contents of most DOS and Windows files. In this instance, the case is insignificant to the processing of these files, but you should keep program commands and options in their original case when you edit any of these files. Many programs are case sensitive in their interpretation of command lines.

Comments in the CONFIG.SYS File

Prior to DOS 5.0, there was no provision for comment lines in the CONFIG.SYS file. Every line of CONFIG.SYS was read and taken to be a command line. DOS would try to interpret all of the information and make use of the items it found. Any text that was not a legitimate command caused an error message to appear on the screen as the file was processed at bootup.

With DOS 5.0 and above, you can type the text **rem** or **REM**, followed by a blank space, to insert a remark or comment in the CONFIG.SYS file. You can also use the rem or REM marker to disable a command line, to change some way in which your system performs, or while testing the process of making changes to your CONFIG.SYS file. Either of these uses for the rem statement are commonly called REMming out or commenting out an active line, or adding a comment to a file. A CONFIG.SYS file with a remark separator and a comment would appear as follows:

```
DEVICE=C:\DOS\HIMEM.SYS
DEVICE=C:\DOS\EMM386.SYS
DOS=HIGH
rem the following line is used for fancy screen attributes
DEVICE=C:\DOS\ANSI.SYS
BREAK=ON
```

If we want to disable the loading of the ANSI.SYS device driver in this CONFIG.SYS file, we simply add rem as the first characters on the line specifying the device driver, as follows:

```
DEVICE=C:\DOS\HIMEM.SYS
DEVICE=C:\DOS\EMM386.SYS
DOS=HIGH
rem the following line is used for fancy screen attributes
rem DEVICE=C:\DOS\ANSI.SYS
rem above line REMmed out for testing
BREAK=ON
```

Notice that we also added a comment line indicating that the ANSI.SYS line was disabled (or "REMmed out") intentionally, and why. Removing the entire line for ANSI.SYS would accomplish the same thing, but it would create more work for us if we wanted to reinstall the device driver later.

Comments in the AUTOEXEC.BAT File

The process for the AUTOEXEC.BAT file is quite similar to that
for the CONFIG.SYS file. The `rem` statement simply disables an
active command line or prefaces a comment, as shown below:

```
ECHO OFF
CLS
PROMPT $p$g
SET PATH=C:\;C:\DOS;C:\WINDOWS;C:\BAT
CALL C:\BAT\NET.BAT
rem CALL C:\BAT\LOGIN.BAT
MENU
```

In this example, `CALL C:\BAT\LOGIN.BAT` is disabled by the `rem`
placed in front of it. Do you notice anything missing from this file?
The comments, perhaps? Yes! Let's fix that:

```
ECHO OFF
CLS
PROMPT $p$g
SET PATH=C:\;C:\DOS;C:\WINDOWS;C:\BAT
CALL C:\BAT\NET.BAT
rem disabling the LOGIN since we are taking this system
rem to another office with different network setups.
rem Manually login instead.
rem CALL C:\BAT\LOGIN.BAT
MENU
```

By substituting a pair of colons (::) for the `rem` characters, you can
take advantage of a recently popular shortcut used for comments in
BATch (.BAT) files. This shortcut can speed up BATch file processing and avoid the possible misinterpretation of the contents of
`rem` lines as commands.

As documented in DOS BATch file documentation, BATch files
are read, interpreted, and acted upon in sequential, line-by-line
order. There are only three types of entries that can appear in the
lines of BATch files: remark lines, DOS commands, and labels.

Labels are short lines of text preceded by a single colon used to identify a grouping of BATch file commands. The colon or double-colon is valid only in BATch files, since labels are indicated by different symbols in CONFIG.SYS files. The CONFIG.SYS labels do not work for BATch files.

DOS must spend time interpreting each line looking for DOS commands to be executed, including those preceded with the rem statement, unless that line is only a label. Label lines are skipped over, so no time is spent interpreting them. Since label lines are not interpreted they can be used instead of rem lines to save time.

To use a label line instead of a rem statement, create the label line as an entirely meaningless one using a pair of colons followed by a blank space. The blank space tends to be a matter of style; it makes it easier to recognize the line as a comment or disabled command line.

This technique also avoids having the line confused as a legitimate working label, and because the colon symbol itself is not a valid label for DOS, it is ignored.

Our example from above can therefore be changed for faster processing and greater clarity to the following:

```
ECHO OFF
CLS
PROMPT $p$g
CALL C:\BAT\NET.BAT
:: disabling the LOGIN since we are taking this system to
:: another office with different network setups. Manually
:: login instead.
:: CALL C:\BAT\LOGIN.BAT
MENU
```

All of your BATch files can and should benefit from these techniques to manage your system configuration properly.

Comments in Windows Files

Microsoft Windows makes the processes of commenting and of disabling lines in its configuration files a bit easier. All of the typical

INI files (such as WIN.INI and SYSTEM.INI) used by Windows programs regard the semicolon (;) as a useless character and skip over lines that begin with it.

A partial WIN.INI file with a comment and a command that has been disabled with a comment is shown below:

```
[windows]
spooler=yes
load=C:\WINDOWS\SYSTEM\POINTER.EXE c:\netscape\tcpman.exe
; COMMENT: I won't be using these features this week...
; nwpopup.exe c:\sndsys\audcntrl.exe C:\DVX\dvwinmon.exe
run=
Beep=yes
NullPort=None
BorderWidth=5
CursorBlinkRate=530
```

In this example, one line is disabled—the one loading NWPOPUP.EXE, AUDCNTRL.EXE, and DVWINMON.EXE. We made the comment above our disabled items obvious, leaving the disabled items intact for replacement later.

 NOTE

You should be aware that Windows is limited to reading only the first 32K of your WIN.INI and SYSTEM.INI files. If these files become too large by the addition of fonts, features, or your comments, some features may not be available within Windows, or you may not be able to run the Windows SETUP program to reconfigure Windows. The solution to this potential problem is to reduce the number of fonts and text and graphics converters, and keep your comments and unneeded lines to a minimum.

Making Changes to the Windows 95/98 Registry

There are several ways to effect changes in the Registry files used by Windows 95/98:

- Using Windows' REGEDIT program
- Working in any number of different dialog boxes from the Start ⇨ Settings ⇨ Taskbar options
- Within the Control Panel
- Changing Properties for Folders, program shortcuts, and so on

Unfortunately, there is no way to temporarily earmark, comment out, or disable entries within the Windows Registry files for later recovery. If you make a change, it is permanent until you manually change it back again. Sometimes, Windows 95 or 98 is smart and changes something back for you by itself.

Your best preventive medicine and eventual recourse in case you make mistakes with the Registry is to make separate backup copies of both Registry files. You may use the Windows 95 REGBACK program, the Windows 98 SCANREGW program, or a Registry change tracking utility like Norton Registry Tracker supplied with the Norton Utilities for Windows.

Making System Changes

By undertaking the discipline of good configuration management, you're in a position to address the questions you need to ask before installing new devices or software:

- Are changes necessary?
- Are the changes going to improve performance or functionality?
- Do you have enough memory or disk space?

- Do you have the right CPU?
- Do you have enough plug-in slots of the right type?
- Do you have enough disk drive mounting slots?
- Will the changes affect other programs or devices?
- Do you need a CD-ROM drive? Sound card? New video card?
- Are enough I/O addresses and IRQ and DMA assignments available?

With your complete system inventory, outside and in, you'll have these questions answered already, or at least you'll have the information to answer them. You'll also be familiar with these items as you find them mentioned on the side panels of most software and hardware packaging.

This is almost enough information for you to decide that your system can accommodate that new graphics or multimedia program you've been wanting to try. But what if you need to get set up for multimedia before you use that program? Few product packages tell you the configuration information you need to know without opening the box and reading the manual, which most stores frown upon before you buy the product. Often, knowing what that information means seems just as elusive.

 Tip

Find a store that has the software or hardware you are interested in already set up and on display for you to try out. Then check the configuration of that system to get better ideas for your own system. Visit the vendor's Web site to check product specifications, FAQs (frequently asked questions), and support information before you buy. You may find that all-important setup tip before you run into installation problems.

Note

These issues of actually preparing for and making changes to your system are where we get to the nuts and bolts or – more appropriately – the switches and jumpers of our system configuration. We will cover these items and what they mean for various devices in the chapters ahead.

Summary

This chapter presents a condensed view of configuration management and the basic procedures that set the groundwork for safe and conflict-free changes. I've discussed some of the simple steps you can take toward positive configuration management: Back up the files critical to running your system, document what's in your system, and keep track of how it changes over time. By doing so, you leave yourself a way to restore the configuration to its previous condition if a change should go wrong, and you get the information necessary for planning future improvements.

Configuration management provides the resolution of any existing conflicts, plus a smooth transition into system software and hardware upgrades with fewer (I hope no) conflicts. As you progress through this book, many more design and implementation details will become evident that indicate the need for the basic steps and tools indicated here. I'll cover the use of these tools and the information they can provide in a subsequent chapter.

Chapter 5

Playing with Plug and Play

We have seen more than our share of technical details by now, and you may be hoping that this chapter is the one that makes it all go away, makes it all better, lets us all sleep at night, wake up refreshed, and enjoy better days ahead. I wish it were so.

At some point, both a complete absence of legacy devices and complete availability of all new systems and devices will have to take place. This point has not been reached yet, but I suspect by the year 2000 there will not be a newly manufactured piece of legacy/ISA PC hardware or software available anywhere. If PnP doesn't fully catch on, we will be revisiting the subject of system configurations again and again.

For the most part, Plug and Play is a wonderful concept. Some day it may even become reality. If it does, this book will be obsolete except for its historical value. Meanwhile, there are and will still be many users and their legacy and PnP devices fighting it out over who gets which resources when and why. For my nickel, I hope someone fixes Plug and Play as we know it so we can get on with the rejoicing.

It will take a complete redesign of most of the PC I/O system as we know it to make Plug and Play a reality. This means that there can be no more jumper- or switch-set legacy devices, at all, anywhere in the system, period — yeah!

This involves a significant effort on the part of all hardware vendors to redesign and replace all the devices they make with PnP-compliant ones. It also means that the system board will have to lose any and all of its 8- and 16-bit ISA slots in favor of PCI slots. Furthermore, it means that any and all software that addresses hardware devices directly will have to work through the services of an updated PnP-compliant operating system. That operating system will have to be aware of or have drivers for every imaginable PC interface device in existence (except, of course, the legacy devices, which would no longer be a part of new systems).

Obviously this is no small task. Hundreds of manufacturers, thousands of products and programmers, and millions of users will be affected in one way or another. Still, the effort is underway. Microsoft is looking forward to and supporting the efforts. Vendors are lining up and catching on. Supporting older, slower legacy devices is costing us all a small fortune in downtime and support.

In the year 2000 or so, many new system users will be happily computing away with Windows 98, 99, or 2000 on new "Octagium Pro 500" systems. They will not have heard of IRQ, DMA, or I/O. They will not have seen an add-in card jumper, DIP-switch, or CMOS setup screen. Don't rejoice too soon. This does not mean that we will have replaced or disposed of *all* of our existing, still working legacy systems and devices. Many of us will still be happily computing away with 1998-vintage systems, dreading the inevitable upgrade costs into new hardware and software.

We are about to explore Plug and Play, and you will see, quite simply, why we still need to attend to some legacy and configuration management issues, until the Utopian glory days of trouble-free personal computing arrives.

Plug and Play: The Solution We've Been Waiting For

The no-conflict, no-hassle configuration solution we think we have been waiting for has rapidly but uneasily come into fruition. COMPAQ , Phoenix Technologies (a primary provider of BIOS for many systems), and Intel are spearheading the effort to design cooperative, integrated PC systems, system and add-in boards, and BIOS to work together intelligently. Microsoft also has significantly bought in to Plug and Play (PnP) with support for it in Windows 95 and 98.

Plug and Play begins at the very basic and lowest level of our PC systems — the system board and BIOS. These must be designed and implemented to work together. The instant we start up a PC system with PnP, this new BIOS (or rather, enhancements to existing BIOS) goes to work detecting devices toward automatic configuration of the system. A full and PnP-only system, without legacy devices, will configure and verify itself and make the expected devices and services available to us without much, if any, thought or effort. But today there is no such thing as a PnP-only system. Legacy devices (COM and LPT ports, for example) still exist, even if they are built into the system boards — though they may be configured by software.

Plug and Play is designed to work with and around existing legacy devices, whether they are ISA, EISA, MicroChannel, PCMCIA, Local Bus, or PCI. During system startup, PnP's device detection begins to detect any and all system devices and resources that are in use. It also determines whether the devices it finds are PnP devices; if not, PnP devices will use the resources available after non-PnP devices are configured. If you add a new non-PnP device that conflicts in any way with an existing PnP device, the existing PnP device will be reconfigured at startup to keep your system working.

Plug and Play devices and BIOS can't do the intelligent configuration work entirely by themselves. The BIOS and hardware only make provisions for detection and configuration; they do not act directly on their capabilities. The amount of time and memory space allowed or acceptable for BIOS to do its job is just not enough. For this, we depend on the strengths and capabilities of a Plug and Play operating system. We don't seem to mind how long it takes to boot up and configure the system, nor how big the programs actually are that must do the work.

Windows 95 and 98 have PnP technology built in to allow automatic configurability during installations, upgrades, and system changes. Windows 95 and 98 will also alert you to any changes in your system, giving you the option of having it reconfigure itself or any PnP hardware, for the system to have access to all of the expected devices and services.

PnP can be the answer to configuration and conflict concerns if your system contains only PnP-compatible devices. If any legacy devices exist, as they certainly will for quite some time, you must still follow the existing standard configuration rules. PnP will not do anything different with or for standard PC port devices, such as the addressing of COM ports, LPT ports, their IRQs, and so on. PnP devices, for the most part, are still expected to use the originally designed and defined PC configuration standards to work properly with software.

In the prior chapters we've discussed "the rules" and some of the traditional configurations that have developed to date to establish a known, workable PC foundation. For now, that foundation is still extremely important and is not to be overlooked in our zeal to arrive at an ideal Plug and Play system.

From this point on, PnP seems to ignore either the rules or prior significant conventions of how we've configured our systems in the past and the software that must use the devices in the system. We are at an interim point in the transition from legacy to full automation that may be worse during this time of change than holding fast to the solid legacy foundation we've built up thus far.

Plug and Play BIOS and Operating Systems

Plug and Play depends on compliant hardware and software routines that can identify PnP hardware devices and control their configuration. PnP BIOS merely makes the few I/O devices typically built into the system board (I/O ports, disk adapters, and so on) PnP-compliant. This means they can be identified and configured by PnP configuration manager software. The BIOS does not actually provide the configuration services — these devices still need an external configuration manager to handle them as PnP-devices.

To date, PnP configuration management is handled only by the operating system. For many of us, this means Microsoft's Windows 95/98, although the current version of IBM's OS/2 is also a PnP-compliant operating system with configuration management capabilities. LINUX and other operating systems are developing PnP support as this book is being written. Oddly enough, version 4.0 of Microsoft Windows NT ("New Technology") lags behind its little brother, Windows 95; it does not have PnP support. Microsoft is supposed to have PnP support in Windows NT, now called Windows 2000, by some time in 1999.

That the operating system carries the bulk of the configuration burden is not necessarily a bad thing. It is far easier to download a new configuration program file for the operating system than it is to update the system BIOS code. Also, the configuration management software is too large to fit into most system ROM chips. Also, to configure additional ROM would take up precious memory addressing space we would rather use for other things.

Whether or not your PC system contains PnP BIOS or has PnP hardware built into the system board, a PnP-compliant operating system such as Windows 95 or 98 is still able to work with add-in PnP hardware devices.

It is within this configuration management software, how it implements the Plug and Play specification and configures hardware devices, that we need to focus our attention. This is where the "work" is done. This software determines the configuration of any ISA/legacy devices, sets off the PnP hardware identification process, and then allocates resources to the PnP devices before the operating system can use them.

We still have to live with how, when, or which PnP hardware wins our identification crapshoot, and thus which device gets configured first. After that, we hope that the configuration management software (our operating system) will be able to make the right configuration assignments. More on this as we go along.

Extended System Configuration Data

Within specific PnP BIOS implementations and during its operation may come a new allocation of memory to what is called the ESCD, or Extended System Configuration Data area. This is an 8K block of RAM located in the upper memory region, often found between E:A000h and E:BFFFh. It is used to store information about PCI and Plug and Play devices. You may notice references to the ESCD during system bootup as PCI and PnP devices are discovered and their initially or previously assigned resources are listed on the screen.

We don't interact directly with this region of memory, but its existence is worthy of note when configuring memory managers or if you ever wonder why a mysterious 8K block of upper memory is not available for loading device drivers or TSR programs into high memory.

Support for and use of the ESCD memory allocation depends on the BIOS. The configuration manager software may often read from, but it may not write to or update the ESCD data directly. Instead, the configuration software typically acts on the hardware devices. The ESCD data is updated on the next system bootup based on the configuration of the hardware it finds, saving and making this data available to further configuration manager operations.

The existence of the ESCD information may or may not save time in loading the operating system, because the BIOS has already discovered and recorded information about PnP devices. Thus, the operating system would not have to discover all of the Plug and Play devices all over again — but some PnP devices may require drivers to be loaded into the operating system first, before PnP discovery and configuration of the device could be done anyway. Certainly the ESCD could be useful where an independent configuration manager, outside of the operating system, is used to support PnP devices.

How Can You Tell if You Have Plug and Play BIOS?

This is an excellent question and one to which there is no obvious answer. During the initial part of bootup, some BIOS will report the existence of their PnP BIOS support and which version of the BIOS is in the system — but most do not. I would have expected this information to be available within most utility programs, such as those from Norton (System Information), Quarterdeck (Manifest) or similar, but this is not the case. There is no standard definition for how or where PnP BIOS is indicated or detected, unless you invoke a specific PnP test or configuration program to look for PnP devices in the system. So far, the most reliable program available is PNPBTST.EXE from the people who should know, BIOS-maker and PnP specification partner, Phoenix Technologies. You can get this program from their Web site at http://www.phoenix.com/products/util.html.

The Legacy and Plug and Play Dilemma

We've come to accept a certain basic configuration for most of the common devices found in a typical PC. In review, this gives us a typical PC system with items and their configuration as listed in Table 5-1 below.

Table 5-1 *Typical Legacy Resource Assignments*

Device	Address	IRQ	DMA	System Device
RAM Refresh		0		Reserved
System Timer	40h	0		Reserved
Keyboard	60h	1		
Cascade for IRQ 8-15		2		Reserved
COM2	2F8h	3		
COM4	2E8h	3		
COM1	3F8h	4		
COM3	2F8h			
LPT2	278h	5		
Sound Card	220h	1, 3, or 5		
Diskette Adapter	3F0h	6	2	
LPT1	378h	7		
Real-Time Clock	70h	8		Reserved
Cascade to IRQ 2		9		
Network Card	280h	10		
SCSI Adapter	330h	11	3 or 5	
PS/2 Mouse Port	64h	12		
Numeric Co-Processor	F0h	13		Reserved
Hard Disk Interface	1F0h	14		
2nd Hard Disk Interface	170h	15		
VGA card	3B0; 3C0			

Understanding that it would be a tremendous effort to redesign the entire PC system as we know it, many of the resources assigned to common PC devices will never be suited to Plug and Play or automatic configuration. A computer simply needs things like its clocks, CPU, and basic low-level items to be left as and where they are, consuming the resources they do, so the computer can do its job — boot up and predictably run certain pieces of software.

Note

Those items that we cannot anticipate or expect to change regardless of legacy, PnP, or other changes in the PC platform are marked as Reserved in the System Device column in Table 5-1.

This leaves us a few devices — mostly those troublesome I/O-things — that could be affected by Plug and Play. The questions then become: Do we want to affect them? Should we affect them? Can we affect them and if so, how? If some of them are not PnP devices, how do we get them to work together?

Plug and Play Doesn't

First, experience and anecdotal references have shown that all too often Plug and Play does not play, or play well, or play as we might expect it to, with our existing systems. We wonder why, after all the hype and technology behind this supposedly marvelous solution to such basic problems, does this technology really not work?

The answers may be solid, logical, and reliable only in very specific cases where a vendor or other very technical people have researched and tested specific cases. For the rest of us — the millions of us who can't get access to all the whiz-bang technical tools and details — the answers are unfortunately more vague and troublesome.

Experience and research into what information is available is very telling, beginning with the Plug and Play specification and how it is designed to work. After the fixed resource and legacy devices are identified, Plug and Play works as follows.

The PnP device identification and resource assignment process, by design, may be thought of as a crapshoot or, as some have expressed it, like a fast game of one-card poker played between devices and the PnP software.

A device's ability to win the crapshoot to be eligible for a spot in the configuration order is at best dependent upon the following variables:

- The speed at which a device can respond to automatic identification processes
- How each PnP BIOS vendor actually wrote its PnP BIOS code
- How each device's PnP hardware and internal programming was designed to work
- System timing considerations
- Location of a PCI device in a particular slot

Once the configuration order is determined by the crapshoot method, a device's resource assignment is dependent upon the following:

- The resources a device is designed to be able to use (vendor programming of the device)
- The resources the operating system or device driver allows a device to use (vendor, driver, and operating system variables)

The crapshoot is repeated at every bootup, and configurations do change and can become more complex as you add new PnP devices to the system. A device's configuration should not change with each bootup, but it might if it has defective internal firmware.

If you're looking for a distinct set of rules for some priority and predetermined resource assignments, you'll be hard pressed to find them. Apparently, neither the vendors nor the Plug and Play specification authors wanted to tie anyone's hands and limit their ability to use whatever resources were available in any order that you could get them.

For the most part, vendors have limited themselves to using resources that only make sense based on legacy rules, tradition, and convention for the particular device of concern. This means that we probably won't see, for example, a VGA card vendor, the device driver programmer, or the PnP operating system folks allowing a VGA card to use assignments typically used by COM or LPT ports, sound cards, or other typical devices.

In most cases you also won't see I/O addresses thrown about and assigned with wild abandon, but you may find IRQ and DMA assignments not falling into place as you might expect. The fact that the configuration can change between system bootups, and when new devices are added, makes PnP all the more interesting and challenging in some cases.

Since for most of us Windows 95 or 98 is our operating system, and it controls and keeps track of the actual PnP device configuration process, the odds in the crapshoot tend to even out to being a little better than playing Russian roulette with a fully loaded gun.

You will usually not (but can) find that your once stable PnP device configurations change when new devices are added. This may become evident when you add a PnP network card and suddenly find that you can't load its new drivers from your CD-ROM drive because the PnP routine has shuffled the CD-ROM interface configuration around, temporarily or permanently disabling the CD-ROM drive.

Plug and Play can outsmart itself on numerous (and as indicated by the PnP BIOS, device driver, and operating system variables above) unpredictable occasions. This is where we enter a new phase of configuration management and have to start loading the dice so we get and retain some of our own control over the configuration again. We'll cover this topic as part of Chapter 7.

Microsoft's PC95 Standard: Defining Compatibility

PC95 was Microsoft's initial answer to, or dictate of, what a properly configured and configurable PC system should have been by the end of 1995 — to work with Windows 95 and similar PnP-compliant operating systems. The PC95 standard was intended to make PCs more affordable, approachable, and easier for non-technical users. This means that there should be no user concerns over I/O addresses, IRQ, DMA, ports, logical devices, and so on, and thus no manual configuration when buying or upgrading a PC system.

To fully meet this goal, all hardware devices would have had to become Plug and Play compatible and be able to be dynamically reconfigured as new devices were added or old ones removed. This includes all hardware, meaning that even disk drives will also have to support configuration changes (such as first, second, or further drive IDs, SCSI device numbers, and so on).

But PC95 is about more than compatibility. Windows 95 and PC95 were designed cooperatively, with the features of Plug and Play, VESA (video modes and performance), automatic power management (to serve the U.S. Environmental Protection Agency's Energy Star program for energy conservation in computing devices), and other new PC device standards in mind. Since Plug and Play was designed to also be compatible with legacy devices, they are likewise covered under the minimum PC95 requirements. To encourage this, Microsoft licensed systems as being "Designed for Windows 95," complete with an identifying logo saying so, if they meet certain minimum requirements.

These requirements were tested with Microsoft's Hardware Compatibility Test for Windows 95. They include CPU type, amount of RAM, video display capabilities, CD-ROM drive performance and capabilities, and multimedia (sound and video playback) capabilities as listed in Table 5-2. To date, the Hardware Compatibility Test is not available to the general public, but we can compare its requirements to a variety of system components to see if they might comply.

Similar testing was provided for software products as well. As many developers have found, there were several issues relating to interoperability between devices and software that have probably allowed several exceptions to the originally stringent tests. For example, software "Designed for Windows 95" had to run on both Windows 95 and Windows NT according to the test criteria. Unfortunately, it is possible to create quite good software for either environment, using the unique features and benefits of a particular environment, that were not available in both operating systems.

Thus, Microsoft had to start issuing exemptions to their own rules for many software products very quickly as Windows 95 came to release and acceptance. No doubt similar exemptions were granted for many hardware systems as well.

Table 5-2 *PC95 System Requirements*

System Components	Minimum Requirements	Recommendations
BIOS	Plug and Play BIOS Version 1.0a with resource readback	PnP with soft-set for all resources
CPU	80386 or equivalent	80486DX-33 or equivalent
RAM	4MB	8MB
Video Adapter	640 × 480 × 256 colors	1024 × 768 × 256 colors
Video Display	640 × 480, color	VESA DDC1/2B standard and Display Power Management Signaling (DPMS) for shutdown
Pointing Device	Dedicated port or integral device	
Parallel Port	Supports compatibility (output only, to printers)	Full IEEE-P1284-I Enhanced Capability Port (ECP) mode and Nibble modes compatibility (bi-directional data transfer)
Serial Port	One; two if mouse uses COM port	16550A or compatible serial I/O chip
Hard Disk	Not required if networked	80-120MB min.; 500+MB recommended
Diskettes	3.5", 1.44MB, providing write-protect signal if diskette not present (for disk presence test)	
Sound		22KHz, 8-bit, mono output only
Labeling	Standardized icons for device plugs for easy identification	
System Board	* Advanced Power Management BIOS interface v1.1; software-controlled power supply power-down * High-speed expansion bus (PCI or VL-bus)	

Continued

Table 5-2 *Continued*

System Components	Minimum Requirements	Recommendations
General		* CD-ROM drive with soft-eject control * SCSI-2 interface * Clearly labeled switches and jumpers on all boards * Plug and Play expansion cards * Standardized cabling that cannot be plugged into the wrong card or device

The PC95 standard, and in essence the Plug and Play standard, was also to provide for several more configuration options than found on standard PC devices. Having more options available provides a great deal more flexibility for adding devices to our system, though most of the popular and commonly desired items may already be provided with an off-the-shelf PC system.

Cross-Reference

Refer to Chapter 2 for the limitations imposed by legacy devices.

Note

If you review Table 5-2 and compare it to your existing system, you may find that except for PnP-BIOS, your system may already be close to meeting the PC95 standard and some of its additional recommendations. If you establish and manage your system's configuration adequately, in essence acting as the Plug and Play manager for your own system, you could at least be "PC94"-compliant without having to replace your system board and other devices.

PnP hardware and software not only address the issues of configurations and avoiding conflicts, they also open the door for several new features to be introduced into our PC systems. These new features extend themselves to both usability and environmental issues.

Energy Conservation

A few years ago, energy conservation was simply considered getting more life out of the batteries in laptop systems. On our desktops, the video monitors, the disk drives, and an otherwise idle system are power hogs. They not only use a lot of electricity, they also generate a lot of heat, which in most cases we eventually remove with air conditioning. The cumulative effects of several dozen PCs running in an office has overburdened the cooling systems in buildings designed before PC systems were in common use. Even with new building designs, PC systems can create a waste of energy overall.

Advanced Power Management in PC systems can be thought of as the ultimate screen saver of the 90s. Instead of displaying flying toasters or psychedelic fish, these new features dim or turn off our monitors, stop our disk drives from spinning, and even put the computer system to "sleep" if we leave our systems inactive for a certain period of time. In essence, we will be saving the environment's batteries.

If you're wondering whether it's better to leave your system on or turn it off between uses, as far as energy conservation is concerned, it is better to turn it off. In terms of wear and tear on cooling fans, drive motors, and power supply components, leaving the system turned on is better. Basically, the choice depends on how often you need access to your system or how long a time there is between system uses. If automatic power control is designed into the system, the electronic circuits will control the power smoothly, preventing the turn-on/turn-off surges that are suspected of causing many system failures.

In reality, the PC95 system need not be completely shut off, so that it can come to life again as you need it. Those items that are shut off internally are protected by the power supply regulators, so there is no great influx of current through the AC power line as there is when you operate that big red ON/OFF switch on the side.

On/Off Control in the Keyboard

Okay, so our friends using Apple Macintoshes will laugh at us for bringing it up, but once we have software control of the power consumption of our system, it's a relatively simple matter to design the ability to monitor the keyboard periodically to see if anyone's pressed a certain key.

Windows 95 and 98 are already designed to shut down the system as part of its exit routine from Windows (although it doesn't go to DOS, as with Windows 3.*x*). When you elect to shut down Windows 95 or 98, you have several options. One options is to restart the system (reboot). Another option is to perform a shutdown, which currently instructs you that it's safe to turn your system off, or in some systems actually does shut down the system.

Because there are no arms, hands, or fingers provided to toggle the big red switch, the shutdown command goes to an electronically controlled power supply. The big red switch may stay ON, but the supply will be turned OFF inside.

To turn the system back on, we need to get access to that internal electronic control, and since the keyboard is close and used most often by users, it seems like an obvious place to put the ON button, just like the Macintosh. Okay, so there's no ON button on your PC keyboard yet, but any key should do!

Accessibility

Windows 95 and 98 provide a set of installable options to make the use of a PC system easier for physically impaired users. Currently these options consist of "sticky" keyboard keys, many special one-key operations, large and high-contrast screen characters, and similar items.

The PC95 standard allows for the interconnection of a variety of devices, some yet to be invented, through a feature and new standard called the ACCESS.bus. These devices may replace or supplement keyboards and pointing devices with special articulation controls, depending on the nature of physical impairment and mobility.

This effort is to be applauded and greatly encouraged throughout the industry, for both hardware and software design. We're all aware of programs that require a mouse, if only because a programmer forgot to include the standard set of alternate keyboard commands for a function or designed a new control whose odd new behavior would take forever to get used to.

There are thousands if not millions in the world who would be able to get a lot more out of life, and put a lot more into it, if only they could use these wonderful PC systems. Developers of hardware and software should be encouraged to ensure accessibility for all current and potential users.

Microsoft's PC97: Compatibility, Performance, and Then Some

Just when we thought our 150MHz Intel Pentium processor in a system with 16MB of RAM was good enough, along comes something newer, faster, and of course, something we don't have now and that our present system may not be upgradeable to.

Microsoft believes that in order to get the full benefits of software and technology, a certain set of minimum speed, RAM, and feature criteria should be met inside the PC hardware. Of course, the software they want you to benefit from would be theirs (ActiveX, MMX-compliant applications, and so on). Intel plays no small hand in this, anticipating that if they help developers create new features and software that users will need or want bigger faster processors, so they do their part, quietly or not, to drive up the minimums as well.

Admittedly, we do get to enjoy some of the benefits of technology's advances, and anything that will keep us away from having to worry about PC resource configuration issues (and also away from bugging all those technical support people) gives us more time to enjoy or produce with our computers.

Table 5-3 below lists the basic performance and feature recommendations and requirements for various Microsoft PC97-compliant systems.

Table 5-3 *Significant System Performance and Feature Requirements for Basic PC97*

Attribute/Feature	Basic PC97	Workstation PC97	Entertainment PC97
Minimum CPU	120 MHz Required	166 MHz Required	166 MHz Required
256K minimum L2 cache	Recommended	Required	Required
Minimum system memory	16MB	32MB	16MB
Advanced Configuration and Power Interface (ACPI) support	Required	Required	Required
Hardware support for OnNow	Required	Required	Required
BIOS support for OnNow (x86-based systems)	Required	Required	Required
System BIOS support for alternate boot devices, for x86-based systems	Required	Required	Required
BIOS boot support for USB keyboard, if USB is the only keyboard	Required	Required	Required
Industrial Design: All expansion slots in the system are accessible for users to insert cards	Required	Required	Required
Industrial Design: Audible noise meets PC97 standards	Recommended	Recommended	Required
All devices and drivers meet PC97 standards	Required	Required	Required
All bus and devices to be Plug and Play compliant	Required	Required	Required
All devices support correct 16-bit decoding for I/O port addresses	Required	Required	Required
Devices and buses support hot plugging if using USB, 1394, or PC Card	Required	Required	Required

Attribute/Feature	Basic PC97	Workstation PC97	Entertainment PC97
The user is protected from incorrectly connecting devices	Required	Required	Required
Minimal user interaction needed to install and configure devices	Required	Required	Required
Device driver and installation meet Windows and Windows NT standards	Required	Required	Required
Standard system board devices use ISA-compatible addresses	Required	Required	Required
Universal Serial Bus with one USB port, minimum	Required	Required	2 USB ports required
Support for other high-speed expansion capabilities (CardBus required for mobile)	Recommended	Recommended	IEEE 1394 Required
If present, PCI bus meets PCI Version 2.1 and higher, plus PC97 requirements	Required	Required	Required
ISA expansion bus	Optional	Optional	Optional
Wireless capabilities in PC system	Recommended	Recommended	Required
Support for installing the operating system	Required	Required	Required
Audio support in PC meets PC97 requirements	Recommended	Recommended	Required
Communications device provided with PC system	Recommended	Required	Required
Display adapter meets PC97 minimum requirement (bpp=bits per pixel, color resolution)	800 × 600 × 16 bpp; (640 × 480 × 8 bpp, small LCD)	1024 × 768 × 16 bpp	1024 × 768 ×16 bpp

Continued

Table 5-3 *Continued*

Attribute/Feature	Basic PC97	Workstation PC97	Entertainment PC97
Support for NTSC or PAL TV output, if no large-screen monitor	Recommended	Recommended	Required
Color monitor supports DDC 2.0 Level B, EDID, and 800 × 600, minimum	Required	Required	Required
System supports MPEG-1 playback	Required	Required	Required
PC97 DVD playback requirements, if PC system includes DVD-Video	Required	Required with DVD-Video	DVD-Video
Support Int 13h Extensions in system and option ROMs	Required	Required	Required
Host controller for storage device meets PC97 requirements, if present	Required	Required	Required
Primary host controller supports bus mastering	Recommended	Required	Required
Hard drive meets PC97 requirements, if present	Required	Required	Required
Media status notification support for removable media	Required	Required	Required
Legacy floppy disk controller built into system	Optional	Optional	Optional
CardBus for high-speed expansion capabilities on mobile PCs	Required	Required	Required
Mobile unit and docking station meet PC97 requirements as a pair	Required		
Docking station meets ACPI requirements	Required		

Attribute/Feature	Basic PC97	Workstation PC97	Entertainment PC97
Docking station meets all Basic PC97 requirements for general devices, expansion cards, system bus, and system board	Required		
Automatic resource assignment and dynamic disable capabilities for mobile/docking station pair	Required		
Automatic resource assignment and dynamic disable capabilities for replacement devices	Required		
"Multimedia PC" minimum requirements	Required	Required	designed to meet PC97 MPC

Data source: Microsoft PC97 Specification

Legacy/ISA Devices Will Be Optional

Hoping to relieve us of one of our biggest headaches — the configuration of legacy devices and finding resources for them — the PC97 specification allows legacy/ISA device capability to be optional. This is in favor of system boards having built-in Plug and Play I/O ports and devices and using only PnP/PCI add-in I/O cards. If this works out well, a lot of us techies will end up as legacy resources too!

Computer Availability On Demand

Of particular note are references in Table 5-3 to something called *OnNow*, which refers to the ability to start our systems as quickly as possible, whether the system is in a power-on but dormant/sleeping state or able to boot up faster from data stored in memory rather than having to load entirely from the hard disk.

Admittedly, as power and speed hungry as we have become, being able to use your computer on demand is probably a good thing. The other advantage to an OnNow system is that there should be less worry about the configuration changing between power-down and power-up times and the not too logical Plug and Play crapshoot of system configuration at startup.

New I/O Connectivity

There didn't seem to be any other place to mention the next few items except in the context of Plug and Play, PC97, and beyond. Ridding ourselves of the common legacy/ISA hassles inside the box and getting more performance and fancier devices to play with can't be accomplished without addressing a few things outside of the box too.

We've probably exhausted ourselves impatiently waiting for sluggish downloads from various Web sites with 28.8 Kbps modem. Even if we've been able to enjoy the speed of ISDN (but not the costs), today's PC I/O connections have reached their limits in terms of satisfying performance.

The PC box is only so big, and when we start adding on musical instrument devices, portable storage units, and begin to dabble with virtual reality, finding the slots and wrestling with all the cabling only goes so far before we need something better.

Three new I/O interfaces, each with its own set of benefits and applications as well as costs, will be appearing on the PC horizon very soon. The Universal Serial Bus (USB) addresses the everyday, low-cost, multiple device attachments most of us will be using everywhere we sit with our desktops or tote our portable systems to. The IEEE-1394 FireWire I/O system allows us to hook up a variety of high speed devices out of sight or at least off our desktops. The Fibre Channel I/O system will service (both internal and external) ultra-high-speed data delivery needs.

Of course, these interfaces feature the ease of Plug and Play, and they give us more I/O speed than we might have ever dreamed of. Personally, I'm really looking forward to the day when I can toss out my serial ports, cables, and switch boxes and use one simple cabling system to hook up all the devices around me, and move them from system to system much more easily than we can today.

Universal Serial Bus

In 1997, we began to see a new breed of peripheral interconnection called the Universal Serial Bus, or USB. This interface will allow hot-plugging (connection or disconnection, as with PC Card devices) of up to 127 I/O devices along a single connection chain. Here again, Apple Macintosh fans may laugh, because the Mac has had features like this all along (plugging the mouse into the keyboard, and the keyboard into the system box, all on one connection, for example), though perhaps it is not as fast or versatile.

Each USB peripheral is by nature a hot-plugged, automatically identified, and configured device that will be detected and have drivers loaded as needed by the operating system. It is truly Plug and Play from the outside in. The system's USB port will require no legacy resources, thus avoiding all possible conflicts. The USB port works as part of the chipset with drivers intended to sense and register devices when they are attached or disconnected. Our first taste of this came with USB drivers for Windows 95 OSR 2 (OEM/manufacturer Service Release #2), and the feature is native to Windows 98 and beyond.

USB is designed to be a low-cost method of providing up to 12Mbps data rates. It serves a wide range of peripheral applications from mice, keyboards, and gaming devices at the low end of the spectrum to phone and compressed audio, video, and data services at the upper end of its useful speed range.

The key features here, in addition to Plug and Play and speed, are both a simple and low-cost implementation. The cabling design eliminates the need for all those 9-25 pin adapters, null modems, and other collective junk hanging around your PCs. Also, the USB port provides power for many low-current devices, so you can probably get rid of a few of those nagging power bricks and stubborn little black wires too. You'll find ISDN or similar low-cost, high-performance network connection devices as well as printers and virtual reality attachments using USB very soon.

IEEE-1394 – FireWire

Talk about fast when it comes to new I/O interfaces and you have to be talking about FireWire, a 400Mbps serial data connection bus (3200Mbps per IEEE-1394b) intended primarily for multimedia peripherals, such as external/portable storage, sound devices, and fast, high-density printers. It's a little too fast for your average keyboard, mouse, printer, or modem applications, but you can expect to see this interface available for systems coming in the next year or so.

FireWire has the capability to handle 1,023 networks of 63 nodes, and each node can contain 281 terabytes (that's a lot) of memory space. Average cabling length is limited to 4.5 meters, but 14 meter cabling is provided for, as well as repeating through each node device to extend the end-to-end distance between farthest devices out to 224 meters. It's not a network solution, but one that does provide extensibility of high-speed peripherals that are otherwise currently limited to distances of a few feet between devices (as with SCSI). No existing network cabling or fiber optic solution delivers this much performance, no matter the distance.

With this Plug-and-Play-compliant interface, once again, legacy/ISA resources won't be a problem, but I suspect we'll face a few more software driver compatibility issues.

Fibre Channel

Briefly, Fibre Channel (it uses copper wire, as the fabric or medium linking items together, not necessarily by fiber optics but that is an optional medium) is a 1 gigabit per second (Gbps) multi-purpose (networking, data bus, and so on) solution for high-speed data access needs. It is being implemented in high-end disk drives, network and server systems, and LAN/MAN data communications paths. You probably won't see much of this on your average desktop system, but it will be part of everyday computing connectivity somewhere in your computing life within the next year.

Microsoft's PC99: Goodbye Legacy

Just when we thought our 233MHz system with 32MB of RAM and 6GB hard drive was good enough, along comes something newer, faster, and of course, something we don't have now and that our present system may not be upgradeable to. Does this lament sound familiar? It should — Microsoft got the two-year itch and still wants more, better, and faster.

The PC99 specification does not appear to be so much about performance and RAM as finally doing away with legacy/ISA devices. *Hurrah* – perhaps. It's very easy to hyperventilate when you look at the technical details and wonder where you're going to get a PC that meets this specification in 1999. Take a deep breath. Remember, it appears that what Microsoft thinks is the desirable minimum specification for today has proven itself to be a forward-looking goal for the next year or two. Thus, PC99 is pushing us toward the goal of what the average PC will (should?) be by the end of 1999 or 2000.

Table 5-4 lists the highlights of basic performance and feature recommendations and requirements for Microsoft PC99-compliant systems.

Table 5-4 *Highlights of the System Performance and Feature Requirements for PC99*

Attribute/Feature	Consumer PC99	Office PC99	Entertainment PC99
Minimum CPU	300MHz (233MHz mobile system)	300MHz (233MHz mobile system)	300MHz
L2 cache minimum	128K	128K	128K
Minimum system memory	32MB	64 MB (32MB mobile system)	32MB

Continued

Table 5-4 *Continued*

Attribute/Feature	Consumer PC99	Office PC99	Entertainment PC99
Advanced Configuration and Power Interface (ACPI) and BIOS support	Renewed specification, including USB keyboard and hub support	Renewed specification, including USB keyboard and hub support	Renewed specification, including USB keyboard and hub support
NO ISA (legacy) Expansion ports			
DVD	Recommended	Recommended	Required
Modem	56 Kbps v.90 modem w/v.250 AT commands; v.80 synchronous access; v.8BIS call progress; or public network (Internet)		56 Kbps v.90 modem w/ v.250 AT commands; v.80 synchronous access; v.8BIS call progress; or public network (Internet)
Network Adapter	Recommended	Required	Recommended
Video	3D Hardware acceleration	3D Hardware acceleration	3D Hardware acceleration
AGP Graphics	Recommended	Recommended	Recommended
Display	Must be compliant with Display Data Channel Standard version 3, level 2B (DDC2B)	Must be compliant with Display Data Channel Standard version 3, level 2B (DDC2B)	Must be compliant with Display Data Channel Standard version 3, level 2B (DDC2B)
PCI	Optional, must be PCI 2.1 compliant	Optional, must be PCI 2.1 compliant	Optional, must be PCI 2.1 compliant
USB	Optional, must be USB 1.0 compliant	Optional, must be USB 1.0 compliant	Optional, must be USB 1.0 compliant
IEEE 1394	Recommended, IEEE P1394.a compliant	Recommended, IEEE P1394.a compliant	
IrDA, FastIR (infrared I/O port)	FastIR required	FastIR required	FastIR required
Device Bay			

Attribute/Feature	Consumer PC99	Office PC99	Entertainment PC99
Printer Ports	ECP mode enabled on all IEEE 1284 compliant printers; daisy-chained ports must answer Plug and Play requests; pass-thru devices must comply with IEEE 1284.3	ECP mode enabled on all IEEE 1284 compliant printers; daisy-chained ports must answer Plug and Play requests; pass-thru devices must comply with IEEE 1284.3	ECP mode enabled on all IEEE 1284 compliant printers; daisy-chained ports must answer Plug and Play requests; pass-thru devices must comply with IEEE 1284.3
All bus and devices to be Plug and Play compliant	Required	Required	Required

Data source: Microsoft PC99 Specification

Note

PC99 dictates that there will be no ISA ports available in compliant systems. Also that there will be *Device Bay* support, a specification for how the system, BIOS, and device drivers will handle addition or removal of pluggable/interchangeable devices, which may be implemented as USB or FireWire devices.

In Chapter 7, I document efforts and results while trying to take an average 1998-vintage PC and make it conform to PC99 standards. As you read through this, you will see that we've already exceeded much of the performance and resource specifications. We have 333, 350, 400, and 450MHz CPUs in new and upgraded systems already. Most of us already have 32MB of RAM, and many of us have 64MB, and serious gamers, developers, and hardcore techies have 96 or 128MB already.

Many of us have or will have 3D graphics accelerators, perhaps not on AGP cards, but the PCI versus AGP debate for best graphics performance is still rambling on. If the goal is to reduce the number and type of devices and configuration issues, having a bus specific to one function, graphics, seems to contradict what I believe are the specification's goals.

It is possible to turn many built-in legacy devices such as COM and LPT ports into Plug and Play ports through BIOS setup settings, so we may have that requirement covered. It is unlikely that these ports will disappear — the x86/PC system BIOS must still provide for these ports for non-Microsoft operating systems and non-driver based modems and hardware.

The USB requirement I agree with 110 percent. In fact, as more devices shift their I/O to USB, we may indeed rid ourselves of the COM and LPT ports, or they will be moved out to USB adapters. Here we will find many practical devices to work with — pointing devices, document scanners, camera interfaces (both portable snapshot varieties and those for PC-to-PC personal communications), and so on.

The requirement for an infrared communications port is somewhat questionable. While a few non-PC devices such as PDAs can use infrared, not much else does, and the port cannot handle connecting with more than one device at a time, as USB does. Similarly, FireWire is best left as the recommendation it is until more popular and consumer market devices are available — not everyone can afford a $2,000 video camera after investing $3,000 in their wonderful new PC.

Who the PC*xx* Specifications Are For

Intel and Microsoft are coauthors of the PC*xx* specifications. The largest target audience and goals have to do with the Windows operating system running on Intel-based platforms. There are no indication that either Sun Microsystems, the LINUX community, Santa Cruz Operation, or Berkeley Software Design have participated in, or will adopt the PC*xx* specifications for their operating systems. At least not as fast as Microsoft would have us believe that PC*xx* will be a reality. Thus, we cannot rule out considerations for other operating systems, and completely, overnight, expect other vendors to fall in line and do away with legacy devices and support for them.

As quick as the UNIX community is at grasping new technologies, and even pushing them, it will take some time for UNIX developments to catch up to and then perhaps exceed the Microsoft desired capabilities. When you have a high-performance environment such as UNIX, you may not need as much horsepower as it takes to make Windows practical. Similarly, the UNIX community is generally more technical, and not as likely to encounter the various configuration problems that PC consumers typically have, so they may not need or want configuration options to disappear so fast.

With Intel openly supporting Red Hat's distribution and developments with LINUX, there may be more support for catching up to some of Microsoft's recommendations, or holding back on dumping legacy/ISA until the UNIX variants are caught up. Imagine what it would be like in the year 2000 if you could not find a new PC system on which you could install and run LINUX because either the devices it supported or the ones you still needed, did not and could not exist on that system. It would obviously be a detriment to Intel to force compliance before all of their interested partners could comply.

Of course everyone wants high performance and reliability. What PC*xx* lacks is coverage of issues concerning hardware, operating system, device driver, and applications stability. Windows environments generally tolerate system interruptions and shutdowns more gracefully than the UNIX operating systems do — and there are reasons for that — good and bad on both sides. I see nothing on the hardware side that would help protect the UNIX environment, while I also see nothing in hardware or the operating system that compels developers, or even Microsoft itself, to protect the operating environment, applications, and end-user data. It is one thing to have the fastest system in the West that turns on instantly — but if it also crashes faster and more often, it may be of little interest to the users.

Summary

We've explored legacy systems, and now Plug and Play, both from its theoretical and practical aspects, and peeked inside the industry's goals and dreams for ideal new PC setups.

If even half of the configuration benefits mentioned become reality in the next year, most of us will be enjoying relatively hassle-free computing. If we begin to see even half of the I/O speed benefits offered, then gaming, Web surfing and other typical PC activities will become more approachable, pleasant, and productive. Still, there are and will be for some time to come, many mysteries and new considerations for how we'll be able to transition to and use all of these technological advances with existing and new PC systems.

Having covered the rules and the promises of things to come, and having gone deeper into the realities we face right now — mixing old and new, understanding how they must be made to work together, and finding some practical examples of common pitfalls and their solutions — it is time to see how some of these things come together before us.

Chapter 6

Windows 95, 98, NT, and the Registry

IN THIS CHAPTER:

- How Plug and Play configures Windows
- What is the Registry?
- A practical view of Registry data
- How your configuration affects the Registry and how the Registry affects your configuration
- How you can affect changes in the Registry
- Don't neglect legacy and the PC foundation

After more than three years of trials and tribulations with Windows 95, "Plug and Pray," new BIOS, bigger hard drives, more memory, faster CPUs, new devices, a variety of new and old system crashes, we see that the legacy of the PC is still with us. It's a technical marvel and a nightmare at the same time, and perhaps somewhat spooky with more window-dressing and more cryptic configuration parameters.

For most of us, the new Windows 95 and 98 are better in a lot of ways than what some of us have had before. I would not credit these operating systems/environments alone with making computing more popular — I believe that our careers, the Internet, and a certain amount of peer pressure have done that. Certainly it is possible to enjoy the Internet and other social and functional computing activities just as much with an Apple Macintosh, a Sun workstation running Solaris, and perhaps even with a WebTV appliance. The PC and Windows have together helped make computing affordable and approachable to the common person. No doubt they have also influenced pricing of other makes of computers, making them more affordable.

For all of that, it appears Windows is here to stay, and so are many of the technical aspects. I will discuss how Windows works with all of the gadgets and configuration details covered so far. I believe it is important for users to understand some of these details, even at a very high level of functionality, action versus reaction, and interactions. In doing so, I hope to debunk some myths about what part of the overall PC system controls what other parts and how you can be sure to know that you have control over the whole system. This chapter may be more the short but sweet side, but it is very much to the point.

For significant detail about Windows and the Registry, you should gather up John Woram's *The Windows 98 Registry* from MIS:Press, Rob Tidrow's *Windows 95 Registry Troubleshooting,* and Brian Livingston's *Windows 98 Secrets* from IDG Books Worldwide. These are all very comprehensive and friendly works covering the Registry issues from stem to stern. You will also find lots of cumulative hints about various unsupported devices at the Windows 95 and 98 Annoyances Web site, `www.annoyances.org,` and many bug and patch notices at `www.bugnet.com.` Combined or separately, all of these works and several other online references, will either help make you an expert or make you wish you'd never asked.

Windows

Windows may still mean different things to different people. Users of Windows 3.*x*, Windows 95, and Windows 98 are all using Windows, regardless of the obvious differences between versions. In the next few months, someone using Windows 2000 will claim to be using Windows as well. It all seems to be a matter of perspective and which version is current in the marketplace. I won't make any assessments about who's right or wrong, who's up-to-date, or who's in the dark ages based on the operating system they use. For the most part, they are all getting done what they need or want to do with a PC system—even if they are running OS/2, Linux, or Solaris.

For our purposes, Windows means Windows 95 or Windows 98, with specific differences called out as necessary. Windows 3.*x* has been considered more of a GUI-atop-DOS than either 95, 98, or NT, and the configuration issues are carried out primarily at the DOS level. Windows NT has been and is significantly different from anything we have known related to a Windows system, although a proper configuration is just as important if not more so. However you look at it, it would seem that the Windows 95/98 family carries with it the best and worst of both worlds, the sum of which may or may not be equal to or greater than the sum of the parts.

As to the question of whether or not Windows 95 and 98 are operating *systems* or merely operating *environments*—YES. Perhaps a strange answer, but those who know me know what I mean—they are a bit of both. I would definitely say that they are indeed operating systems, certainly much more than merely shells or pretty faces atop a command-line-limited operating system and environment such as DOS.

Why are Windows 95 and 98 operating systems? The purpose of an operating system is to bridge the functionality and services of a computer system's hardware to applications programs that a user interacts with. An operating environment merely provides some form of navigation and interaction between a user and applications. Windows does indeed do much more than (as well as) that.

Yes, initially a PC system boots up into a DOS command-line interface providing access to some or all of the hardware devices in a system. Yes, you could do a lot with a PC system from just this interface. You could even presumably run the old DESQview environment or the Windows 3.*x* GUI atop this DOS. Yet, when

Windows 95 or 98 begins to load, DOS becomes almost a thing of the past. COMMAND.COM, the DOS command-line shell, is removed from memory and replaced with the Windows hardware drivers, memory management, kernel, and a significant graphical user-interface.

Because of some new hardware implementations, certain hardware devices may not be available to the DOS command-line environment that are readily or only available within the Windows environment. We have all but done away with DOS-level drivers for PCMCIA/PC Card devices. Also, I have yet to see DOS-level drivers for USB and FireWire devices.

Windows is providing operating system features, and thus it qualifies as such. It goes deeper than that as far as who is watching over the hardware, CPU, and shared environment, providing referee and monitoring functions so that applications do not have to watch out for each other as much (if they ever did before). Of course, we still have a lot of bad hardware and bad code to be watched after and something has to do it. DOS didn't have to do much of it because it was a single-task system. Windows 3.*x* did not do it. DESQ view did not do it.

I will take exception to considerations for how much things like network connectivity, Web browsing, telephony, applications functionality, and so on should be considered as or exclusive to the operating system. Windows has yet to prove that it plays well with other standard network environments without some third-party help (IPv6, IPsec, NFS, Novell's NDS, and so on). Internet Explorer doesn't always handle Web activities the same way other browsers do. Regardless of whether pieces of it are separate or buried in the operating system, it is not a requirement for making hardware functionality available to applications programs — it is an application. Modifying Java and pushing ActiveX on the Web has not done great things for global access to Internet resources — Linux, Solaris, and other UNIX systems can't play ActiveX — and users in these environments are not or possibly cannot change to Windows just because it is popular. There are probably other more subtle examples, but the context is pretty well established.

So, if we base the issues of an operating system on making hardware functionality available to applications, we are in the proper context to go forward into how the operating system and hardware interact.

How Windows Deals with Hardware

If it has not been made clear before now, this is the place to assert that Windows, as an operating system, does not determine the hardware configuration. Windows does contain a few services that facilitate or allow for some hardware configuration, but that is not its job. As with other operating systems, Windows is supposed to be provided with properly functioning hardware and then determines whether it can work with the hardware as provided, or not — and will hopefully provide us with status messages about its use of the hardware one way or the other.

That Windows is a "Plug and Play operating system" means only that it is designed to accept or adapt to the hardware configuration it is provided with once the system BIOS has done its job of detecting and dealing with the hardware configuration. That is the job of a Plug and Play BIOS — to figure out what is what and make it presentable to the operating system. That you can actually "Plug and Play" different hardware devices with the power ON in some cases (hot-plugging/unplugging devices) is one of the further benefits of both the BIOS and the operating system. They usually can, or at least should, play well together. In this context, the operating system facilitates being able to either dynamically load and unload from memory or to reconfigure device drivers as needed to suit changing hardware. This is a good operating system feature.

If Windows were not a Plug and Play operating system, all hardware would have to be known to the BIOS at startup, and nothing could be changed without manual configuration changes to the operating system (à la DOS and Windows 3.*x*). This would include providing any necessary drivers at the DOS-level and doing any hot-plugging before the rest of the operating system or environment loaded and ran.

The key message here is that Windows is driven by BIOS and, if available, Plug and Play functionality provided first by the hardware and second by integrated features of the operating system. This is a good thing. It means that hardware development and advancement can be done more or less independent of a single (operating system) vendor. This independence also gives us choices that lead to economic value. It also means that the operating system vendor cannot force users to change hardware with every change in the operating system. Because we continue to invest in faster CPUs and more drive space, it might seem like Microsoft is dictating those upgrades with Windows, but it would be foolish for Microsoft to assume that it can *actually* dictate such things lest it isolate tens of millions of consumers. We also have to consider that Intel and several dozen software publishers also contribute significantly to driving up hardware demands. They are all in business to make money, and as long as we participate in the cycle of supply and demand, the gluttony goes on.

That some independence remains between hardware, operating systems, and software also clearly presents some challenges. Having advanced hardware support capabilities through Plug and Play, PCI, and the operating system is a tremendous advantage. Having to consider the millions of PCs that do not have such advancements, and which leave us with the burden of legacy/ISA issues, keeps these advancements from reaching their goals and our expectations. Having to keep a BIOS feature and operating system compatible with the abundance of legacy/ISA systems and hardware is like running a Ferrari on rutted, muddy horse-and-buggy paths. You have a vehicle designed for high-performance operation on an improved platform, yet it has to crawl along in first gear, navigating carefully around every puddle and protruding field stone.

Microsoft has made a few attempts at shunning legacy, or at least the BIOS, with Windows NT. It had hoped to at least work around BIOS, ignoring it where it could, and even encouraged trying to have a BIOS that would get out of the way so that the operating system could displace its functions. The Windows NT HAL, or

Hardware Abstraction Layer, is the result of this half-successful attempt to ignore the machine and let the operating system rule. To this day, HAL has not replaced BIOS, and NT 4.0 has also not fully adopted Plug and Play technology — but then neither has any other significant multitasking operating system. Holding such an advancement back is a market that will not let go of what it has.

The downside to the advancements thus far is that some of the operating system's interaction with hardware must remain tied to the older technology used for several years by millions of people. Furthermore, much of the older technology is still being sold today. If there is money to be made with something, people will keep making it. As discussed earlier in this book, significant advancement like shunning legacy devices would have significant economic impact on millions of people. We have a balancing act to deal with — the costs of changing out and discarding legacy components with only marginal resale or recycling value must be weighed against the costs of frustration, lack of performance, lack of compatibility, and support efforts maintaining older devices.

As with cars and roads, nothing happens overnight. We adapted to superhighways, unleaded gas, and catalytic converters, scrapped and recycled what we could of older vehicles, and went on with life. So it will eventually be with computers and their operating systems. When enough old computers become dumpster food and are replaced by sleek, shiny new models, we will be able to make yet another leap ahead in configuration and usability. I do not believe that it will be the operating system leading the charge toward better configuration and usability, but rather the cost of system flexibility and user frustration with technical things.

So, just how does Windows interact with hardware and why?

BIOS & Plug and Play Revisited

Windows only knows what the hardware makes available or "tells" Windows it has to work with. First, the system BIOS goes through its Power On Self Test to survey the system for functional hardware devices. This information is stored in low memory for an operating system to gather up and process.

If Plug and Play BIOS does not exist, the operating system has only the hardware configuration it can determine from legacy devices to use. If Plug and Play BIOS exists, it takes additional steps to pick up the information the legacy BIOS found, and it moves ahead from where it left off—identifying Plug and Play devices and figuring out what can be configured to use the resources that the legacy devices are not using. In effect, Plug and Play BIOS negotiates with the Plug and Play hardware to establish a working configuration.

The resulting configuration is saved for the operating system to interrogate. If Plug and Play BIOS exists, the operating system has only to import all of the configuration settings found, configure drivers accordingly, and then, if there are unique Windows devices to be configured, fit them into what remains. In the absence of Plug and Play BIOS, the operating system has to provide the Plug and Play configuration functions, then pass the information on for driver configuration, and then let Windows-specific devices have their chance at getting resources. Occasionally, there may be DOS-level Plug and Play drivers used to activate PnP devices that may not have operating system support.

What we end up with is an operating system capable of dealing with dynamic hardware configuration data at bootup and later with certain types of truly Plug and Play devices. The former seems almost easy and obvious — read what's there, configure, load up, and go. The latter is quite a feat and is a credit to how versatile Windows can be. Through technology like USB and PC Card, devices and their drivers can be changed on-the-fly. These changes alert the operating system, which briefly halts normal operations to consider the new or removed hardware. Then, the operating system allows for reconfiguring, loading or unloading device drivers as needed, and gets back into the game with a different configuration.

Legacy devices never could (and never will) support this kind of dynamic presence and operation. Of course, the PCI and AGP bus devices, though they are Plug and Play devices, are not hot-swappable — the hardware is inconveniently internal to the system, and the connection design does not allow for hot-plugging and unplugging without potential damage to the system or the device. We need technologies like USB and PC Card to provide for these advanced features.

Once a device is in the Windows configuration, Windows must deal with it as-is. Without Plug and Play and hot-plug technologies, there would be tremendous opportunities for conflicts to be introduced into the operating system, bringing it to a halt more often than not. Enough of that happens with bad programs and poor memory management already. So, Plug and Play has to be able to prevent conflicts before they have to be resolved. Thus it must know, record, and make available all configuration information at all times. It must control the devices and not deliver a bad configuration to the operating system. The operating system therefore does not and cannot be in control of the hardware.

At this point it is safe to assert then that the Device Manager is not really or totally a device *manager* at all. What you may see of the operating system that appears to be in control of the hardware is actually Plug and Play services. It may be hard to separate the two aspects and acquire this perception once you are inside Windows, but that's the way it is. If Device Manager is allowed to let you change any resource settings that Windows knows, then that is all you are changing — the settings of what Windows might know about a device — it does not change the actual device configuration or resources used. Any hardware configuration changes will have to be performed manually, as on legacy devices, or by Plug and Play, which may or may not be able to change certain devices on the fly while things are in use and running (thus possibly requiring a reboot).

Why does Windows need to know all of this stuff about hardware at all?

We certainly want applications to make use of the features of the hardware we have. Being an operating system, Windows is responsible for supporting or denying what we want applications software to do with the hardware. The operating system enables us to perform various functions, and it also serves to protect us (users and applications) from performing various functions, such as:

- Displaying information at a proper but no higher resolution than a video card and its driver supports

- Ensuring that the storage system stores and allows retrieval of files and that proper file sharing or protection is available as needed

- Refereeing which application gets to use single-task devices such as modems, audio cards, printers, scanners, and so on

The operating system adapts various hardware specifics into common commands and functions that all applications can use without regard for which make or model of hardware is in the system. Unfortunately, the operating system has to be keenly aware of the hardware details, and it sometimes misses the mark by not fully qualifying all aspects of the hardware as part of an entire system rather than discrete devices.

You will see evidence of such discrepancies quite often with PCs such as various IBM, Hewlett-Packard, or COMPAQ models that do customized things with otherwise generic video and sound chips built into them. If you install a generic version of Windows, you find that you lose the functionality of one device or another. The solution is to find and install the original manufacturer-specific driver for that particular hardware. You would hope that Windows would identify what make or model of system you have to install the correct feature-specific drivers for that system. While the PC manufacturers and Microsoft have tried to work these problems out with vendor (OEM) specific versions of Windows, the companies can't seem to keep up with each other.

What Windows Remembers

If you venture into Windows Device Manager while running in Safe Mode, you'll probably see a lot of devices you either may not have known were in your system or features you thought you had gotten rid of. Windows remembers or stores in the Registry details about almost every device and piece of software that was ever installed on the system. In Safe Mode, very few devices are loaded or used. In Normal mode, Windows determines which devices are still active, usually the last or highest order entry, loads only those drivers, and shows only those items in the Device Manager reports. Occasionally, Safe Mode is handy for tracking what has happened to a system over the course of time. However, it also reveals that there is a trail of messy crumbs left in the system that we may stumble over from time to time. It's okay that the older unused items are in the Registry, so long as device drivers and such that are not needed are also not loaded into memory when we don't need them. Unfortunately though, this is not always the case.

One of the reasons for the unused device information being left behind is that, unlike within the operating system, there is no simple programmatic delete function for the Registry. It is possible to add or modify Registry entries, but getting rid of them means a larger task of exporting entire pieces of its structure, modifying them, and putting them back without the unused device info. Because of this, the Registry may appear to be a one-way or write-once, read-many, delete-never database — and that's what makes it so interesting, if you like that sort of thing. If you're wondering why the Registry is so big, this is it — like an elephant, it never forgets, and its size seems comparable to its evolution.

If you're wondering about those "IRQ holder for PCI steering" things that appear to share legacy IRQs, these are virtual IRQ settings, bridging a PCI interrupt to the legacy side of the system. They themselves are not conflicts. Rather, they are a software function to make it appear that a PCI device is using a legacy/ISA IRQ.

How Windows Gets Confused

If you've ever seen the yellow exclamation point or a red X next to a device in the Device Manager report, you know that it probably means something is wrong in the system. What you're seeing is the result of an analysis that Windows has run based on Plug and

Play data and the lack of ability to load a device driver for a specific device.

The exclamation point means that Windows has compared device settings and encountered a resource conflict, which may or may not render a device unusable. This is at the very least a warning. Some conflicts are allowed because they may not actually be conflicts — such as when a sound card is configured to use IRQ 7 when this IRQ is also assigned to an LPT port. Since LPT ports rarely if ever use the IRQ line, the sound card may function just fine on the same IRQ.

The red X means that either a serious resource conflict exists, or for reasons of memory or hardware configuration, the driver for the device could not get control of the device, or it could not be loaded into memory to function correctly. This is not a warning. It is an indication of a real problem. These special labels on devices in the list may indicate very different problems:

- A critical resource conflict occurred, and this device was not important enough or did not need to be loaded soon enough to get the resource allocation before another got it.

- The device is not configured as PnP, or Windows was told it was.

- The device has failed.

- There is some programmatic failure with the device driver.

This diagnostic information is stored in the Registry and may be recorded as a device driver load failure in the BOOTLOG.TXT file for system management purposes.

You may also encounter system information reports from Microsoft's MSINFO32 program or other programs that show multiple devices sharing the same IRQs, though Device Manager shows no conflict at all. Some apparent resource sharing is allowed. This may be if an IRQ is assigned to a PCI bus device and also apparently to an ISA bus device. Since the buses are electrically and logically separate, and IRQs are handled quite differently between the PCI and ISA bus, an apparent sharing rather than a conflict is possible. Sharing is not possible when a PCI device may have its IRQ logically mapped also to the ISA bus for backward compatibility for older programs or device drivers.

What confuses Windows, or us about Windows, is when it hangs onto a resource setting even though we have added or changed things and expect that Plug and Play has caught up and changed things accordingly. Device or system information programs will show the old settings and possibly conflicts, but Windows has evaluated the situation and determined that there are no conflicts. Basically, many PnP devices will hold their original resource settings unless something forces them to change. That something can be a PnP device that cannot be configured to use any other resources, thus the PnP process has to make something budge (but may not actually do so). That something can also be resetting the NVRAM or PnP settings through the BIOS/CMOS setup program, forcing the PnP process to renegotiate and reset device resources from scratch. This is the best way to get PnP to clean up its act.

All the information about devices that we can view in Windows comes from either of two sources. The information is either extracted from the current and Registry settings, or it is instrumented or detected by a system information program that can "see through" Windows and the Registry, going directly to the device to determine what is going on. Comparing the two can be a real eye-opener — and if there are differences, this should alert you to reset the PnP information immediately to get a more accurate picture of a possible configuration situation.

Good or bad, Windows 95 and 98 allow utility software to get some access to the hardware, which is good for us in this case and is further proof that the operating system does not fully own or control the hardware. Under Windows NT, direct access to the hardware is nearly impossible, unless someone creates a device driver that is specific to direct hardware information-gathering and diagnostics, which may render the device unavailable to the operating system for normal use. To take some or all of the mystery out of hardware configuration processes and utilities, most programs prefer or require that you work at the DOS level, to eliminate any of the variables or isolation that the Windows environment puts between the hardware and the utilities.

Many of the Plug and Play hardware devices retain their resources configuration without Windows being loaded, so we can get a pretty good picture of what the overall hardware configuration really is under DOS. This allows us a good comparison between a non-Windows and a Windows environment. Some devices, such as Winmodems do not retain or provide a DOS-level configuration, making it impossible to detect these devices or assess their configuration outside Windows. Similarly, infrared I/O ports may not indicate any configuration information under DOS, but mysteriously seem to own COM2 or another port assignment under Windows. With some systems, you can disable or preassign the infrared (IR) port configuration in the CMOS/BIOS setup program to try to get it out of the way, but somehow Windows may still find the port and provide it with a logical assignment, resources and all. This is a good point to remember when you're tracking down an elusive conflict.

What Is the Registry?

In a nutshell (and quite over-simplified), the Registry consists of proprietary Microsoft database files in Windows 95, Windows 98, and Windows NT (with important differences between them) to supplement and in most, but not all cases, replace the old Windows 3.*x* INI and CFG files. In many cases, a lot of the INI file information is duplicated in both INI and Registry files. INI files still exist in both operating systems for backward compatibility with older Windows software that still uses them. (For example, Qualcomm's Eudora e-mail program uses the same EUDORA.INI file for all Windows versions.)

In the case of Windows 95 and 98, the Registry database exists as two files, SYSTEM.DAT and USER.DAT. Each contains both static and dynamic system- and user-specific information relating to the system hardware, software, and various environmental configuration items. SYSTEM.DAT contains common system information that does not usually change between different user logons. USER.DAT contains various bits of user-specific information. The Registry contains a lot more information than any prior collection of INI files ever did. Because Windows 95/98 provides 32-bit program support, inter-application communications, and maintains hardware, network, and applications configuration data, and many other types of information, the amount of information it contains as a whole is staggering. If you are into complex data structures, the Registry is a fun place to dig around (and please do). The more the world outside of Microsoft knows about this little gem, the better for all of us.

Much of the information is either cryptic or basically useless to most of us Windows users. What you might expect to find as far as I/O port information is not obvious within the Registry. Instead, that information is coded into binary or hexadecimal numbers, and you must know a lot of details about how to first find and then interpret the information. This is at least one reason why mere mortals have to use system information tools, such as Windows Device Manager, to obtain system configuration details.

Windows 98 handles the USER.DAT differently than Windows 95 does. If you use different logon user names, Windows 98 automatically keeps separate USER.DAT files for each user, in different PROFILE directories for each user name. To get this same feature under Windows 95, you must select Passwords in the Control Panel and then select the option of users not sharing the same profiles. Then you are prompted about different user profiles at startup. If there is only one user of the system, there is only one USER.DAT and it is kept in the \WINDOWS directory.

Windows 98 also provides some features that Windows 95 did not have. Specifically, Windows 98 comes with the SCANREGW program. This program has several purposes. The first of which is to automatically scan for errors and optimize the Registry files when Windows loads. During this process it also makes a single Windows CAB-file backup of the SYSTEM.DAT and USER.DAT files, among others, if so configured. This backup process creates and maintains up to five different consecutive backup files.

f the SCANREGW program is possible by
at?—the C:\WINDOWS\SCANREG.INI file of all
_g_. Whether or not SCANREGW runs during system startup
is controlled by the Autoscan= parameter under [Options] in the
C:\MSDOS.SYS file. By default, the parameter is set to 1 to run
the scan every time. You can also invoke this process at any time by
using Explorer to navigate into the Windows directory and clicking
on the SCANREGW. You may be familiar with SCANREGW's
operation if you have ever seen its blue-screen "registry corrupt"
message when it runs during startup of Windows 98—typically
caused by a system, CPU, memory, or disk drive reliability problem.

Windows 95 users are not so lucky. Its "registry corrupt" messages are presented on the plain black DOS screen, and they offer
no recourse but to fix possible problems and reload the operating
system, reinstalling first with the existing Registry files in place.
Failing that, you must manually delete the old Registry files, and
then rename using the one and only backup Registry file set (.DA0
extension), or delete both the USER.DAT and USER.DA0 and
both SYSTEM.DAT and SYSTEM.DA0 and start Windows from
scratch again. This is obviously a bit complex, changing attributes,
deleting, and copying files, and so on. The closest thing Windows
95 users have to Windows 98's SCANREGW program are two
separate utilities—RegClean, which also requires an OLE driver in
OADIST2.EXE, both from Microsoft, and CFGBACK.EXE,
which is located on the Windows 95 distribution CD in
\OTHER\MISC\CFGBACK. Neither of these are automatic, nor do they
check for or report on any errors.

Several third-party freeware and Shareware Registry utilities
exist that also provide Registry and other critical file backups. The
Norton Utilities also provides Registry and system cross-checking
with its WinDoctor program. WinDoctor surveys the Registry and
your file system, checking Shortcut (LNK) files and file associations
for matches, excess Registry entries, and so on, and it can fix most
discrepancies and delete unnecessary Registry entries.

What's in the Registry?

These files combined contain at least three elements for each piece of information represented. The first is hierarchical key value (an HKEY-prefixed data field) that you might otherwise refer to as the pointer or index field. The second is the data definition or attribute (defining what the data type actually is within the HKEY reference). The third is the actual data value itself.

There are six primary or top-level keys:

- HKEY_CLASSES_ROOT (HKCR)
- HKEY_CURRENT_USER (HKCU)
- HKEY_LOCAL_MACHINE (HKLM)
- HKEY_USERS (HKU)
- HKEY_CURRENT_CONFIG (HKCC)
- HKEY_DYN_DATA (HKDD)

These keys may be seen in Figure 6-1 or by running the REGEDIT program provided with Windows 95/98/NT.

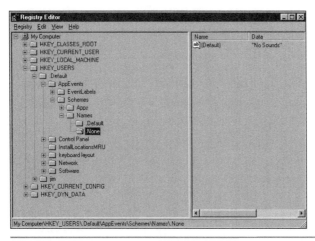

Figure 6-1 *Basic Microsoft REGEDIT program dialog box*

If you venture further into the Registry with the REGEDIT program and expand the key views available (double-click a key or click the [+] box), it will seem as though you are peeling back layers of a very large and complex onion. (Yes, some of us have shed a few tears in this process too!) What you will find are sometimes obvious and logical (but most often cryptic and daunting) names, labels, and data values.

Interestingly enough, you will eventually encounter what appears to be duplicated data values under two or more keys, at different layers. You may at first think that this is the reason your Registry files are so large (my SYSTEM.DAT file routinely tops 1MB in file size). In fact, if you change one of the values and then recheck other duplicate entries, you will notice that the apparently duplicate values have changed as well. What's going on here?

Not only is the Registry hierarchical in structure, it is also referential. That is, there can be and often are many different pointers or keys that refer to the exact same data points. This is one reason why, aside from the proprietary nature of the Registry, no one can describe exactly what the Registry data structures appear like. Thus, you will probably never see a database utility to convert Registry data into Microsoft Access, Excel, xBase, or other common data formats, because it simply and practically cannot be done.

Although there are duplicate references aplenty in the Registry, there are also non-duplicate entries that can contain the same or similar data. Thus, changing one value may not change all or more than one value. How do you know? Without significant research into every key and value, this question may remain unanswered for some time to come.

Registry data includes but is not limited to the following types of data:

- Basic and detailed system information
- Installed hardware devices
- Hardware configurations

- Installed software
- Software registration information
- Software configuration
- Application and file type associations
- Fonts and display information
- Desktop configuration
- Regional information
- Accessibility options
- User information including desktop profiles and preferences
- Application and file use history

Basically, you name it—if it has anything to do with your system, chances are some reference to it is in the Registry. Oddly enough, much of the information we're looking for in the context of this book is not obviously in the Registry, including but not limited to what we might expect of this large configuration database— IRQ, DMA, and I/O information as Windows sees it. Device resource information is encoded into the Data fields of various attributes. This data contains information that first describes the type and size of the data to follow, and then the data. Viewing this data in a meaningful fashion is the job of system information software, rather than trying to manually decode all of this information.

A Practical View of Registry Data

In actual use, each data value is referenced by or organized with at least one, and in most cases several, sub-levels of keys until the data value is accessed. Thus, a single data value, such as which port my mouse is attached to, may appear several layers down into the Registry hierarchy, as shown in Figure 6-2.

```
HKEY_LOCAL_MACHINE\SOFTWARE\Logitech\MouseWare\Current
Version\COM1
```

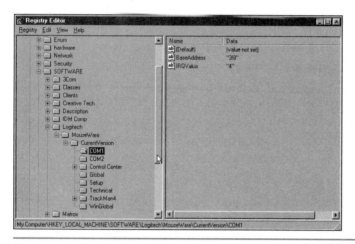

Figure 6-2 *The Registry Editor dialog box showing mouse port values*

Only in this key field, by the way, can I find any reference to legacy hardware port values (3F8 and IRQ4) for the COM1 I/O port. These are absolute/direct hardware values and, as we have discussed previously, would be different if logical COM1 were assigned (by the BIOS) to a different port address or IRQ assignment.

The COM1 port is also listed under two other system configuration keys, as shown in Figures 6-3 and 6-4, but you will notice that in neither of these listings will you see a reference to I/O addresses or IRQ assignments.

What we seem to be able to draw from this lack of conclusive legacy device information is that the port enumeration process (something Plug and Play and Windows 95/98 do internally) that associates ports with some predefined PnP device label (per Figure 6-3) would have to know or be told what COM1 or other devices mean or physically are in terms of addressing, IRQ, and if applicable, DMA.

It also shows, as illustrated in Figure 6-4, that the serialcomm device that Windows 95 knows as COM1 is indeed related to a data value of COM1 and similarly that the serialcomm device COM2 relates to a value of COM2.

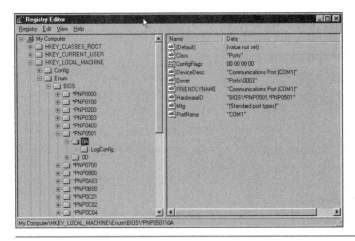

Figure 6-3 *The Registry Editor dialog box showing enumerated port values*

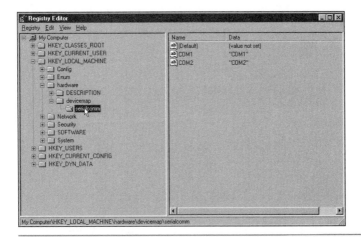

Figure 6-4 *REGEDIT dialog box showing serialcomm values*

If you delve further into Plug and Play (Chapter 5) and the Registry, you will find that Plug and Play defines many device types and their hardware values during its discovery processes and provides references to them for the operating system's use. Practically and realistically, we simply install a modem via the Control Panel, and then we select that modem from within our application's device list by some name or another—foregoing port assignments, and so on. If you thought the logical-versus-physical device translations that BIOS does was complicated, PnP just added at least one if not two more layers of translations to the process of simply getting a piece of software to talk to a piece of hardware. What happened to the good old days when computer techies wrote their own programs in BASIC or assembly language to directly address either a simple logical device or the actual hardware itself?

How Your Configuration Affects the Registry and How the Registry Affects Your Configuration

Your system configuration, as detected and set by the following items, has a tremendous effect on the Registry:

- Bootup/BIOS
- PnP BIOS/ESCD
- Windows SETUP
- Windows Add New Hardware
- PC Card/PCMCIA
- Windows 95/98 PnP Configuration Manager

The Registry does not affect the configuration; it merely stores it and makes the info available to the software and services.

The limited changes you can make to the hardware information stored within the Registry do not activate the Configuration Manager to make changes to the hardware configuration. If you change the Registry, you are only changing the stored information, not the device itself. Microsoft's preferred access into various Registry data is to use the Control Panel and other user-level controls, such as those built into the Explorer dialog boxes. Further, upon a restart of the system, the information may be changed back to the prior values discovered to exist in the hardware if you did not otherwise manually change the hardware to match the new Registry values.

How You Can Effect Changes in the Registry

I've shown a few screen shots from our use of the REGEDIT program, if only to display data points and illustrate the complexity (and sometimes the lack of data) in the Registry.

While there are times that REGEDIT is the most appropriate or only tool available to work directly with the Registry data (for example, to forcibly extract or change application data or to remove lingering application references after deleting or uninstalling a piece of hardware or software), REGEDIT may be too cumbersome or risky to use on a regular basis.

 Caution

As with any major or minor configuration change, other utilities and diagnostics that work with Plug and Play and hardware devices can either affect the Registry or make changes that cause the Registry to get out-of-sync with the actual system and make the system unusable. It can and probably will happen to you if you tinker with the system enough times.

Thus, *BACKUP* the Registry files before working with any configuration items. This means make copies of the SYSTEM.DAT and USER.DAT files to a safe place, preferably a bootable diskette. Merely exporting the Registry data does not make a backup suitable for full recovery purposes. Also, copy the DOS ATTRIB.EXE file to the diskette so that you can unlock the .DAT files in the C:\WINDOWS directory. This allows the backup files to be copied back over the corrupted ones.

Tip

If you have to boot from a rescue diskette or to the "Command Prompt" or otherwise copy Registry files because Windows 95 will not run, you need to unlock the existing SYSTEM.DAT and USER.DAT files, by removing their Read-Only file attributes. This is accomplished by using the DOS ATTRIB program, with the following command-lines:

```
ATTRIB -r -a -s -h C:\<windows>\SYSTEM.DAT
[Enter]
ATTRIB -r -a -s -h C:\<windows>\USER.DAT [Enter]
```

(where <windows> = your active Windows 95/98 location)

You may also need to remove the attributes in the same way to gain access to these files for copying to another directory or a diskette or to put them back later. A simpler way to do this is to use the CFGBACK (95), SCANREGW (98), or a third-party utility to archive the Registry.

Easier Tools to Use for Most Registry Work

Instead of using the REGEDIT program to directly and with considerable risk edit the Registry (since there is no means to "comment-out" or temporarily alter a Registry value for later editing), Windows provides more practical and suitable tools. Backup files of Registry data, SYSTEM.DA0, and USER.DA0 are made by Windows 95 as it starts up and discovers changed data. Otherwise, you have to backup the data with the Windows 95 CFGBACK program. (Available with the Windows 95 Resource Kit and on the Windows 95 CD under OTHER\MISC\CFGBACK.) Or use one of the third-party Registry backup utilities.

We can also affect the Registry indirectly when we start up our system, because a hardware detection process runs then, and a similar detection process occurs when new PnP devices or PC Card (PCMCIA) devices are added. In Windows 95 OSR2 and

Windows 98, the Registry also gets updated when you add or remove USB devices, because they are truly Plug and Play. We can also invoke this process with the Add New Hardware applet in the Control Panel.

The Control Panel is also the home to many other applets (little applications) that present and allow changes to Registry data in a context more appropriate to an end-user view of the system components. The standard Control Panel applets in a typical Windows 95 installation are:

- 32-Bit ODBC
- Accessibility Options
- Add New Hardware
- Add/Remove Programs
- Date/Time
- Display
- Fonts
- Joystick
- Keyboard
- Mail
- Modems
- Mouse
- Multimedia
- Network
- Passwords
- Printers
- Regional Settings
- Sounds
- System
- Telephony

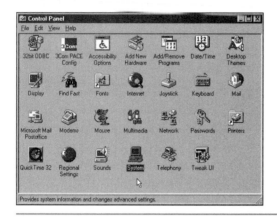

Figure 6-5 *The Windows Control Panel with additional features*

Typically, you might find yourself interacting with Add New Hardware, Date/Time, Display, Modems and Printers, and little else.

The most powerful of the applets is System, which contains a Device Manager tab (see Figures 6-6 and 6-7) to access hardware settings. This is our direct access to the Plug and Play Configuration Manager that is so important to PnP devices and PnP BIOS working with Windows 95/98.

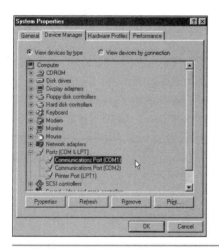

Figure 6-6 *The Device Manager dialog box*

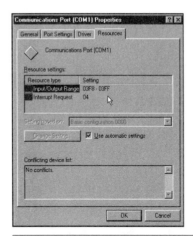

Figure 6-7 *The Resources dialog box for COM1*

Changing settings in a device's Resources tab may or may not actually reconfigure the device — certainly not legacy/ISA (fixed-setting or jumper or switch set devices, that you must physically change by hand) or those devices that require special device-specific configuration software. Many Plug and Play devices also cannot be either fully or partially reconfigured in the Resources tab, especially those devices that must have their own special settings in order for the system to function (certain aspects of disk drive and video adapters for example are expected to have fixed assignments — remember the rules).

Similar to the Registry's multiple access points to the same or similar data values, the Modems applet also gives us access to the same COM port resource settings you might also access through the Device Manager. So, if it's easier for you to think in terms of your modem when considering COM port values rather than the COM port itself, Windows 95 gives you the option to approach the hardware from a different context.

Microsoft also provides a very powerful and practical utility called TweakUI. The Windows 95 version is available from Microsoft's Web site at `www.microsoft.com/windows/download/ tweakui.exe`. Windows 98 users can find TweakUI on the Windows 98 CD-ROM under `\tools\reskit\powertoy`.

TweakUI provides access to several desktop, mouse, and other settings, normally resident but practically inaccessible within the Registry, that can enhance the way Windows 95/98 behaves. None of the features available within TweakUI affects hardware device configurations however.

If you have a portable/laptop system or if your desktop has a PCMCIA/PC Card interface on it, the system configuration can change when PC Cards are inserted or removed. Similarly, docked and undocked portable systems also affect the system configuration because a docking station may contain additional network cards, parallel, or serial ports that are not part of the original/bare portable configuration.

At this point, I won't go into detail about the different resources and values you can access for the various hardware devices in your system. As you'll see in the next section, the Registry and its access methods (REGEDIT or the Control Panel) do not give us access to all of the foundation elements we need to deal with to establish and maintain a proper system configuration. Also, some points are better illustrated in Chapter 7, which covers typical conflicts and their resolutions.

Don't Neglect Legacy and the PC Foundation

It bears repeating here that as good as Plug and Play and Windows 95/98's configuration detection and setting features are, they cannot handle the settings for or resolve conflicts with legacy/ISA devices. If the basic system and its devices are not configured properly, no amount of software or fancy user interface or complex Registry data or tools are going to do any good. Also, from Chapter 5, remember that Plug and Play does not always play by the expected or desired standard configuration rules for basic PC devices.

Certainly, as your system boots up, the PnP BIOS detects devices, and as Windows 95 or 98 starts up, many devices are determined and configured for us automatically. Sometimes the devices aren't really configured by as much as they are reported to the Registry and Windows 95/98 for what they are, so programs can access them. What's really happening is that Windows 95/98 is being configured to work with the devices found. The devices are not being configured to suit Windows 95/98, because device drivers are used to match specific devices to the Windows environment and functions. Devices are identified and reported in terms of predefined PnP device types and attributes rather than discrete hardware devices (those with addresses, IRQ and DMA assignments). If the hardware devices are configured incorrectly, Windows 95/98 will be configured incorrectly; some things just may not work as we would expect them to.

Changing devices at the Device Manager level may not always affect a change to the hardware — unless the device is a PnP device or otherwise allows the internal Configuration Manager (Resources dialog box) to change the resources. Again, typically, this only reconfigures Windows, and we still have to deal with configuring the hardware. This is why Windows 95/98 will present a dialog box telling you to shut down your system, reconfigure the device manually, and start up again for changes made to many legacy and some PnP devices. So much for Plug and Play — you do the work, and the operating system might be able to figure it out after the fact. As discussed in Chapter 5, we may not want Plug and Play to do some of these configuration things for us anyway.

For example, if COM1 is misconfigured and there is only one COM port in the system, and that port is (improperly, for being the only COM port) addressed as 3E8h (the COM3 address) using IRQ 4, Plug and Play and Windows 95/98 will simply accept this port assignment and go about their merry way. If you use the Device Manager to tell Windows 95/98 that COM1 should be addressed as 3F8h, suddenly the port will become unusable (and the device's dialog box will indicate so), because you have not actually changed the port's settings, just those in Windows 95/98. More confusion. Your misconfigured system (because the COM port itself is misaddressed, mismatching physical versus logical assignments) is now doubly misconfigured because the operating system doesn't match the prior (incorrect) BIOS/logical device assignment.

Yes, Windows 95/98 and the device attached to the COM port may work just fine in a misconfigured system, if the misconfiguration is compensated for by misconfiguring Windows, but this only complicates future upgrade and maintenance issues you will more than likely encounter through the life of your PC system.

Use or Avoid the Registry for Configuration Management?

The PnP device discovery and configuration routines and the ESCD are responsible for providing the initial system hardware configuration information. If you're hoping to use the Registry to alter or correct a system configuration issue, such as a misassigned COM port address or IRQ, you may have figured out that this isn't the place to do it. The Registry and the tools that can affect it inside the operating system are not as effective as providing a good configuration before the operating system loads up. They deal with what they are told; they do not make any attempt to inform of or perform a configuration correction. It may be obvious that Windows 95/98 actually allows the use of a misconfigured system, by compensating for the misconfiguration. This may help you get some work done now, but it does not help you later on.

Note

To illustrate this point, if you do operate with a currently mis-configured system under Windows 95/98, using our example of COM1 being misaddressed (at 3E8h), and assign or change applications to use a modem on that COM1 port as-is, then later add another COM port, addressed (properly) as COM1 or COM2, thereby changing the prior COM1 assignment to become COM2 (remembering our logical rules from before), the application that used a modem on (the prior) COM1 will suddenly find no modem on COM1 and fail.

Although Windows 95/98 allows you to alter what it shows and stores for hardware resource settings, the Registry and REGEDIT applications are obviously not the place for altering your system hardware configuration — not the least because they do not actually have any control over the hardware. Neither are the Device Manager or any other context-sensitive approaches (such as the Modems applet to access COM port settings) the appropriate place to manage your PC's configuration. For at least this reason, the whole of this book and all of the technology from "PC Day One" and beyond must still be attended to. We must manage our own PCs and, as a result, the operating system and applications that use the hardware. We cannot count on the hardware, operating system, or software to do that for us.

It is imperative to understand that PnP and the operating system react more to what is than they proactively establish or correct things to what should be, all legacy/ISA, customary/traditional issues considered.

Instead, the physical system configuration drives or determines how and what the operating system will find to work with. This may not be what we expected of Plug and Play, but then most of us are not, and will not be, working with pure Plug and Play systems just yet. When we do, we will have more information available to save us some time and point us in the right direction. By the time we do have 100 percent PnP systems and no legacy devices to contend with, perhaps too all of the software vendors will fall into better compliance and leave the configuration of devices up to the operating system rather than propagating the need to worry about hardware details.

Summary

Certainly Plug and Play and the Registry have a tremendous influence on our systems, but they are not the exclusive or pivotal points of reference for new PC configuration issues that we have been seeking.

Having discovered that it is rarely if ever effective to go to the Registry to resolve system configuration and conflict issues, and quite possibly detrimental to your system if you do, it's probably time to consider just how we actually do address these issues in our current systems and look ahead to enhancements and expansions.

Now that we've followed the rules and technology advancements, it's time to go on to show the configurations and some significant upgrade examples, trying to take a typical system into at least 1999 standards and perhaps beyond to the year 2000.

Chapter 7

Progressing to PC99

One of my goals with this edition was to see how far I could push the average off-the-shelf collection of PC parts from using legacy devices into being a 100 percent non-legacy system. The promise is there — Plug and Play, PCI, USB — theoretically it could be done. This chapter is about trying to get there. Our goal is to do away with anything that has a jumper, switch, or custom configuration software, and let the fixed configuration of the device, or Plug and Play, take over. This is required by the PC99 specification, with legacy devices optional but preferably avoided.

There are a few challenges to fulfilling this goal, not the least of which is finding enough of the right non-legacy devices in the local stores to make it possible. You might think that because I'm in the heart of Silicon Valley I would have been practically tripping over USB and FireWire devices as I walked from the parking lots into the local computer stores. And you'd think that all of the legacy devices would be sitting on the bargain basement, 90 percent off tables.

Unfortunately, euphoria and techno-snobbery have not taken over the off-the-shelf consumer PC market. Instead, I had to look carefully through the same old collection of legacy ISA and current

PCI devices just to find the USB devices. When I could not find some of the USB devices I wanted for the PCs, I ended up in the aisle of Apple Macintosh accessories. I was almost embarrassed to be shopping among the Mac supplies for hardware I would be using on my PC. However, remembering that Apple not only was among the first to ignore the old hard drive interfaces in favor of SCSI devices, but gave us the Apple Serial Bus (likely an inspiration to USB) and a few other innovations we're now appreciating with the PC as well, I didn't feel too bad. I was also calmed by the fact that Mac users have to go to the PC aisle to get PCI devices, and they stand around the same memory, CPU, and disk drive aisles as the rest of us. I found little or nothing for FireWire or FibreChannel devices — they are just not priced for or required by the consumer market yet. When I build a full high-end server room and a video editing studio, I'll be back!

What I could not find in the stores I had to go out hat in hand to borrow from a few vendors. Fortunately, a few were more than willing to help out — presumably to give their investment in USB development a little extra marketing push. The vendors need this new technology to be accepted for them to succeed. Acceptance partially means that you can get your average, outside the margins press guy to use and like the products and tell others. They did not let me down, and I hope I don't let them down either!

What are we waiting for? We've been shopping. The office looks like Christmas exploded early with all of the shipping boxes, packing, instruction manuals, and shiny new toys. Let's get to it!

Our Legacy Guinea Pig

This project started out with an average 1997-vintage Pentium PC system. What's it got?

- Socket 7 Pentium system board
- Cyrix 233MHz CPU
- 32MB of RAM — EDO DIMMs

- Matrox Millenium PCI video card
- Creative Labs Sound Blaster 16 ISA sound card and analog speakers
- External USR Courier V. Everything modem on the built-in COM2 port
- Logitech TrackMan Marble on the built-in COM1 port
- Palm Pilot cradle on add-in COM 4 port
- Quantum hard drive and CD-ROM drive on IDE interface
- Adaptec AHA-1540 SCSI Adapter for SCSI CD-writer
- 3Com Etherlink III ISA network card
- UMAX parallel port-interfaced scanner on the built-in LPT1 port
- Generic 20-inch VGA monitor

At various times I would rotate out system boards as I upgraded one or the other, so this system has been everything from a 120MHz Pentium up to the present state. The system board is equipped with a PS/2 mouse port, which I simply chose not to use, even though the TrackMan would connect to it just fine. The system board documentation also claimed to have a USB port on it, but there is no connector for the add-on USB paddle-board to connect to, and there's no way to enable the port in the BIOS.

The challenge appears to be to get rid of the obvious legacy devices—the COM port devices, the sound card, the network card, and the scanner. This should free up some resources, which of course we may not need if the legacy devices disappear. The disappearance of legacy devices begs a new question: If we do away with legacy devices, why do we need all of the remaining free legacy resources? Will IRQs, DMA, and addresses go away?

Answer: Most devices will move off to the PCI bus IRQ, DMA, and I/O address space—as if it can handle any more than the three to five devices we can fill our slots with. Others will move off to AGP or USB. There is or will be only one AGP port until PCI makes another leap forward and AGP, like the VESA Local Bus, fades as quickly as it came about. USB allows for 127 devices, but it uses only one set of conventional system board device resources. This transition will give us more resources for new Plug and Play devices, if there ever are any. After all, how many serial port devices, printers, scanners, cameras, and so on can one person have and use on a PC at a time? So, you'll probably wonder why we're doing this as we go along.

The Legacy PC As-Is

Table 7-1 shows the configuration details of the system we started out with. Nothing spectacular here, and really very little reason to upgrade it if we're satisfied that we have enough devices to play with and don't need any more performance. Since IRQs are typically the rarest resource and toughest to configure around, the list is ordered by IRQ number.

Table 7-1 *Mixed Legacy and Plug and Play System Resource Usage*

Device	Address	IRQ	DMA
System Timer		0	
Keyboard		1	
*		2	
Modem – COM2 (ISA)	2F8h	3	
Pilot – COM4 (ISA)	2E8h	3	
Mouse – COM1 (ISA)	3F8h	4	
* – COM3 (ISA)	3E8h	4	
Sound Card (ISA)	220h	5	1
Diskette Interface	3F6h	6	
Scanner – LPT 1	378h	7	3 (ECP)
Clock/Calendar		8	
3Com NIC (ISA)	280h	9	
Adaptec SCSI (ISA)	330h	10	
Video Card (PCI)	3B0h/3C0h	11	
* PS/2 Mouse Port		12	

Device	Address	IRQ	DMA
CPU/FPU		13	
Primary IDE	1F0h	14	
Secondary IDE	170h	15	

= Not used

This configuration is not bad, but it appears that perhaps only IRQ 2 may be available. You will notice that I am sharing IRQ 3 between COM 2 and COM4, but I've always been careful to avoid using the modem when working with the Pilot. I use a network printer, but a local device could be plugged into the scanner's pass-thru parallel port to make things seem a bit more normal. I have a few IRQs left, which is good only if the devices I might add can use the ones that are available. Unfortunately, IRQs 2 and 9 are troublesome or unusable for some devices. Also, Windows 95/98 will almost always find the PS/2 mouse port and IRQ, even if disabled in CMOS/BIOS setup and in Device Manager. We'll keep this table in mind as we move things off to USB or other I/O methods.

The Non-Legacy Options

As I scoured the stores and the Web for nifty things that someone might eventually want or need to use, or things that would be suitable to replace legacy devices, I didn't find anything that was *really* compelling, except perhaps a faster scanner. Anyone who has used a parallel port interfaced scanner and then used one that is connected to a SCSI port will tell you that there is a world of difference. SCSI is simply faster. I'm a little superstitious about keeping only storage devices on my SCSI ports, so a USB scanner seemed the most compelling item. Digital cameras also intrigued me, because I telecommute and would like to video conference occasionally. However, like parallel port-interfaced scanners, parallel port cameras left me with clunky images.

I dug back a little in my experiences and remembered the high-tech VP I worked for that wanted all of the extra gadgets he could get his hands on connected to his PC. That included an infrared I/O port, his Pilot cradle, two (yes, TWO) printers, and a parallel interface digital camera. Most troublesome in this case was supporting three parallel I/O devices — actually getting Windows 95 to recognize a port at 3BCh and work with a supposed IRQ conflict.

I figured if I could come up with a way to give this VP everything he could ever want, without my having to spend hours configuring everything, I'd have succeeded. I decided that I'd keep my average system somewhat modest, but able to depend on USB for most future expansions for those gotta-have-it-all folks. Despite the lack of USB devices available in the stores, I actually had more check marked items on my shopping list than items left unchecked when I was through. Again, I avoided FireWire intentionally — devices and the interface are too expensive, and it would not offer anything practical for us yet.

USB Capability

The first thing I needed was USB capability. Because Windows 95 retail version and OSR1 do not support USB, and Windows 98 had just been released, well, I had to use the latest operating system. So that was the first upgrade. Luckily it was a good experience.

My system board did not support USB, so I had two options — a PCI USB expansion card provided by ADS or a new system board. (They also sent a PCMCIA/PC Card version which I have yet to try in my laptop.) MSI Computer had just sent me their MS-5169 board to try out, though it was an ATX format board and used DIMMs for the memory, and I was still stuck in AT-style casings with SIMMs. I eventually bit the bullet, bought an ATX case and a couple of DIMMs, and went whole hog. The results are parallel to the PCI USB expansion card experience, but the MSI board also provided an AGP port, which let me convert the video from PCI to AGP and free up a slot that I needed to use. Check off two items from the shopping list!

Either way — PCI expansion card or system board USB ports — you get two USB ports to work with. Two USB ports is not a lot considering that the interface is capable of addressing and supporting 127 different devices, which is why the next thing on the list is a USB hub.

USB Hubs

In my search for USB devices on the Web, I ran across a couple of firms that offered USB monitors. I knew that they don't use the USB port for video, and I learned that USB is used to provide Plug and Play information and PC-based monitor configuration features. A monitor from ADi also provided a four-port powered USB hub internally. This, I thought, was the way to go — you need a monitor anyway, and if it has a hub, you save having to add one more external widget to get in the way.

USB ports and hubs are an interesting subject. This is where you really start to learn or need to learn about some of USB's features and properties. Hubs may or may not provide power to the ports you connect devices to. Hubs are almost useless if they do not provide power, unless you have all externally powered, or high-power USB devices with their own power supply. The USB specification indicates that no device or port shall allow for more than 25 watts of power drain per port — a whopping 5 amps at 5 volts. There is *no* way that the hubs I encountered, or their power supplies, could handle a single 25-watt load, much less four or eight 25-watt devices. That would be 100 to 200 watts, or 20–40 amps of current.

The power supply for one hub I have is rated for only 2.5 amps/12 watts. Some of that capacity is consumed by the hub's own internal circuits. Something is obviously wrong with the USB spec. The typical low-power devices I encountered draw less than 0.5 amps, so four of them connected to a hub, plus the hub's power consumption, seems to make more sense.

Each hub must have its own power supply, even if it is a non-powered hub, which does not provide power to devices connected to its ports. Again, those can only be self-powered or high-power USB devices that require too much power to be supplied by the hub. The USB port on your PC or an add-in card should be a powered port.

Check the specifications carefully. In these cases the power supplied comes from the same source that supplies your system board. So, if you have a defective or shorted USB device or cable, you will shut down your system. It is best if you connect only powered hubs to the system's USB ports, to avoid whole system shutdowns.

Hubs are also not allowed to pass power cumulatively from one to the other. A unique cable connector is used for hub to port connections, and it does not have power wires in it. Devices and USB ports use a four-wire cable and the plug is flat or rectangular compared to the two-wire hub-to-port connection, which on the hub is more square.

So, when you're shopping for USB devices, check their power consumption. Then, when you select a hub, remember to check the capacity of the power supply. Do some arithmetic and make sure that the hub power supply is adequate to handle all the devices you can plug into it. Add up either the watts or the amps. If you can't directly match the figures, calculate a common rating value. All devices run at 5 volts. Multiply 5 volts by the current in amps to arrive at the available or required wattage, or divide the wattage by 5 to arrive at the current drain or capacity.

ADi stepped up to the task and later helped me with a couple of troubling USB issues. Check off one 19-inch monitor with a fabulous picture *and* a built-in powered USB hub! Later, I purchased an additional four-port powered USB hub (selected from the Macintosh aisle at the computer store). So, hubs get a second check mark on the list.

USB Devices

Our USB hub search already provided us with a USB monitor, an added bonus that also furthers our Plug and Play capability and compliance goal. The big step is to see which of the legacy devices we can displace or add with non-legacy devices — USB or otherwise. Our targets are the mouse, the modem, the sound card, the network card, and if possible, the Palm Pilot cradle.

Essential Upgrades

Eliminating the pointing device from COM1/IRQ4 and not using the PS/2 port/IRQ 12 wasn't as ideal as I wanted it to be. I'm a trackball user—specifically Logitech's TrackMan Marble. The Marble was not available in USB. Because most folks are mouse users, and Microsoft had just introduced its WheelMouse in a USB version, that was it. One USB mouse checked off on the shopping list, and our first legacy resource is free.

Changing the modem was an easy choice. I'm a diehard USRobotics user, and they now have a USB version. One more check mark on the shopping list, and COM2/IRQ 3 is free.

Next on the list is dumping the old legacy Sound Blaster. There are lots of choices here—from myriad PCI cards to only a couple of USB speaker options. I acquired a set of Labtec LCS-1040 USB speakers that provide the functions of a sound card inside the speakers. As a backup, I also picked up a PCI sound card. Check off the sound card and IRQ 5 and DMA 1 which it used.

Though I could have done so, I elected not to try a USB network interface. It just seemed a bit silly to fill up a 12MB pipe with all of that data should I eventually convert the network to 100BaseT from 10BaseT. I opted to finally put my 3Com Fast EtherLink 10/100 PCI Plug and Play card to use in the system, knowing that USB was certainly a viable option. Keep in mind that there are USB networking products out there for those who just need to hook up a couple of machines for sharing files, printers, or playing games, but who do not need full 10BaseT or TCP/IP and other features. This also frees up an I/O address, and we'll see about the IRQ later.

I had to relent a little by keeping an active COM port rather than tossing out my current Palm Pilot for a new version. I could have opted for a USB-interfaced COM port adapter, and I may still do that, but because I've freed up the need for the two add-on ports, and the remaining two are built into the system board, I left them. The most I could hope for in a new version of the Pilot would be to go with infrared connectivity, and most systems support infrared ports only as COM ports anyway, so I would not have gained anything by changing this device at this point. When they put USB into a Pilot, I'll go for it — maybe by 2000?

I could have gone for a USB keyboard to make the PC more Mac-like, but there were no USB keyboards for the PC on the shelf. Also, since I scrounge endlessly to find any and all variants of the old Northgate Omnikey keyboards for all of my systems, I was hesitant to take on a new keyboard in the middle of a major writing project. A USB keyboard may have added some to the Plug and Play equation, but it would have done nothing to free up legacy resources. Well, okay, IRQ 1 would have become available, but that IRQ is permanently wired to the system's keyboard I/O port, which you cannot disable, and the IRQ is not available for other devices anyway.

Optional Upgrades

Next, I considered the items or functions that would benefit from higher performance and those items or functions that were desirable and could be added to round out the system features. Again, without any legacy issues whatsoever.

I was running out of disk space, and being disappointed with the performance of even UltraDMA33 IDE drives, I went whole hog and converted everything to WideSCSI. Well, almost everything. The CD-ROM writer and a second SCSI CD-ROM to replace the IDE CD-ROM drive stayed on the SCSI-2 side of a new Adaptec AHA-2940W applied to the PCI bus. The IDE disk drive was replaced by a single 9GB Quantum device. It would appear that I've opened up at least one more IRQ, 11 this time, and an I/O address. I also give up the IDE interfaces at 1F0h and 170h, and their IRQs 14 and 15. I can disable these in CMOS/BIOS setup, but Windows may find them anyway and require me to disable these specifically in Device Manager.

The scanner on the parallel port could stay there or not, because most people maintain their local printer and port anyway. However, faster was more appealing, and I couldn't resist checking out the new H-P 6250C with USB. I'm glad I did. Follow that up with a color printer on USB, and I'm really good to go for those holiday pictures!

Ah, pictures. Well, this could go a couple of different ways. FireWire is the right option for full motion video off of a camcorder, but at $1,000 to $2,000 a whack for a decent camera, plus the expense of a FireWire interface card, I said no, not this year. The next, more modest options were either a digital snapshot camera or a small PC video camera. All of the commonly available consumer cameras still use serial ports to transfer the data, which means both slow and legacy for $400 to $800. Hey, catch up, guys! This left me with a small but impressive handful of USB PC video cameras with USB ports. The most available choices were the ViCam from Vista Imaging, the C-It camera from Xirlink, and the WebCam from Creative Labs. I've had all three to play with and compare — very cool. While not portable nor Christmas dinner portrait quality, these are great items!

I couldn't resist trying an AGP video card. We've got an avid 3D-gaming expert in-house, and I wanted to show him up once I cranked up the new system board. As it turns out, once we got done adding up all of the devices, we were beginning to run out of PCI ports, and the AGP video card was just the thing we needed to make room, sort of.

USB Device Issues

I've already touched on some of the characteristics of USB devices, but there is more than power consumption to consider when working with USB ports, hubs, devices, and their device drivers.

Drivers First

One of the first problems I encountered when I began to set everything up was probably typical of most initial new toy experiences. The first thing you do is rip open the box, grab the widget, unwrap it, and plug it in. Wrong. That does not work with most USB devices, because even Windows 98 does not have an adequate compliment of drivers to handle all of the new things that are being released. So, at least in the case of USB, *stop* and read the manual, or at least get out the CD and install the drivers first, before you plug the unit in. You will not damage anything by plugging the device in first without the drivers, but Windows will appear to be confused, try to identify the device, and then ignore it. Windows definitely needs the drivers for the device in order for it to identify it properly and do the Plug and Play thing to load the device driver and enable it.

Marginal Devices

The second problem is a little more baffling technically. One of the cameras I tested, an early but still production version, absolutely fails to be identified when plugged into the ADi monitor's hub. Windows acts normally for a second, aware from the USB port that something has changed, but then it ignores the device as if nothing ever happened. This camera similarly does not work on another monitor's hubs. However, another similar vintage camera does work fine with the monitor's hub, and the troublesome camera works great on both the system's USB port and the extra hub I have. Go figure. The high-level technical response, without taking everything into the lab with all of the scopes and signal analyzers, is that we may find that some devices have marginal signal quality. I can accept this for some of the very early devices whose stock should have been exhausted well before you read this. It's my impression that USB product vendors will be eager to please you, and they will replace any questionable devices.

Power Glitches

The third problem is more baffling yet, and it proves my last point. Under any and all circumstances, the Hewlett-Packard scanner worked flawlessly on any port or hub I connected it to. The darned scanner is *so* nice that I hope Santa lets me keep it. However, one day I was messing with the disk drives and cross-connected the diskette drive power plug, shorting either the 5- or 12-volt line to ground. (Sound of fans and drives winding down — *rats!*) Well, one replacement power supply later (I'm really going to rewire these things with fuses someday), and the system is back up. Well, all except for the scanner. No matter what I did or what USB port I plugged it into, the scanner could not be identified by Windows 98, though Windows acted like it knew something changed on the USB ports. Then, to make matters worse, the system hung up—no toggling of the NumLock LED, no Ctrl+Alt+Del—the system required a hard reset, without the scanner connected, to come back to life. Without the scanner connected, all ports, hubs, and devices worked just fine.

After a couple of technical support sessions it was decided we'd replace the scanner, and the bad one would go to the lab for detailed tests. A new scanner arrived and worked flawlessly. The bad one was checked out and apparently worked fine at the lab. One of those *weird* problems we'll never know the answer to.

This last issue does point out that any device bus is vulnerable to power supply problems, and, as with the primary USB ports on the system board that take power from the same supply as everything else, you have to be careful about what you're doing at every step. For this reason, I recommend that you use an external USB hub for all devices to isolate the devices and the system from each other.

High-Speed or Low-Speed?

In addition to low-power (bus-powered) and high-power (self-powered) USB devices, there are both high- and low-speed devices. Low-speed devices are typically items like mice, keyboards, and classic serial I/O ports that do not need to transfer massive amounts of data, nor at high-speed. High-speed devices are typically items such as scanners, printers, cameras, and networked devices. There are no options for the type or speed of device you get, nor are there issues of the hub or port speeds. USB identifies and automatically changes speed as needed for each device.

High-speed may only be an issue, as with the flaky camera, if signal cables are not of high enough quality for the speed of the device or the length of the cable used, or if the device uses marginal chips. You won't know what's what without trial-and-error between different ports or systems, and using the diagnostics that come with the device, if any.

Why Change to Non-Legacy if Things Are Working Okay?

We're looking ahead here. Ahead to the day when a replacement system board or new system, the operating system, some piece of software, a new device, or an old type of device, is not available with any type of legacy support at all. That day is coming. It may be mid-1999, late-1999, or after we've survived the Year 2000 issues.

If your system is already at or close to the limit of available resources, you don't have a choice. Either dump a device or upgrade. This day is looming ahead for many of us already.

Apart from the inevitable, performance is always an issue. Having the latest 450MHz Pentium-II system sitting in your den with your activity held back by a nibble-mode parallel port scanner can be a bit cumbersome. Even if we don't care that the scanner is slow, when we need to telecommute and video conference, this means multi-tasking. Productivity is shot to pieces if you are stuck waiting for the printer or some other I/O activity. Speedier devices mean you can get back to work quicker, or you can play more enjoyably.

I don't think the basic serial port will ever disappear completely, or as soon as some might hope. Too many things still use it. I am surprised that digital snapshot cameras still use serial ports . . .what's up with that? Apple's computers have never had a native parallel port. They use a serial port, SCSI, or AppleTalk network instead. The PC world's answer to the parallel port has been to try to enhance it with three different feature/function methods that have not really caught on. Why bother anymore.

There are some hitches in some of these new things, mainly with how the software, drivers, or the operating system handle certain devices or tasks. Most PC camera software will only allow one such device to be active at a time, even if you use separate and different programs and devices. Thus, you cannot have a camera on the front door and another on the pool and watch what's going on at both locations at the same time.

If your camera uses the TWAIN driver, only one of these devices can be used at a time. This means that you cannot have the (TWAIN) camera active and use your scanner at the same time — bummer.

I'm sure that some of these bumps will be ironed out soon. Until they are, and by the time they are, there is and will be a lot of benefit to be had from these new devices.

Jim's New Improved 1999 PC

Despite the little bumps and diversions in our journey to create a 100 percent non-legacy system, I think things turned out pretty well. Let's see how well by looking at Table 7-2 to see what has become of the resource usage.

Table 7-2 *Resource Usage Resulting from Our Non-Legacy Upgrade*

Device	Address	IRQ	DMA
System Timer		0	
Keyboard		1	
Not used		2	
Disabled – COM2	2F8h	3	
Removed – COM4			
Pilot – COM1	3F8h	4	
Removed – COM3			
Not used		5	
Diskette Interface	3F6h	6	
Not used – LPT 1	378h	7	3 (ECP)
Clock/Calendar		8	
3Com NIC	DF00h (PCI)	9 (PCI steering)	
Adaptec SCSI	D800h (PCI)	10 (PCI steering)	
USB Host	(PCI)	11	
Disabled – PS/2 Mouse Port		12	
CPU/FPU		13	
Disabled – Primary IDE	1F0h	14	
Video Card (PCI)	3B0h/3C0h	15	
Mouse	USB	USB	USB
Sound	USB	USB	USB
Scanner	USB	USB	USB

From the table, it appears that I have a number of free resources — IRQs 3 (if I disable COM2), 5, 12, and 14. Notice that in this new configuration, the video card was reconfigured (automatically) to use IRQ 15 instead of 11, and USB took IRQ 11.

I may or may not have also opened up IRQs 9 and 10, but I have noted that these are occupied with the 3Com network card and the Adaptec SCSI host adapter, and I noted PCI bridge for each. These are more formally listed as IRQ holder for PCI steering, which in Windows and PCI terms means that this IRQ has been reserved for a PCI device, but if an ISA device that uses this IRQ is installed later, the Plug and Play routine will disable, reconfigure the PCI device to another IRQ, then re-enable the PCI device. This is what Plug and Play and PCI are all about — the ability to be reconfigured around non-configurable or non-Plug and Play devices. IRQ 7 is available if we don't need or use the printer port, which is typical with shared network devices.

With four available IRQs (possibly four with IRQ 2 still open), we should have no problem configuring and installing legacy devices as needed, or configuring and installing new Plug and Play devices with fear of running out of resources.

Adding the USB I/O ports (2) consumes no more legacy resources than a single IRQ (11). USB now handles five devices, the mouse, sound features, modem, camera, and scanner, all with one resource. Giving up one IRQ for a possible 127 new devices is pretty impressive. Intel has reportedly hooked up a total of 111 USB devices to one system — incredible. If we added a FireWire adapter, we'd have to give up one more resource, but the performance exceeds USB, and the expansion benefits are similar, so we'd gain several more devices per consumed resource.

When USB Is Not the Best Solution

There are certain things that may not be ready for a changeover to USB. The USB sound system performance was not acceptable for catching the first sound bytes of WAV files, and short WAV files were completely lost. This is apparently due to latency or the delay in queuing up, enabling, and placing the data on the USB or having it processed by the speakers. When you're used to the Microsoft ding and similar sounds that alert you to various system events, and instead you get no sound other than a tick noise, it's a little annoying. Once the USB speakers catch up, the sound is as crisp as any audio setup, but "...'ve got mail" is definitely not acceptable.

When Even the Updated PC Is Not Enough

Off came the USB speakers to be replaced by a new Diamond S70 PCI audio card, *but* the original system board has only 4 PCI slots, and they were taken by the network adapter, video card, SCSI, and USB card. Yikes!

This was the perfect time to give the new Socket 7 ATX-style system board with AGP video and 2 built-in USB ports from MSI Computer a go. AMD had sent me their K6-2/350 chip to check out in the board, but I did have to contribute a new ATX-style case and get some DIMMs for RAM. I would gain back two PCI ports in one shot with this upgrade, opening up one PCI slot by removing the PCI USB adapter and another by replacing the PCI video card with an AGP version.

Our final resource use is detailed in Table 7-3, with the whole configuration as:

- Super Socket 7 Pentium system board — ATX-style
- AMD K6-2/350MHz CPU
- 128MB of SDRAM DIMMs
- Diamond Viper 550 AGP w/16MB of video RAM
- Diamond Sonic S70 PCI audio card
- ADi 19-inch VGA monitor with USB hub
- Hewlett-Packard 6250C scanner on USB
- External USR 56K modem on USB
- Microsoft IntelliMouse on USB

- Xirlink and/or Vicam digital camera on USB
- Quantum WideSCSI hard drive, SCSI CD-ROM and CD-writer on PCI host adapter
- 3Com FastEtherlink PCI network card
- Palm Pilot cradle on built-in COM 1 port

Table 7-3 *The Resource Usage Resulting from Our System Board Upgrade*

Device	Address	IRQ	DMA
System Timer		0	
Keyboard		1	
Not used		2	
Not used – COM2	2F8h	3	
Removed – COM4			
Pilot – COM1	3F8h	4	
Removed – COM3			
Sound (PCI)	DC00h	5 (PCI steering)	1
Diskette Interface	3F6h	6	
Not used – LPT 1	378h	7	3 (ECP)
Clock/Calendar		8	
3Com NIC	DF00h (PCI)	9 (PCI steering)	
Adaptec SCSI	D800h (PCI)	10 (PCI steering)	
USB Host	(PCI)	11	
Disabled – available		12	
CPU/FPU		13	
Disabled – available		14	
Video Card (AGP)	3B0h/3C0h	15	

In Table 7-3, we still have but a few free resources left. The PCI sound card took back IRQ 5 and DMA 1, leaving IRQs 3 (if we disable COM2), 12, and 14. At this point, it is to our advantage to use USB devices when we need to add features to our system.

What We Gained

Now that we have a high-performance 2D/3D video card, plenty of RAM, and a faster CPU, the next step may be into more interactive gaming. Quake II works well on the system, as do the virtual car racing games. (I get killed frequently in Quake, and I've messed up so many virtual race cars that someone ought to take my driver's license away!) A USB force-feedback game accessory would be an excellent addition to this system.

Remember, I started out with a slow performing scanner and all legacy I/O devices. With this upgrade, I've eliminated all but one legacy device, which could also be displaced with a USB serial port adapter. This adapter could also be used for the legacy modem, saving the expense of changing to a USB modem. It's interesting to note that the USB modem creates a presence as a virtual COM3 port, which does not show up as a COM port at all in Device Manager. I've upgraded to provide faster scanning, a digital camera, faster 3D graphics, and the ability to add just about any device we want without concern for legacy configuration issues.

I've also met most if not all of the PC99 specifications — complete Plug and Play compliance. So, our upgraded PC is ready for the Year 2000. Or is it?

Speaking of the Year 2000

It is important to make sure our system is Year 2000 compliant, and to start checking applications and our data for compliance. There are dozens of tools to check the system hardware, BIOS, and operating system. Checking applications and data is another challenge. If you or your company have not started investigating this issue, it may be too late.

Checking your system for Year 2000 compliance is essential. If your system clock chip, BIOS, or operating system do not update properly, or if they do not properly recognize dates into the year 2000 and beyond, many of your applications and much of your data will have problems. Dozens of Y2K test programs are available on the Internet—from the National Software Testing Laboratories' YMark2000 freeware (for personal use) from www.nstl.com, to the new Norton 2000, of which a demo is available from www.symantec.com.

You can remedy the BIOS Year 2000 calendar errors with a BIOS update or any of a few software products that perform the same functions as a BIOS update does. Doren Rosenthal's R-Y2KFIX.EXE program that we've included on this book's companion CD-ROM is a great little application to make sure your DOS or Windows 95/98 system is good for the Year 2000. I use it on a couple of older 486 and early Pentium systems here in the raisin patch, and it's great. If you have any questions or problems with R-Y2KFIX on a particular system, let Doren know, and he'll fix it!

If your system is okay for the Year 2000, or once you've made it okay with a BIOS or software fix, you must audit or check your applications and data for compliance. The most important software to check are tax and financial applications, and anything that works with dates in the data—spreadsheets, business forecasts, inventory, and so on. Failing to deal properly with the Year 2000 and beyond can wreak havoc in your personal and business operations. Data files, macros, and customized programs must be checked for the proper expression and use of the Century and Year information. Two-digit year expressions are no longer adequate. If your programs think that a date is in the year 1900 instead of 2000, things can really get out of whack fast.

Begin your Year 2000 research at one of the original Year 2000 Web sites, www.year2000.com. From there, you will find references to various Y2K system test and calendar repair software options, myriad details on corporate/enterprise Y2K tools, and a lot of general information on various applications.

After you are fully indoctrinated into the Y2K flurry, you'll want to go to the Web sites for your PC system and application vendors and look up their Year 2000 issues. They can advise you on the Y2K compliance of their products, BIOS updates, application versions and updates, and more.

Beyond the technicalities and software details, Year 2000 compliance issues also contain many legal and social implications. Beware of sticker shock when it comes to fixing some Year 2000 issues. Many Year 2000-related vendors are focusing on corporate level customers and their budgets, and they involve thousands of dollars for various alternatives and services, which is shock enough. Failure to comply could cost you more than just money. You must protect yourself legally as well as financially. The best advice I can give is to get aware and be aware of all of the angles — the obvious and not so obvious ones. If the potential loss of business due to noncompliance doesn't get you down, the cost of proving compliance or failing to prove it may have far-reaching effects beyond the turnover to a new 00 year.

If the end of the world is really coming, we might not care so much about our computers, but on the good chance that life will indeed continue into the next millenium and beyond, be prepared; your boss will probably e-mail your to-do list the same as always, expecting you to get it done, Year 2000 bug or not!

Summary

I hope this chapter has been as enlightening about the new expansion capabilities and configuration relief for you as it was fun for me to implement. I always like implementing new gadgets and technologies that truly add value to the computing experience.

Of all the technologies available, I believe USB holds the most promise for the average PC user. Aside from the technical advantages, USB brings us some nice new devices that are within our reach. Many of them have practical and fun uses — some that were not possible without complicated customized interfaces, awkward use of the parallel port, or simply not offered because there was no suitable way to get the device connected to the PC.

I also hope that there are more and plentiful USB gadgets for everyone to buy and use in the coming months. It's about time we got beyond talking about Plug and Play, and began to enjoy it. Now we can. Just remember to install the software drivers first, be careful of power glitches, hubs, and cables. Experiment a little, and have fun with it all.

I expect that by Christmas 1999, you'll have created a 100 percent non-legacy system that is Year 2000 compliant and ready to accept all of the new gadgets that you'll be presented with. And I expect you'll enjoy them all well beyond 2000!

Chapter 8

Tools, Tips, and Tricks

IN THIS CHAPTER:

- What system information tools can show you
- What system information tools *cannot* show you and why
- Why we get confused about Windows 95/98 device details
- Using system information tools
- Managing a Windows configuration
- Getting better technical support

This chapter covers using system information tools for collecting and sorting the myriad technical details you or someone else might need to know about your system. These tools will help us complete the configuration management we've been discussing all along. I'll discuss the software that shows what resources are in use in a typical system configuration. There is also information that most software and hardware companies ask for when you call technical support. We'll also cover some other handy software tools that make dealing with your computing environment a lot more pleasant.

You might already know that your system is a 486 or Pentium-something, that it has a bunch of memory, a big hard drive, a high-speed 33.6 fax modem, and that it connects to some kind of network in your office. You might even know what kind of hard drive you have, what brand of fax modem is installed, and what type of network you're connected to. However, when you call for technical support and they start playing Twenty Questions about addresses, IRQs and such, you might be hard-pressed to answer these questions accurately. Using the tools discussed in this chapter, you'll have the answers.

What if You Don't Know What Your Configuration Is?

There are numerous software tools available that detect and report tremendous amounts of information about PC systems. Some of these tools simply report on the items found in the low memory area, ports, video modes, disk drives, and so on without actually testing for the presence of these devices. There is a difference. The low memory shows what the system BIOS finds during Power-On Self-Test. POST only knows about the few basic PC devices. It can also identify newer devices that look like legacy devices (SCSI adapters and drives that behave as standard hard drives through their own on-card BIOS, for instance.) POST does not know how to identify sound cards, internal modems (except that they can appear as COM ports, without Plug and Play turning them on), proprietary CD-ROM interfaces, network cards, and so on.

Advanced system information tools — the ones you really need to use — show the generic details about PC ports and devices (including what their IRQ and DMA assignments are or should be). They also show the details about many add-in devices and new features (such as identifying the PCI bus, PC Card/PCMCIA devices, advanced video cards and their features, sound cards, network cards, and so on).

Of the many software tools available, only a few are aware of a significant number of specific hardware items by generic type and specific brand and model. These tools can accurately identify addresses, IRQs, and DMA assignments. One of these tools, Watergate Software's PC-Doctor program, is provided in an evaluation version on the diskette included with this book.

As good as any software program may be — and many are very good and can save you a lot of work — there are some cases in which it is necessary to inspect the hardware physically to determine specific jumper or switch settings. Table 8-1 lists the general types of information we *can* get and the information we *cannot* get from system information software.

Limitations to Obtaining System Information

This section contains a little bad news and some good news about the various technical advances we've made with PCs, and how we have to deal with them, if we can, in terms of system information.

As noted in the table above, a lot of the system information you might want or expect to find out about your system is impossible, or at the very least impractical, to obtain. Until Plug and Play and PCI came along, there was no easy way to get consistent information about many generic and specific system components. For instance, it was hard to determine the manufacturer, make, and model of the system board, a diskette drive, a hard disk drive adapter, or the serial and parallel I/O ports.

Generic devices such as I/O ports are for the most part just that — generic. While it is possible to determine what kind of serial I/O port might be there (the original 8250 and AT's 16450, or the much touted 16550A UAR/T serial port chip), determining if the entire port card is made by Acme or Smith or Sunshine is not possible, and in most cases, not necessary.

System boards have no unique identifiers, and there is no way to provide them, unless the information is written into the BIOS chip. Even at that, the information is not always in the same place or the same format. Awareness and reporting of specific system boards is usually only possible if the board manufacturer has told the software developer what information is stored where that might uniquely identify the board as theirs. As an example, I've got a system board that was manufactured by Micronics, a well-known system board firm. That board was available as a generic board with Micronics

Table 8-1 *Configuration Information You Can and Cannot Get*

Information Type	Generic Information	Vendor Specific Information	Unavailable Information
System Manufacturer	None	Usually read from the BIOS (see "Limitations to Obtaining System Information" below)	
Machine Type	PC, PC/XT, PCjr, PC/AT, (generic AT, includes 80286, 80386, 80486, and Pentium)		
System Board Data Bus Type	ISA, EISA, Local Bus, or PCI		
CPU Type	i8086, i8088, NEC v20, NEC v30, i80286, i80386, i80386sx, i80386dx, i80486sx, i80486dx, i80486dx2, i80486dx2, i80486slc, Pentium; AMD, and Cyrix upgrade chips by model #		
CPU Manufacturer	Intel, NEC, AMD, Cyrix		AMD (see "Limitations to Obtaining System Information" below)
NPU (math chip)	Intel i8087, i80287, i80387, Cyrix, and AMD (usually integrated with CPU)	Weitek; other non-Intel math chip	
Base Memory	0–640K		
Extended Memory	Up to 16MB in AT-class systems. Up to 25256MB in in many 386, 486, and Pentium systems	Greater than 64MB can be identified with specific system manufacturer support	(see "Limitations to Obtaining System Information" below)
Expanded Memory	Amount of memory and the software device driver version	EMS board manufacturer	

Information Type	Generic Information	Vendor Specific Information	Unavailable Information
Shadowing/Cache	No generic info, except CPU cache for Intel 486+ parts	Vendor-specific chip and system board chipset information can be developed	Special-case shadowing or cache cache functions where system manufacturer no longer exists to support this
BIOS Information		Any available internal information if presented and the software knows how to read from BIOS chip	
Keyboard	Keyboard type		
Video Card	Monochrome, CGA, EGA, VGA	Video card make, model, BIOS, video RAM, with vendor support or generic VESA VBE presence	Monitor size, type, mode, display content
Serial Ports	Logical device assignment; hardware address: IRQ	Generic UART chip type as 8250, 16450, 16550, and 16550A; SMC and National Semiconductor parts	Generic chip manufacturers
Parallel Ports	Logical device assignment; hardware address: IRQ	SMC or National Semiconductor parts; enhanced modes	Generic chip manufacturers
Diskette Drives	Presence and drive letter assignment for: 160K, 180K, 360K, 720K, 1.2m, 1.44MB, 2.88MB		Diskette size

Continued

Table 8-1 *Continued*

Information Type	Generic Information	Vendor Specific Information	Unavailable Information
Hard Drives	Presence, logical drive letter, and capacity	SCSI & IDE: Drive geometry, firmware version and manufacturer; yields only physical and logical parameters unless translated by controller	MFM/RLL drives: drive manufacturer
SCSI Devices	Drive presence only if assigned logical device (drive letter) driver; attached device type; SCSI ID#; host adapter address, IRQ, DMA	Host adapter manufacturer information; Adaptec parts/interfaces; ASPI	
CD-ROM Drives	Drive presence only as DOS logical; drive letter (all via MSCDEX driver program)	Specific device driver or drive ID support per vendor	Disk content type
Pointing Device	Presence; 2/3 button	Manufacturer details only if specific driver and device supported	
Game Port	Port presence		Joystick or device type
Network		Specific vendor/protocol support required for presence, IRQ, boot ROM, DMA, card make/model	
Sound Cards		Creative Labs, MediaVision, Sierra Semiconductor, Aria, Roland MIDI, Microsoft Sound System; ESS chipsets; Crystal chipsets	

identification written into the BIOS chip, and was used by Gateway 2000 where it had a Gateway 2000 identification string written into the BIOS. The identity of the board could be changed by merely writing a new BIOS file into the BIOS ROM on the board, though it worked exactly the same either way, and it used the same parts and upgrade components.

While you won't find this type of identity crisis happening between systems from Hewlett-Packard, COMPAQ, IBM, or other big names that make their own boards, this type of cross-use but private-label identification of commonly available components happens daily in the PC business. Thus, if you think it makes much of a difference whether you bought a Pentium system that says Acme, Smith, or Bill's Computer Emporium on the front, where each of these manufacturers used the exact same Asus, Opti, Sunshine, or even Intel system boards, it doesn't in most cases. The differences should be subtle and left (we hope) only to the BIOS.

What you really need to know about a system board has to do with CPU, chipset, cache RAM, and BIOS. Most CPUs are easily identified with software. Chip sets were not identifiable until recently when they began to identify themselves through Plug and Play. BIOS is similarly difficult to identify unless the software programmer knows what to search for, and where, in the BIOS chip, to tell the difference between AMI, Award, COMPAQ, Hewlett-Packard, Microid Research, Phoenix, and other BIOS sources, though some of this also may be determined by Plug and Play. Cache RAM was also difficult to identify until recently, when the newer Intel chipsets made it easier to detect and test for the amount of cache RAM installed. You may not get all of these nice features with "off-shore" BIOS and chips. Knowing what kind of RAM you have is now equally important when you are either upgrading a system or replacing it and hoping to reuse your old RAM. Programs can't tell you the physical details of your RAM (SIMM or DIMM, parity or not), but some programs do identify the electronic type — Fast Page Mode, EDO, or Static DRAM.

There are many, many cases where the original equipment manufacturer (OEM) or system designer has provided for certain capabilities outside the original design standards for PC, XT, or AT systems. Also, new standards are introduced on a regular basis. This is a constant challenge for software programmers. In order to detect and report on the capabilities of newer and special devices, the system information software programmer must obtain detailed information about any and all PC systems and devices from the equipment designers. With this information, the software may then be enhanced to make use of this specific information. This is no small challenge. Advances in technology seem to happen at a faster and faster pace all the time.

Getting updated software into the hands of all users is a tremendous task, and it's not always as responsive as we might like it to be. Yet, being aware of these limitations is good information to have as you inspect your system configuration using these tools.

Things were a little easier when we had IBM PCs and only IBM PCs to deal with. Things were even fairly easy for a while when there were only IBM PC/AT systems and a few clones. When different hard drives, sound cards, and memory types came along, things only started to get complicated. When 386 and 486 systems rolled out, EISA, SCSI, network cards, advanced video features, and then Microsoft Windows became popular, it seemed that personal computing was going to become rocket science.

This is indeed why Microsoft, a software firm, began working more and more with hardware developers to create standards for system devices and information. It is also why hardware vendors looked to each other for cooperative solutions so their products wouldn't fight one another when they got into our systems. Of course, the skyrocketing prices of technical support had no small influence on everyone seeking mutually agreeable solutions, either. Cooperation between all of these commercial interests makes it easier for Microsoft to create and maintain its operating systems and featured software products, and it makes it easier for the manufacturers to design and sell newer and better I/O devices. Believe it or not, some things in this area of technology are getting easier for us.

The end result may seem a bit confusing from our aspect as users, because we find ourselves digging around on the Internet looking for the latest driver files to support our new toys. But the very existence of the Internet, and more cooperation between hardware and software vendors, creates better support of one form or another, and hopefully a reduction in the need to provide more and more costly hands-on support by phone. We no longer have to wait for a new driver diskette to be shipped to our homes or offices. We can worry less about most hardware and software updates creating problems for us.

However, we still have to keep ourselves aware of the limited resources we have available inside the PC box and how to make the best use of them.

Keeping Some Parts a Secret

It is impossible for software to read the labels or to penetrate the depth of many chips and features inside our PCs. Some information about a feature or component may be completely unavailable, except by visual inspection of the components involved. This is due to proprietary designs, manufacturing license agreements, various legalities, or design limitations.

Some manufacturers want their devices to appear to be generic devices, or possibly even to look like someone else's device. This is the case for some early microprocessors (many of AMD's chips, specifically, as well as various levels of Cyrix, TI, and IBM chips).

You might also notice that even if your sound card is not a Creative Labs Sound Blaster, the system information you get tells you that it is a Sound Blaster, or perhaps that it is Sound Blaster-compatible — if only because it acts like a Sound Blaster card.

No Two System Setup Programs Are the Same

While many users would like to have a single software tool that would let them edit or save all of the system setup information stored in CMOS RAM, this little gem has been and probably will be unobtainable.

This information, consisting primarily of date, time, video display type, amount of memory, hard drive types, and diskette drive information, is usually accessible at the time you start up your system ("Press ESC to enter SETUP") or by a special Setup program provided with the system.

Very little of this information is common between systems, and that which is common represents a few of the basic features you could change in the IBM PC/AT system. Still fewer bits of information resemble the limited options we had with tiny switches or jumpers on PC and XT systems.

With Phoenix, Award, American Megatrends, and Microid Research publishing variants of BIOS for U.S. and foreign PC makers, and IBM, Hewlett-Packard, COMPAQ, and just about every major PC manufacturer creating their own BIOS and setup features, we now have to deal with highly customized system setup information. They are all very different from each other.

System designers may use the system setup program and CMOS memory to control and hold information about many things that the PC, XT, and AT systems never had, such as:

- CPU caches
- Memory and I/O timing
- Bus clock speed and turbo mode
- Daylight savings time
- Enhanced disk drives
- Newer I/O ports (EPP, ECP, Infrared, USB, and so on)
- PC Card/PCMCIA devices
- PCI bus configurations
- Energy savings/power management

This information is not only newer and different from that of the AT-standard information; it is not stored the same way in all systems. Since systems change so frequently, with new features added or some taken away, it is nearly impossible to provide a single independent setup program for today's PC systems. I don't believe anyone has tried. It would be a frustrating and never-ending task.

> **Note**
>
> There is nothing worse than having your system crash and not being able to access its setup information to get it going again. If your system came with a special SETUP program diskette, make backup copies of it right now! Some systems let you make SETUP diskettes from within the SETUP or system utilities programs – do it now!

All the Memory That's Fit to Use but Not Detect

The IBM-PC/AT system established a standard for identifying system memory up to 16MB. Many systems now hold and address 256MB or more of memory, well beyond the original PC/AT standard. Handling larger amounts of RAM often requires nonstandard customizations to the system BIOS, as well as other system design considerations. Because it is a customized situation, identifying this much memory requires utility and information program designers to work closely with the system manufacturers so they can learn how to detect and test such tremendous amounts of RAM. Microsoft's HIMEM.SYS and similar memory management utilities go the extra megabyte, so to speak, to get as much information from BIOS, system, and chipset vendors as possible so that memory utilities become aware and make use of all the memory that the system has.

The same situation is true for various external or level two (L2) caches and other memory control parameters that are not covered by existing design standards.

DOS Device Drivers Thwart Device Detection

One of the most common causes for a piece of system information software to miss the identification of a piece of hardware, or its IRQ or DMA usage, is the existence of a device driver program. Device drivers for DOS and Windows 3.*x* systems are typically loaded and run on your system through the CONFIG.SYS file when the system starts up. While these drivers may be essential to the functionality of your system or a specific device for normal, workaday applications, they can hide or intercept the hardware details necessary for a proper identification.

If your choice of system information software misses detecting a device that you know is in your system and working properly, try using the software after starting your system without device drivers. (In versions of DOS from 5.0 on, pressing the F5 key when the screen indicates Starting MS-DOS or Loading PC-DOS will bypass the loading of device drivers at bootup.) Conversely, some devices require that a device driver is loaded at startup before the device becomes active and available for detection.

Similarly, if you run any of these programs under Windows or OS/2, the reported system information can change significantly, because these environments place several device drivers and their own device control programs between the hardware and application programs. Be aware that since system information programs are designed to interface with the hardware directly for proper detection, the use of such programs and their results may be unpredictable, or may cause Windows or OS/2 to crash or lock up.

Keeping Up with the Joneses

As PC systems and add-in devices are developed and introduced to the market so rapidly, few if any software programmers can detect the new features and devices. Nor can they update their software fast enough for their most recent devices' software to always be available in programs on store shelves or direct from the software producer. It's important to understand that if you have a piece of hardware that was just designed in June 1997, and you are using software that was updated even as recently as March 1997, there's a very good chance that the new hardware will not be identified by the old software. As magical as software is, it still hasn't been able to overcome the time-space continuum. (Okay, so Einstein, Newton, and Murphy do have something to do with computers.)

Software that can identify the new data buses, and the devices connected to them, is under constant development and will appear with time. It is likely that more software will also identify Plug and Play BIOS and PnP devices and their configuration separately from the system and applications software that uses them.

These limitations do not have a tremendous impact on our configuration work. Those items we have the most trouble with still use the original IRQ, DMA, and address resources we have become familiar with; detecting activity on or the use of these resources is fairly standard as PCs go. For finding and reporting these resources, we'll see how to use and explore system information software.

Keeping up with all of the various vendor developments has always confounded us amidst the promises of Windows 95/98/NT. Simply stated, it is not possible for two simultaneous but separately developed pieces of hardware or software to stay completely in synch or aware of the other development's work, especially when one is released before the other. I guess that's what keeps some of us in business — just trying to catch up!

Only Plug and Play Knows for Sure, and Why Windows Doesn't

As we've seen throughout this book, there are a lot of places different bits of information come into the picture. The trouble is that many of us seem to depend on Windows to know what's what when sometimes it doesn't know what's what, at least not when we want it to. To reiterate points made in earlier chapters — Windows only knows what the BIOS (standard and PnP) tells it or, more specifically, what Windows learns from the BIOS as it discovers new hardware. Windows does *not* control the hardware configuration, but it maintains a lot more information about it than might be obvious.

Once you think about it, because of the way things are built to work with Windows, the operating system (or the operating environment parts we see) really has no business dealing with the hardware, and it is amazing that we should be able to get any hardware information from it at all. Windows also depends on device drivers to simply provide services from a device, regardless of its configuration. For instance:

- **For disk drives.** Well, here I'm quite disappointed because almost any program can know more about the disk drives, either IDE or SCSI, than Windows tells us. But perhaps it's proof that the O/S does not need to know if the drive is a Quantum or a Seagate, is on the SCSI or IDE port, or how that port is addressed. The operating system simply needs to know that it has a file system to work with — hardware be damned.

- **For modems.** Only the TAPI driver really needs to have any connection with the hardware, and that, often as not, through a modem or serial port device driver that is intimate with the hardware configuration. This is why you may never know for sure what, if any, standard COM port your Winmodem may be assigned to — it's really none of our business — or is it? The only thing communications and fax programs want to know is that there is a way to get like-data between two different systems.

- **For networks.** Only the protocol layer (TCP/IP, IPX/SPX, NetBEUI, and so on) needs to have any connection with the network interface, and that can be through other drivers such as the PPPMAC services for dial-up networking, or NDIS or similar driver layers that eventually connect to a network card driver, which then knows the hardware specifics. Again, applications typically only want to know that there is a file system to get and store data with, or a way to connect to other systems to transfer data back and forth.

- **For multimedia.** Video, sound, and so on — the environment and its applications only need to know that there is a compatible-something out there to output (display or make noise) some data to, or get data from (audio or images.) Thus, which IRQ or DMA something uses is not necessarily important.

These are probably the most common examples of things we concern ourselves with the configuration of, but the operating system shouldn't have to. However, and therefore, we have device drivers and BIOS to handle hardware for us — and those are the places we should be looking to get information.

Although Microsoft has tried to eliminate the need for a system BIOS altogether in their partially successful efforts with Windows NT, their hardware abstraction layer, and their Windows Driver Model, until we see a significant change in equalizing hardware platforms, eliminating all differences between chipsets, memory handling, and so on (which is *extremely* doubtful), the only standards or common ground we have to know which hardware is which are the BIOS and Plug and Play device identifications.

Most of the PC industry has agreed on the use of the BIOS for providing the initial hardware configuration, despite what Microsoft thinks or has tried to do about it. At least the industry giants— COMPAQ, Hewlett-Packard, Novell, Phoenix, Intel, and such— have been working together to keep this much of the PC somewhat under control. And they have some incentive to do so, because Sun, Novell, and others have a stake in operating systems that also run on PCs. It's hard enough getting one operating system vendor (Microsoft) to work with the systems that currently exist. Getting three or four major operating system companies to agree on what a new PC architecture should look like without a BIOS could be beneficial overall. However, many others depend on having a PC standard as well. We still have hundreds of other hardware and software manufacturers to contend with — so BIOS it is for the time being.

One interesting aspect we've discovered about Windows is that it does seem to have a memory of sorts for things that are or have been in our systems. This memory is called the Registry. It's something we know keeps growing as we use our system, but we can't quite seem to figure out why it never shrinks, especially if we've removed things from the system.

In normal use, we don't have instant recall access to this memory — we have to go into Safe Mode and view the System ⇨ Device Manager dialog boxes to see what's back there. When you look at the Device Manager in the Registry, when operating Windows in Safe Mode, you may see all sorts of interesting devices that you either never knew you had, or know you don't have. This would be the case if you got a used system with Windows 95/98 installed on it, or if the folks who built your system did so using other hardware and then reconfigured it to your specifications. Unfortunately, no one has yet exploited the Registry's "Safe Mode memory" for tracking what was or what has changed. Perhaps someday they will.

The perspective we need to have at this point is that Windows will only tell us part of the story — an important part, but not all of the story. We need better tools than Windows has to tell us what is really going on sometimes. That's what the next sections are all about.

Gathering Hardware Configuration Information

In this section, you learn about the types and variety of information you can obtain about your PC system, using system information or hardware configuration reporting software. With an understanding of the limitations of this type of software and the limitations imposed through some hardware designs, you may find yourself either overwhelmed or disappointed with the information reported to you.

Our primary concerns are the system resources of IRQ, DMA, and I/O address assignments. In most of the system information programs available, at least the I/O address assignment of many common devices is not reported, simply because it has been taken for granted that a specific device always uses a specific address, and this configuration resource cannot be changed. If some of these fixed configuration items could be changed, our task of configuration management would become many times more difficult. Having some known, standard, unchanging devices makes our job easier in some ways, even though it may appear to limit other configuration options.

Information to the Rescue

Two very helpful programs are included on the CD-ROM provided with this book: an evaluation copy of Watergate Software's PC-Doctor for DOS, and a full shareware copy of Doren Rosenthal's RCR, or Rosenthal Conflict Resolver.

PC-Doctor provides a wealth of information about your system, including our three critical hardware configuration resources — IRQ, DMA, and I/O — within a very simple menu-driven interface. It allows you to save the information to disk, or you can print it out.

RCR works with your system interactively as you use it to determine any and all detectable IRQ activity. It's a little more technical to use than most typical information programs, but that's where its value lies.

Using PC-Doctor

PC-Doctor (PCDR) contains the system information gathering part of Watergate Software's products, which are used by technicians, power users, and PC system and device manufacturers. It is a powerful tool that addresses your system hardware and devices directly and specifically to obtain detailed device identification information.

PC-Doctor cannot be run under Windows. Running it under Windows might cause your system to freeze or crash because of the low-level technical functions it performs. This is a concern when using this or any similar system information utilities. Conflicts occur with the device drivers or the memory protection used in Windows 3.*x*, Windows 95/98, or Windows NT).

This unpredictable behavior might not be destructive, but it is annoying. This behavior is usually caused by a poorly designed device installed in your system which mistakenly responds to program instructions for another device that the program is trying to detect.

Installing and Running PC-Doctor from the CD-ROM

PC-Doctor comes with a small handful of support files on the CD-ROM with this book, and is ready to use. To keep the program handy and easy to use, you should make a new subdirectory for it and copy the files from the CD-ROM to your hard drive.

PC-Doctor is designed to be run under DOS only, not in a DOS box or from the MS-DOS Prompt under any version of Windows or OS/2. You can perform the installation in a DOS session, but you should reboot your system and stop at a DOS prompt to run the program.

Nearly any plain DOS-only bootup situation will allow you to run this program and gather the necessary system information. This means you should boot up with a minimum of device drivers (preferably none) from CONFIG.SYS or AUTOEXEC.BAT. For DOS and Windows 3.x systems, this means you should press F5 when you see the "Starting MS-DOS" prompt on your screen. For Windows 95 systems, press F8 when you see the "Starting Windows 95" prompt on your screen, and then select the Safe Mode command-prompt only menu item. These will leave you at a bare-bones DOS prompt.

If you do not have adequate free DOS RAM to load the program or its support files, you may receive a message indicating so, and the program will prompt you to exit. Do so, and then reboot the system as previously prescribed.

If you require the information from SCSI, sound, or network cards, you should load only the drivers needed to activate these cards and no more (eliminate SmartDrive or other caching programs, special video mode drivers, SETVER, SHARE, and so on from your CONFIG.SYS and AUTOEXEC.BAT files, and reboot).

Note

This version is intended for demonstration and evaluation purposes only. If you need to use this tool regularly, you must purchase a full version from Watergate Software. The price is quite reasonable for the features you receive.

1. Start at your root directory:

   ```
   cd\[Enter]
   ```

2. Create a new subdirectory for PC-Doctor on your hard drive. Assuming your hard drive is C:, type:

   ```
   md PCDR[Enter]
   ```

3. Copy the PC-Doctor files from the CD-ROM. Assuming your floppy drive is A:, type:

   ```
   copy <CD-ROM>\PCDR\*.* c:\PCDR [Enter]
   ```

 Note

Files saved on CD-ROMs are provided with the Read-Only DOS file attribute. When you copy files from a CD-ROM, this attribute remains with the files that are copied. In order to move or delete files from the destination drive you copied them to, this attribute must be changed. To remove the attribute under Windows 95/98/NT Explorer, navigate to the location of the files, right-click each file, and select Properties from the menu presented. In the dialog box that displays, clear the Read only option, click OK, and then delete or move the files as needed.

4. Change to the new subdirectory:

   ```
   cd \PCDR [Enter]
   ```

5. Run the main program file (again, not in a DOS-session under Windows or OS/2, but booted to DOS only or with a DOS diskette only):

   ```
   pcdr [Enter]
   ```

The first time you run PC-Doctor, it tells you that it is initializing and checks itself for viruses. The initial screen is shown in Figure 8-1:

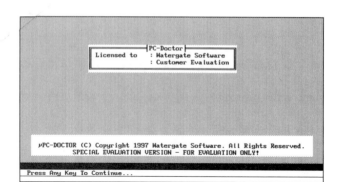

Figure 8-1 *PC-Doctor opening screen*

6. Press Enter for the next screen, shown in Figure 8-2:

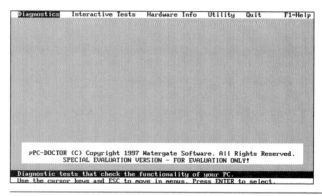

Figure 8-2 *PC-Doctor title screen*

7. Press Enter for the next screen (Figure 8-3):

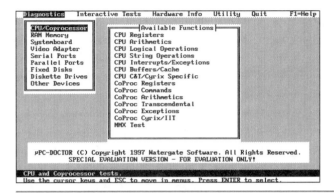

Figure 8-3 *PC-Doctor Diagnostics menu*

Note

This version of PC-Doctor provides system information functions only. Selecting a diagnostic program will provide only a descriptive display screen.

8. Press the right arrow cursor key twice for the Hardware Information drop-down menu, shown in Figure 8-4:

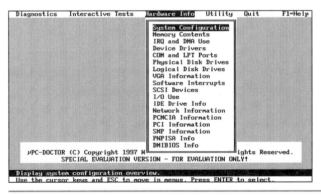

Figure 8-4 *PC-Doctor hardware information menu*

The most critical information reports for our conflict and configuration concerns are the System Configuration, IRQ and DMA Use, COM and LPT Ports, and I/O Use selections.

What Could Go Wrong

While PC-Doctor has undergone extensive and very detailed and careful development so that it behaves well with all known hardware and system configurations, there are always a few systems, configurations, or unusual pieces of hardware that do not conform to expected and standard hardware design and operations. Encountering problems with non-standard hardware can occur with all products of this nature (DiagSoft's QAPlus-family, Eurosoft's PC-Check, NAI's PC Medic, and so on). If the process of gathering information about your system becomes very frustrating as different devices respond poorly to being interrogated for their information, you may wish to consult with a PC technician or your system vendor for assistance.

Any unpredictable behaviors or unusual results that occur when you run programs like PC-Doctor usually happen when IRQ or DMA assignment detection is performed, but they may also occur when gathering any type of low-level technical information. By unusual or erratic behavior, I mean that the system locks up or reboots, or the screen blanks out. (I've never yet seen such a program destroy data, format a hard drive, or corrupt system setup information, though I'm sure it is possible under the wrong circumstances.)

Erratic behavior is possible because the program must actually control the specific device to get an interrupt or DMA reaction from it, or to confirm the specific identity of a device. If another device conflicts with the one you are trying to detect, or if the detected device is unusual in some way, erratic program behavior is possible.

With over 50 (100?) million different PC systems in use, it is not possible to be aware of, much less absolutely prevent, something from going wrong at some time, which is probably why you bought this book in the first place.

System Information

The PC-Doctor system configuration report is one of our first lines of defense in system conflict battles. Without knowing the basic contents or inventory of devices installed in your system, no configuration can be made conflict-free, except by luck or trial and error.

Figures 8-5 and 8-6 illustrate a typical system hardware configuration report. Details of each line item reported (not all are shown) are given in Table 8-2.

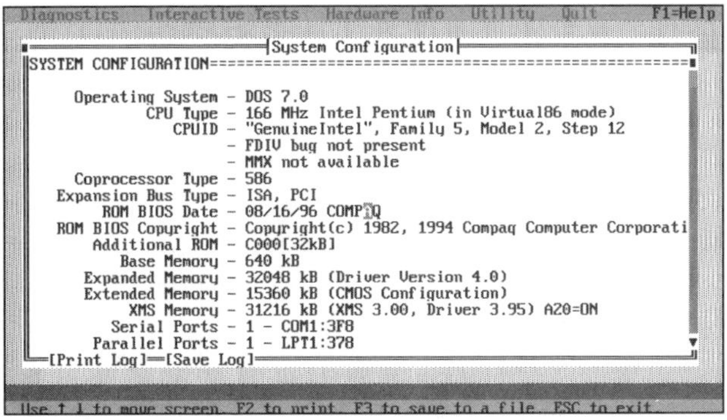

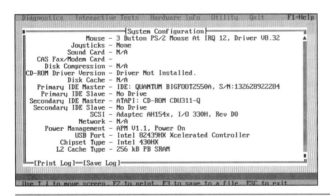

Figure 8-5 *First page of PCDR System Configuration report*

Figure 8-6 *Second page of PCDR System Configuration report*

Table 8-2 *Description of PCDR System Configuration Report Contents*

Information Attribute	Value
Operating System	The version of DOS the system is currently running.
CPU Type	Speed, brand, and model of the CPU chip.
CPUID	The internal CPU chip identification code (typically applicable only to Intel CPUs).

Continued

Table 8-2 *Continued*

Information Attribute	Value
Coprocessor Type	Brand and model of the math chip.
Expansion Bus Type	Indicates all known I/O buses.
ROM BIOS Date	Date, if known, of the BIOS ROM chip/contents.
ROM BIOS Copyright	Copyright date of the ROM BIOS chip/contents.
Additional ROM	Addresses of other ROM chips (usually from video and disk adapters).
Base Memory	The amount of RAM allocated for DOS use. Typically 640K, but may be 512K for AT systems, or less for PC and XT systems.
Expanded Memory	The amount of LIMS-EMS memory currently managed in the system.
Extended Memory	The amount of RAM in the system beyond the 640K for DOS (reported from the system CMOS setup RAM).
XMS Memory	The amount of memory managed by HIMEM.SYS or equivalent.
Serial Ports	Indicates number of ports, logical (COM) assignment, and physical addresses for each logical COM port.
Parallel Ports	Indicates number of ports, logical (LPT) assignment, and physical addresses for each logical LPT port.
Video Adapter	The type of adapter (Monochrome, CGA, EGA, VGA, and so on), and the video chip type if known/detected.
Fixed Disk Drives	The size of each detected hard drive.
Floppy Disk Drives	The number and type of each detected diskette drive.
Mouse	The type of mouse, if driver is present.
Joystick	Indicates presence of a game port.
Sound Card	Indicates model and address of known/detected sound cards.
CAS Fax/Modem Card	Indicates presence/type of modem card if detected.
Disk Compression	Reports type of disk compression used on current hard disk drive.
CD-ROM Driver Version	Indicates driver type/version if installed.
Disk Cache	Indicates type and size of disk cache installed and running (SmartDrive, and so on).
Primary IDE Master	Type and size of drive attached as Master on first hard drive adapter.
Primary IDE Slave	Type and size of drive attached as Slave on first hard drive adapter.
Secondary IDE Master	Type and size of drive attached as Master on second hard drive adapter.

Information Attribute	Value
Secondary IDE Slave	Type and size of drive attached as Slave on second hard drive adapter.
SCSI	Type of SCSI adapter, if known (usually requires ASPI or CAM driver in CONFIG.SYS).
Network	Indicates presence and type of network adapter (usually requires driver to be loaded and running in DOS).
Power Management	Indicates presence and status of energy saver features of the system BIOS.
USB Port	Indicates presence and type of a Universal Serial Bus adapter.
Chipset Type	Indicates the type of system board chip set.
L2 Cache Type	Size and type of External CPU cache.

Memory Contents

The Memory Contents screen indicates the amount, type, and free/available RAM, and the address and purpose of BIOS ROMs contained in the system. See Figures 8-7 and 8-8.

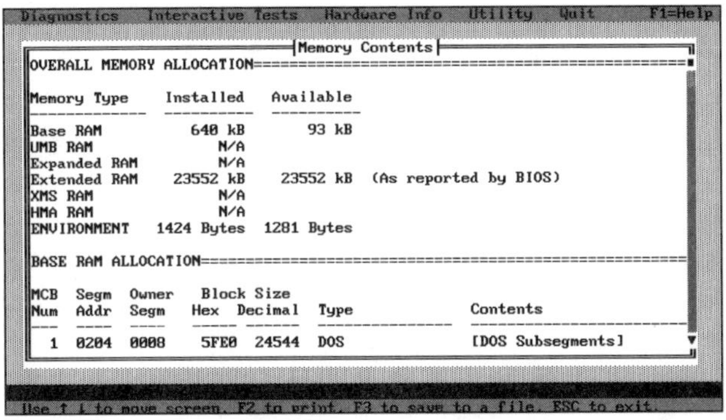

Figure 8-7 *DOS Memory Contents display*

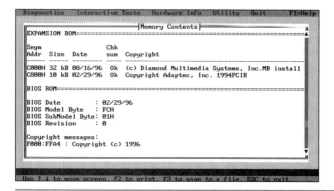

Figure 8-8 *ROM Memory Contents display*

IRQ and DMA Use

Two of the most important hardware resources in your system configuration are reported in the IRQ and DMA Use screens. Two screens full of information are shown to give you an illustration of these resources. The first page is shown in Figure 8-9.

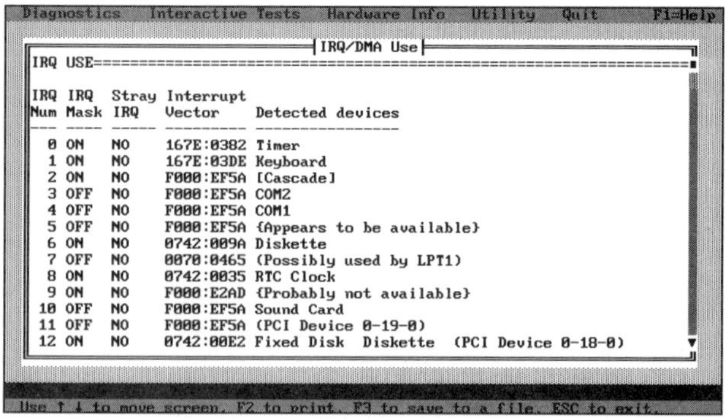

Figure 8-9 *First page of the PCDR IRQ and DMA report*

- **Hardware IRQ** lines are listed in numeric order, with some additional technical information, prior to identifying the actual device known to be using the IRQ.

- The **IRQ Mask** column indicates whether or not handling of the respective IRQ is masked or filtered by another program that is monitoring it.

■ The **Stray IRQ** column indicates if there was activity detected on an IRQ line from any unknown sources. This could indicate a possible conflict with another (unknown) device, or hardware failure that is falsely sending IRQ activity to the CPU.

■ The **Interrupt Vector** column shows the memory address of the software program or routine that is handling the I/O for the respective device listed.

■ Notice that IRQ 7 indicates "(Possibly in use by LPT1)." The word "possibly" is used because, without a loopback test connector, it is normally not possible for software alone to trigger input or detectable activity on the LPT ports. (Contact Watergate Software at http://www.ws.com or 510-654-5182 for information on obtaining a full version of PC-Doctor and the loopback test plugs.) The loopback plug drawings are also included in the appendices if you wish to build your own.

■ IRQs listed as "(Appears to be available)" did not have any interrupt activity from any known, standard, or specially supported devices.

The second screen (Figure 8-10) indicates if there were any problems with any of the IRQ lines. In this case, there were no problems.

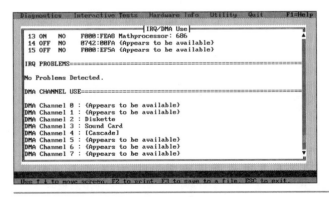

Figure 8-10 *Second page of the PCDR IRQ and DMA report*

All eight DMA channels are listed in this report, indicating which device uses a specific channel, or that a channel is possibly available, as shown by the "(Appears to be available)" text next to a DMA channel. In this report, only three DMA channels are in use — 2, 3, and 4. DMA 4 is shown as [Cascade] or otherwise unavailable, because this channel is used to link the second of two DMA controllers to the first. You might also expect to see one or two functions of your sound card using DMA channels. (A sound card has been detected in this system, but its specific DMA activity cannot be determined unless the driver for the card is installed and running.)

Device Drivers

The device drivers report from PCDR provides information that is technically interesting and functional for programmers, but is perhaps too detailed for most users. The exception occurs when this information is pertinent to technical support transactions when troubleshooting a software configuration or function. The items reported are defined below (see Figure 8-11).

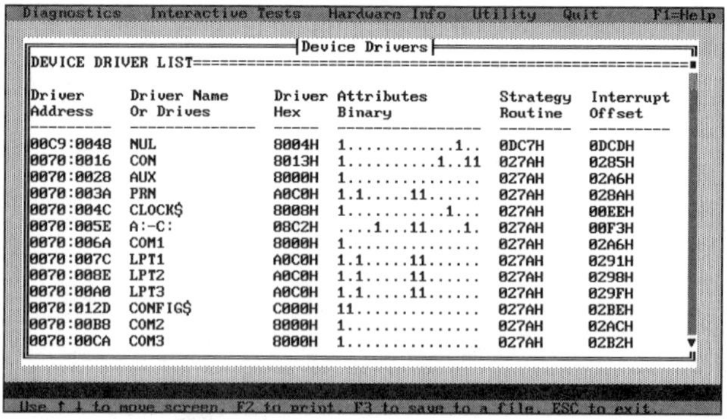

Figure 8-11 *PCDR DOS Device Drivers report*

- **Driver Address**: This column indicates the actual memory address that the device driver has been loaded into and occupies as it runs.

- **Driver Name or Logical Drives**: This column indicates the internal process, device, or program name of the device driver, or the logical designation for disk drives found.

- **Driver Attributes**: These columns indicate what type the device driver is by the numerical value assigned to the type of device. A 1 in the first column indicates that the device is a character device, handling data one character at a time, and the absence of a 1 (an implied 0) indicates that it handles data in blocks.

- **Strategy Routine**: Numeric values representing how DOS handles the device's I/O operations (not much value to us here).

- **Interrupt Offset**: The location of the software interrupt service routine that is responsible for handling I/O for this device.

COM and LPT Ports

Perhaps the most popular reason to go digging for information about your system is to figure out what the heck is going on with COM ports. This and the IRQ and DMA Use reports will be the most useful in such endeavors, and will illustrate quite clearly the relationship between physical addresses (3F8h) and logical port assignments (COM1). From the information given in previous chapters, you will be able to determine if these physical versus logical port assignments are correct. (Sorry folks, the software has not yet been written that highlights this information for you.) See Figure 8-12.

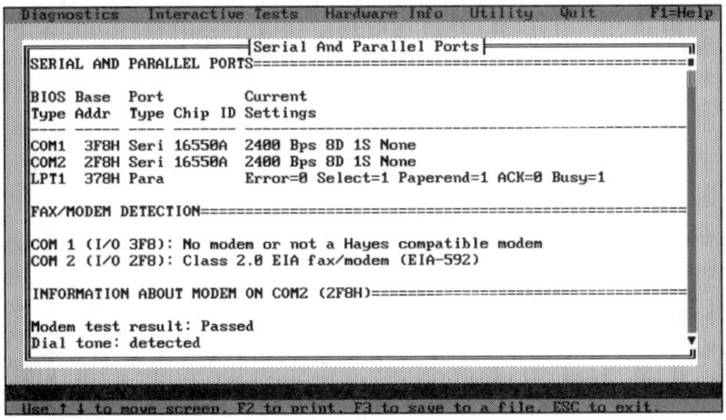

Figure 8-12 *Serial and parallel port information*

This particular system has only two COM ports. They are addressed correctly for a proper physical versus logical association, and the associations match the proper IRQs for these two ports (see also Figure 8-12).

The information given in this report consists of:

- **BIOS Type**: The logical device designation given the port by the BIOS at bootup.

- **Base Address**: The physical address, assigned to the logical device name of the detected port.

- **Port Type**: A description of the port (serial or parallel).

- **Chip ID**: The type of chip detected on the serial port(s). This is important information for high-speed COM port (modem) use. No specific chip type is associated with parallel/LPT ports.

- **Current Settings**: The initial speed and data bit settings for serial ports (this does not reflect the maximum capability of the port) and the status of signal lines of parallel ports.

Note

You must consult the IRQ and DMA Use report to cross-reference serial and parallel port IRQ assignments with the physical and logical COM and LPT port assignments.

This screen also shows under "Fax/Modem Detection" the results of the program's attempt to detect and identify what type of modem might be present on your system, and what port it is associated with. The next screen goes on to query the modem for more specific internal information.

Note

Don't be surprised if your modem doesn't show up here! Some Plug and Play modems may not actually show up with a COM port or IRQ assignment until they are actually initialized and configured by a Plug and Play operating system, such as Windows 95.

Also, to specifically detect the presence of a mouse, your mouse driver must be loaded (in CONFIG.SYS or AUTOEXEC.BAT).

The serial and parallel (COM and LPT) report will also provide a summary of the information from any modems detected on the available COM ports, as seen in Figure 8-13.

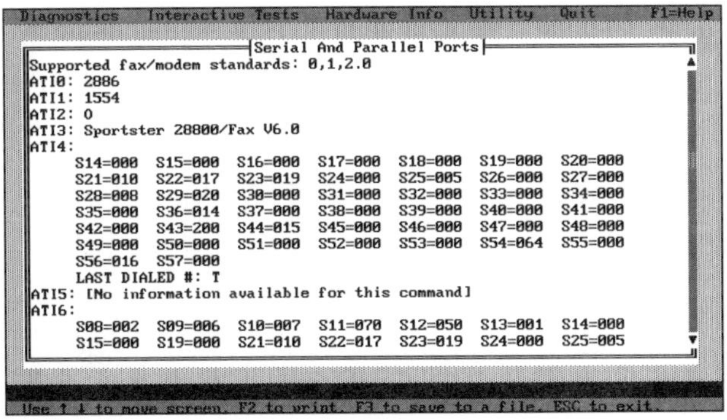

Figure 8-13 *Modem information from COM2 port*

Physical Disk Drives

This report gives us details about the physical disk drives in the system. The report, shown in Figure 8-14, is an example from a system with a 1GB SCSI hard drive, in which the SCSI host adapter provides a special translation for large drives. (I know it's a SCSI drive because it's my system. If we were to run and look at the IDE Drive Info report on this system, we'd also see that there are no IDE drives in this machine.)

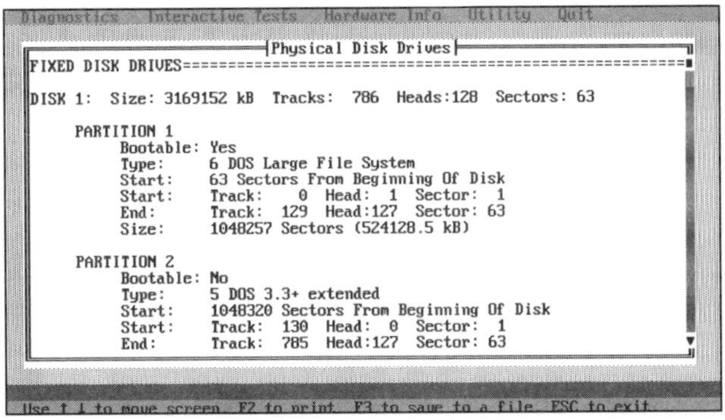

Figure 8-14 *PCDR Fixed Disk Drives report (SCSI drive without ASPI driver)*

The Fixed Disk report for an IDE drive in Figure 8-15 looks very similar to the report for the SCSI drive. DOS doesn't know the difference at this point, and it shouldn't; physical disks are handled by the system BIOS. Logical disks, as we'll see next, are created from physical disks, and likewise display no clues about whether or not the drive is a SCSI or IDE device. There is no indication of the CMOS setup drive type, as this now varies greatly between systems and BIOS.

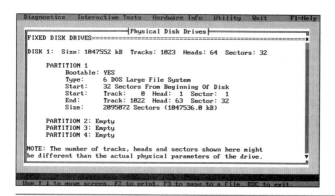

Figure 8-15 *PCDR Fixed Disk Drives report (IDE drive)*

Logical Disk Drives

This report, shown in Figure 8-16, displays the way DOS views the disk drives in your system, by drive letter, and gives us further details.

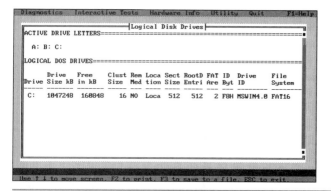

Figure 8-16 *Logical Disk Drives*

In the Logical Disk Drives report, we see that drive C: is the only active hard drive, with the following DOS partition parameters:

- **Drive**: The DOS drive letter. CD-ROM drives, if active through MSCDEX, and mapped network drives, are assigned DOS drive letters too.

- **Drive Size**: The actual capacity of the drive, displayed in bytes.

- **Free in kB**: The amount of the drive, in bytes, that is still free for storing more information.

- **Clust Size (Cluster Size)**: The number of sectors per disk cluster — in this case, there are 16 (512 byte, see Sect Size below) sectors per cluster. A cluster is the minimum DOS file allocation size measurement unit.

- **Rem Med (Removable Media)**: Does this drive support removable media? In this case, no.

- **Location**: Is this a local or network drive? In this case, local. Otherwise, perhaps a network or externally shared drive.

- **Sect Size (Sector Size)**: The size of discrete disk sectors. Almost always 512 bytes.

- **RootD Entri (Root Directory Entries)**: The maximum number of entries that can be listed in the drive's root directory, including files and subdirectory entries. (Even if you have a lot of your drive space free according to DOS, if you have 512 entries in your root directory, the drive is full and cannot hold any more data in the root directory, nor can it allow the creation of any more subdirectories off the root directory.)

- **Fat Are (# of FAT Areas)**: Most/all DOS hard drives have two File Allocation Tables, as does this one.

- **ID Byt (ID Byte)**: The DOS drive identifier byte information. Not a critical configuration concern.

- **Drive ID**: The volume identification type (not the volume label) assigned to this drive.

- **File System**: In this case, as with most drives partitioned and formatted with DOS versions later than 5.0, FAT-16, indicating that the maximum number of File Allocation entries is defined by a 16-bit number.

VGA Information

Just about everything you ever wanted to know about your VGA card, and then some, is listed in this report. See Figure 8-17.

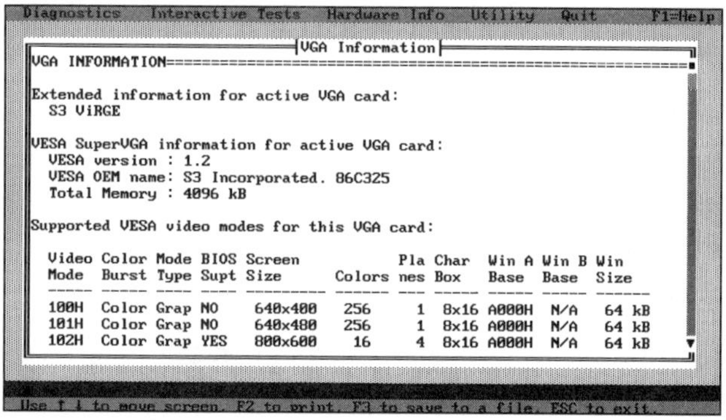
Diagnostics Interactive Tests Hardware Info Utility Quit F1=Help

VGA Information

VGA INFORMATION

Extended information for active VGA card:
S3 ViRGE

VESA SuperVGA information for active VGA card:
VESA version : 1.2
VESA OEM name: S3 Incorporated. 86C325
Total Memory : 4096 kB

Supported VESA video modes for this VGA card:

Video Mode	Color Burst	Mode Type	BIOS Supt	Screen Size	Colors	Pla nes	Char Box	Win A Base	Win B Base	Win Size
100H	Color	Grap	NO	640x400	256	1	8x16	A000H	N/A	64 kB
101H	Color	Grap	NO	640x480	256	1	8x16	A000H	N/A	64 kB
102H	Color	Grap	YES	800x600	16	4	8x16	A000H	N/A	64 kB

Use ↑ ↓ to move screen. F2 to print. F3 to save to a file. ESC to exit.

Figure 8-17 *VGA Information report*

Although not reported in this case, the card is a Diamond Stealth 3D 3000, which uses the S3 ViRGE chipset, contains 4MB of video memory, and supports VESA BIOS version 1.2 functions.

SCSI

The SCSI device report (Figure 8-18) requires an active ASPI (Advanced SCSI Peripheral Interface) drive, and is relatively simple at this level, telling us what the devices are in order of their SCSI unit ID numbers.

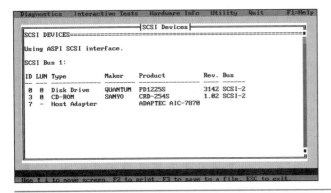

Figure 8-18 *SCSI Devices report*

I/O Use

While it's normally a risky venture to have a program simply walk through a range of addresses to see if they are occupied or not, PC-Doctor is the first program I've seen do this without regularly crashing the system. Unlike other efforts to produce a similar report, this function does not attempt to specifically identify what devices occupy what addresses; it merely reports that an address is probably occupied by something. It is as accurate as I can determine from knowledge of this system, and other system information.

Figure 8-19 shows the legend to the various contents of the I/O address range, and the beginning I/O address range contents. Figures 8-20 and 8-21 show the I/O address range with occupied addresses.

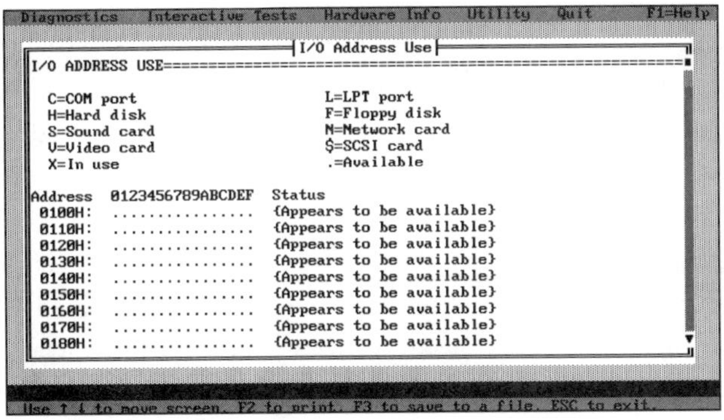

Figure 8-19 *I/O Use Map, first page*

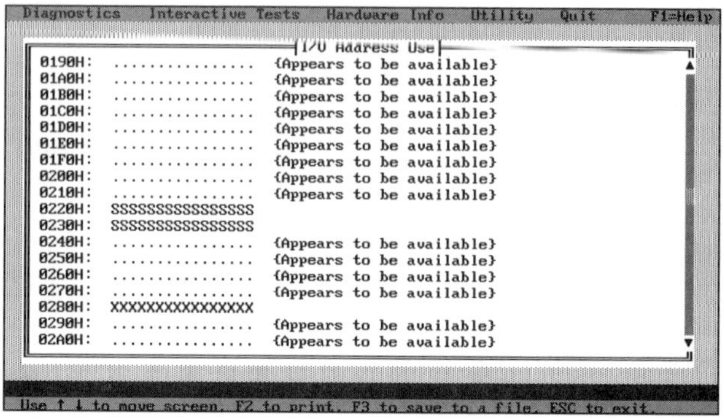

Figure 8-20 *I/O Use Map, second page*

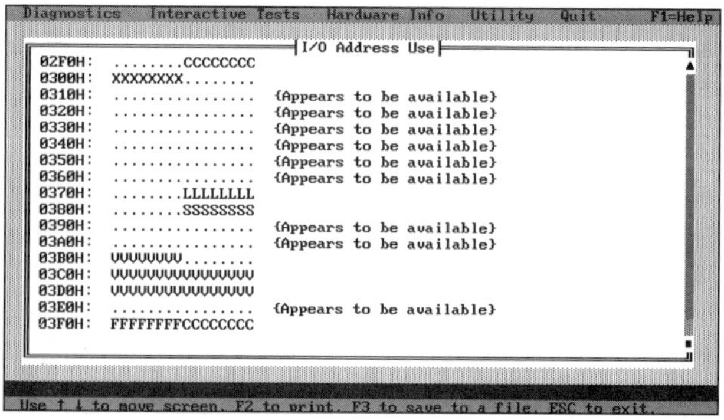

Figure 8-21 *I/O Use Map, third page*

The pages of this report list memory addresses in order from 0000h to 03Ffh. This is the range where I/O devices are to be found. If a type of device (though not a specific device) is known to occupy an address, this is referenced by letters shown in the header of the first page of the report. Unknown but in-use addresses are flagged with the letter *X*.

You may assume from this list that addresses without any flags (see the "Appears to be available" Status listing) may be available for your use to configure new I/O devices. However, you must be aware of the full address range a device uses, and of the I/O addresses that have been predefined for other known devices. (Yes, we're back to all those rules again.)

IDE Drive Info

The next two report screens (Figures 8-22 and 8-23) show you the results of asking any IDE drives found on the system to report what they are with the "Read Drive ID" command available with IDE devices.

Here we have our IDE hard drive and IDE CD-ROM drive baring their most intimate internal details.

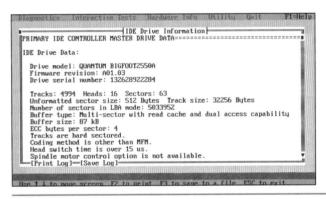

Figure 8-22 *IDE Drive Information report, first page*

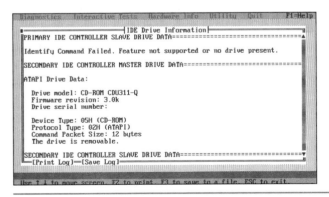

Figure 8-23 *IDE Drive Info report, second page*

PCI Configuration

This selection within PC-Doctor provides basic information about the PCI bus and installed PCI components in your system. The PCI bus helps integrate a number of devices within the system board construction itself, reducing the need for a variety of add-in cards. Even though you may not have any PCI add-in cards plugged into your system, you may still have some PCI devices listed in this report. The information provided in this report (see Figure 8-24) is described below.

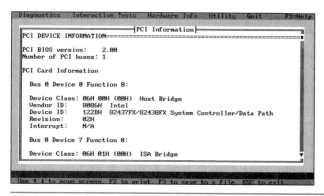

Figure 8-24 *PC-Doctor PCI Information*

The first PCI information screen gives us the bare essentials of our PCI BIOS support, and begins to list PCI devices in the order they appear, the PCI chipset being a mandatory item for other PCI devices to exist.

The second PCI information screen (Figure 8-25) shows us a lot of detail, but most importantly the specific presence of the types of PCI devices in the system, starting with the integrated IDE drive adapter interface, then on to the add-in SCSI card.

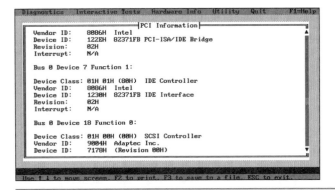

Figure 8-25 *PC-Doctor PCI Information, second page*

The third PCI information screen (Figure 8-26) completes the SCSI information and shows us the PCI video card information.

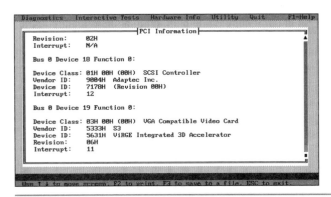

Figure 8-26 *PC-Doctor PCI Information, third page*

 Note

The latest evaluation and regular retail versions of PC-Doctor for DOS include additional information reports covering PNP/ISA configuration, SMP (Symmetric Multi-Processor systems), and DMIBIOS (Desktop Management Information) support. Typical Plug and Play information can also be obtained through PC-Doctor for Windows, as seen in Figures 8-27 through Figure 8-34. The version available and distributed with this book may contain additional information options for which we did not provide screen shots. I hope this additional information is equally or more useful to you.

PC-Doctor for Windows

This section provides a brief overview of the system information available from PC-Doctor for Windows (Figure 8-27), another full-featured Windows 3.*x* and Windows 95/98 diagnostic and information product.

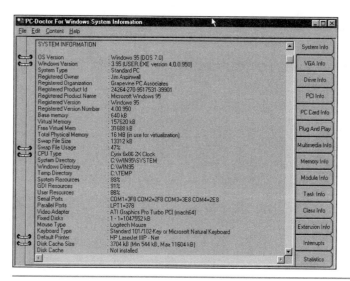

Figure 8-27 *PC-Doctor for Windows System Info report*

PC-Doctor for Windows appears to know a lot more about your system than the DOS version in Figure 8-28 and subsequent screens, mostly due to the fact that there have to be so many device-specific drivers loaded and running for Windows to function.

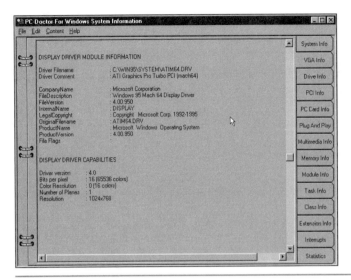

Figure 8-28 *PC-Doctor for Windows VGA Info report*

Of course, one thing we don't see is a listing of our precious resources — IRQ, DMA, and I/O — but we will.

And the disk drive information looks pretty familiar (Figure 8-29).

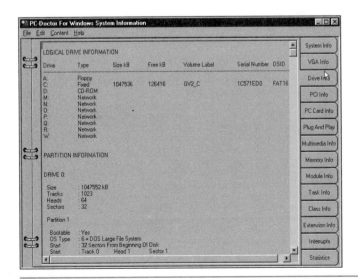

Figure 8-29 *PC-Doctor for Windows Drive Info report*

As does the PCI information (Figure 8-30).

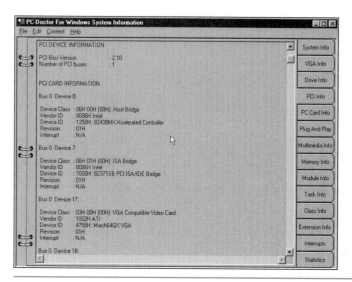

Figure 8-30 *PC-Doctor for Windows PCI Info report*

Then we get to the "good stuff"—everything Windows 95/98 knows and can tell us about Plug and Play devices and resources. The inevitable IRQ and DMA assignments are shown in Figure 8-31.

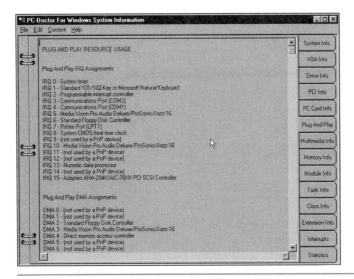

Figure 8-31 *PC-Doctor for Windows Plug and Play Info report, showing IRQ and DMA assignments*

Then we see the addresses assigned to all the expected devices, from the bottom of memory on up as shown in Figure 8-32.

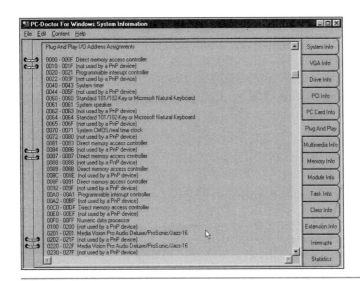

Figure 8-32 *PC-Doctor for Windows Plug and Play Info report, showing memory address usage*

Then we begin to see the upper memory details, including video RAM and device BIOS regions (see Figure 8-33).

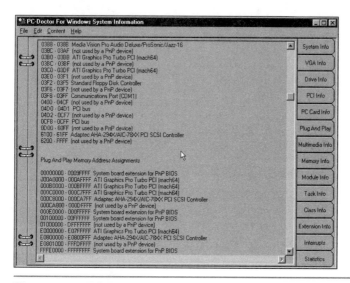

Figure 8-33 *PC-Doctor for Windows Plug and Play Info report, showing the upper memory area*

And finally (though there are more pages to this report), we see details about each device that Plug and Play has identified. Note that even a legacy ISA device is reported. Whether or not a device is specifically PnP-compatible or PnP-supported, PnP must still identify it and the resources used before it can configure the real PnP devices (see Figure 8-34).

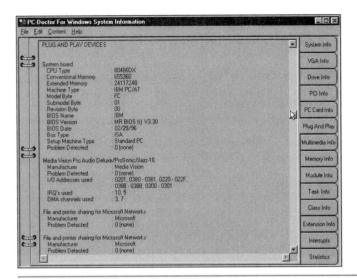

Figure 8-34 *PC-Doctor for Windows Plug and Play Info report, showing Plug and Play and legacy device information*

Rosenthal Utilities

Doren Rosenthal found the first edition of *IRQ, DMA & I/O* in the course of his work creating his conflict detection and resolution software, RCR. I'm sure I didn't help him technically, because he's a programmer, but I certainly provided some validation to the work at hand. He was kind enough to mention the book in the document file for his utility program. We've been comparing a lot of notes ever since. The results of the tests I've done with his programs, and how they operate, convinced me that they deserve more than a little mention in this book.

The highlight of Doren's utilities for me is RCR, or the Rosenthal Conflict Resolver program (RCR.EXE) and his System Monitor, SYSMON.EXE, both of which are on the CD-ROM accompanying this book, with some of his other works.

RCR

RCR runs and functions like no typical DOS utility program, and it performs two functions. First, it is designed to run as part of the boot, or perhaps as a pre-boot operation, so that it can absolutely track all system IRQ and DMA activity. It does this by working off a special diskette that the program creates for you, which is then used to pre-boot the system; thus, it does not interfere with your hard drive in any way.

The big difference here is that RCR is actively monitoring IRQ and DMA incidents as they happen, as you use your system, regardless of what device causes the signals to happen. This is significantly different from most diagnostic and information programs, which merely inspect any devices found in the system and tickle them to see what activity they generate.

At least one of the benefits with RCR is that Plug and Play devices, and even some of those elusive soft-configured sound cards we mentioned before, can change their configuration as different programs use them. A game program may set up and use a sound card in very different ways than the card's drivers might set the card up for use under Windows. As you use the system and devices under any and all imaginable conditions, you will likely discover that a device uses more resources than you thought. Still more configuration mysteries unraveled all the time!

The second function of RCR is a real-time indicator of IRQ and DMA activity. You can start and use this real-time indicator at any time (provided you've booted with that special diskette) as a TSR in your AUTOEXEC.BAT file if you wish, or later on (but it is most useful in TSR mode). In its real-time display mode, RCR shows you when an IRQ or DMA line goes active, and leaves an indication turned on if any of the lines has ever been activated (should you happen to blink and miss the real-time activity).

Even without the TSR portion running, RCR logs all IRQ and DMA activity to a file for later inspection, also by the RCR utility program. The point here is to have the pre-boot activity monitor running and logging activities while you merrily exercise any and all parts of your system to their fullest.

Finally, after you've done all of your tests, run games, run network applications, used the CD-ROM drive and sound card, and so on, you can inspect the RCR.DAT logfile that the program created to see what activity happened, or you can run RCR to display the file contents itself.

RCR and the techniques used above are intended for troubleshooting and tracking down mysteriously active conflicts you can't find any other way—or finding the easy problems more easily. It is not intended for everyday use.

System Monitor

SYSMON is intended to be used every time you start your system. It runs once to get a profile of the system, which it logs to your disk drive. It can be run again at any time to log if anything has changed since the last time it was run.

SYSMON is a perfect daily configuration tracking tool that can be used to log the system before and after software or hardware installations, so you can review the log to look for any changes in the configuration. You never know when adding a sound card may rearrange your network card or how software handles these changes unless you have this kind of information. Even changing the order in which you load drivers and resident programs can be detected and give clues about why something suddenly doesn't work right.

This is a great tool for system installation and technical support people who want to get a snapshot of how they left the system, then come back and compare the configurations for any changes that may have happened, and gain clues as to why the system crashed.

The logfile is fairly technical and extensive, so it's not exactly for the average user to enjoy, but a technician looking for the mysterious bug will enjoy the details that are recorded.

Using RCR and System Monitor Together

RCR and System Monitor also work together to form a very comprehensive record of system configurations and activities, combining the configuration report with the IRQ and DMA activity report. Using them together makes a very powerful troubleshooting tool set. Here's how I do it:

1. Run the RCR program (in DOS, or in a DOS box) and allow it to make a special boot diskette.

2. Put SYSMON.EXE into the beginning of your AUTOEXEC. BAT file — edit the file so it looks something like this:

```
C:\RCR\SYSMON (first line of AUTOEXEC.BAT)
ECHO OFF (the rest of AUTOEXEC.BAT)
CLS
PROMPT $p$g
SET PATH=......
```

3. Reboot the system with the special RCR diskette in place, allowing it to load the piece of code that does the IRQ and DMA monitoring processes. The bootup then progresses normally through loading boot information: CONFIG.SYS, DOS, and AUTOEXEC.BAT.

4. Run your system through all of its normal paces: play games, run Windows, surf the Web, play a CD-ROM, and so on.

5. When you think you've done enough exercising your mouse, video card, disk drives, sound card, network card and modem, and even run Windows (3.*x* or 95), it's time to get out of Windows (do a Shutdown or Restart under Windows 95), stopping at a DOS prompt if you can, to manually run the SYSMON program again. Or, you can run SYSMON at any later time to see the log file, or view SYSMON.DAT with a text editor.

Also unlike other DOS-based utilities, Doren's program survives quite nicely and does not disturb Windows 3.*x* or Windows 95/98, to the extent that opening a DOS-window under Windows 95/98 shows you the RCR on-screen activity monitor as you're working away. Thus, my AUTOEXEC.BAT file ends up looking something like:

```
SYSMON
RCR
```

```
ECHO OFF
CLS
LH C:\WINDOWS\COMMAND\DOSKEY /INSERT
```

With this AUTOEXEC.BAT file, SYSMON is logging all of the activity that's going on with the system; I get the RCR activity monitor during any DOS sessions I call up.

RCR and SYSMON report the software interrupts in use by various programs and drivers, giving you some further clues about what program or device might be causing the unknown interrupt activity.

The real value here is that RCR is not just looking for and testing the IRQ and DMA lines of known, detected I/O devices. It detects and records any and all IRQ and DMA line activity that occurs as you use the system, making sure you know if an IRQ or DMA line was in use, even if you don't know what device may have caused it. Just the trick for those elusive conflicts you either didn't know you had, or couldn't find otherwise.

Doren's other utilities are equally as innovative and interesting to work with, as you'll see if you spend any time with them. He's also got a hardware-based IRQ and DMA indicator card available, which will give you a real-time visual indication of what's going on with the system as you're poking around. It's a lot cheaper and simpler than using an oscilloscope or logic analyzer, and you can see all of the signals happening at once.

The best part about Doren's tools is that they are shareware, meaning they are freely available and quite inexpensive (though he does have to charge a reasonable fee if you want to order the hardware IRQ/DMA indicator card separately). For the latest news and files from Doren, check out his Web site at `http://slonet.org/~doren/`.

Managing the Configuration of Microsoft Windows

There are at least two major hassles when dealing with Windows in any version or configuration — managing its configuration, and adding or removing installed programs. The tools we'll be looking at in this section provide a tremendous amount of support for you and your Windows configurations.

The following sections are only brief highlights of some exceptional tools to help you with Windows woes, as we don't intend to cover the vast realm of Windows configurations. These highlights should give you some incentive to consider these tools for your own use. After all, once you have your system hardware configuration perfected, it may be time to do something about the on-screen environment you work with.

Adding and Removing Software

As you may know, simply deleting a desktop object or a program icon from Windows does not remove that program or all the files it added to your system. After upgrading or changing to a new program, or trying to delete an old one, you don't always know which files it installed onto your system, or what changes were made to your WIN.INI or SYSTEM.INI files. Removing an old program can be tedious work, and may leave behind several megabytes of unused files. The Remove-It utility from Quarterdeck helps you manage this situation.

Remove-IT

There are a lot of uninstall utilities around for Windows. These utilities keep track of all of the files, Windows program groups, and subdirectories that are placed on your system when a new application is installed. If you later decide to remove a particular program, the uninstall utility remembers everything that was installed and can delete it from your system. This process prevents a lot of disk drive clutter left by program files that are no longer needed.

Since installing a program under Windows, especially Windows 95, involves more than just copying some files to your hard disk and creating a desktop icon, we could all use a little help monitoring the process and getting out of it if we don't like the software later on. Many software packages provide their own uninstall routines—

which is good, since they know what they installed where in the first place, and the chances are that we don't and won't. Windows 95 will also track a lot of software installations, but this is the environment we might also be a little suspicious of, so we'd like some third-party validation of what's going on.

The problem with many uninstall products is that they just track what happens during the immediate installation process. If a reboot is involved, they can't pick up the pieces and finish the installation logging process. Further, a lot of programs make Registry and file system changes during their first use, after the installation, and tracking those changes has never been a strength of other products. Some utility products track Registry changes by simply making a backup of the entire Registry — thus, when you want to remove a product whose install you tracked, the program will put back an *old* copy of the Registry, causing you to lose the *many* other changes that occurred in the meantime. Not good. Remove-IT is much more surgical and accurate about its installation and Registry tracking.

You may have guessed that I've spent more than a little time working with Remove-IT, originally from Vertisoft Systems, Inc., and I believe it's at the top of its class for utilities of its kind. Remove-IT is not just a utility to track and help you remove software installations. It also tracks almost every file on your system for use, or lack of it, and for duplications and mixed versions of files that may be causing a variety of obscure conflicts on your system. This tracking activity will tell you what files are junk or excess, and if they can be deleted, without impairing the operation of your system.

Ideally, a utility that tracks software installations and system changes should be installed and used immediately after you have done a fresh Windows installation and before installing all of your applications, so that you have an installation log of everything on your system. If you've decided to use one of these utilities on an existing and fully loaded Windows installation, some of these programs can still survey your disk drives to locate the bits and pieces of installed applications.

As indicated in Figure 8-35, Remove-IT includes many useful features, many quite pertinent to Windows Registry management, including:

- **Cleanup Coach**: A wizard-driven process to clean up the junk files and Registry entries on your system
- **Quick Clean**: A preconfigured search and junk removal process
- **Remove-IT**: The main function—remove unwanted applications, completely, or archive them for later re-installation
- **Clean-IT**: User-driven junk removal feature, as provided by Cleanup Coach and Quick Clean, which searches the Registry for orphaned and unused data that can be removed
- **Find-IT**: A duplicate file finder
- **Watch-IT**: Configure the file and program items to monitor on your system
- **Reinstall-IT**: Reinstall a stored, removed application
- **Store-IT**: Store an application
- **Move-IT**: Move an application from one drive/directory to another, including Registry and desktop references
- **Transfer-IT**: Create a self-installing removed application archive
- **Recover-IT**: Create an emergency recovery boot disk
- **Report-IT**: Comprehensive reports on the status of your system files and Registry

As with any resident program that works in the background on your system, such as Microsoft's own FindFast disk content indexing program, utility software that monitors your system for changes and records what's going on is admittedly going to use up a little CPU time and disk space. Just like backups, defragmenters, disk and file system testers, and anti-virus scanners, Remove-IT needs a little (very little) time of its own to survey and log your current system

Figure 8-35 *Remove-IT's main screen*

and software installations. Let it do so. The power of this program to keep track of your system's software configurations, and to remove cleanly excess bits you don't want is well worth the few minutes you let the program run to do its job. If you do not let Remove-IT monitor your system, some of the features, especially the surgical removal of applications, will not be as effective.

Remove-IT provides the basics of what an uninstall utility can do, and it has a lot of additional features, including keeping track of whether or not certain device drivers and font files are used. If you want, you can remove files that are historically never used. Why waste precious disk drive space? The benefits do not stop here. If you would rather not completely uninstall a seldom-used application, you can have Remove-IT do an archived removal of an application by compressing and backing up all of an application's files, making them available for later use, but saving some disk space in the meantime.

Of the many features of Remove-IT, Cleanup Coach, Quick Clean, and Clean-IT proper are the biggest assets for Registry maintenance, but we must not overlook two other very strong features of the product; Remove-IT proper and Move-IT. Remove-IT will thoroughly clean out any application you select, including installed and Registry entries added or changed later. The removal has two options — simply removing/deleting an application for good, or storing it away in a compressed archive, in case you want to get the application back later. This can save the hassle of a complete reinstall, and is one way to conserve disk space for seldom used applications.

Move-IT

Move-IT is especially handy when managing disk space, changing or adding disk drives, and so on. These days you simply cannot copy and delete or move an application subdirectory from one place to another and have the application work right after the move; file and directory moves do nothing to alter the associated Registry entries and desktop shortcuts. Move-IT handles all of that for you in a few simple steps.

Caution

Users should thoroughly read and understand the README files and manuals included with this and all similar utilities before deleting/archiving any files from Windows 3.*x* applications that you may still be running under Windows 95. INI files and many Windows 3.*x* .VXD, .386, .DLL, and .DRV files may still be valid and necessary for your applications.

I know — reading the manual is a pain sometimes, but some are well written, informative, and occasionally even educational. It's hard to know what level of user to write for or how much information to provide when doing product manuals and help files, but believe me, we do try!

So, now that you've got your software inventoried and logged, let's look at the next level of utility we'll need.

Reckoning with the Windows Registry

The Registry may be the eighth wonder of the (computing) world, and with that wonderment comes still more questions, including "How the heck do I deal with this thing?"

First of all, try not to, but with anything PC-related, we know that any and all aspects of the system will require our attention from time to time. Thus, there are a few utilities to highlight that will help you with your Registry experiences.

Second, sort out what you need to do, but as is always recommended, keep backups. To that end, we come to our first set of Registry utilities, those that provide regular backup services for the Registry and other critical system files. Among these are:

- **RegEditX**: Extended RegEdit featuring a history of editing sessions

- **RegRepair 2000**: Repair damaged system and Registry files in Windows 95 and Windows 98

- **WinRescue 95**: Backup the critical files your Windows 95 installation needs to survive

- **WinRescue 98**: Backup the critical files your Windows 98 installation needs to survive

- **WinSafe98**: Plan ahead to recuperate from a crash with your vital Windows 98 files

- **VT RegMAN**: Registry backup tool tracks your activities so you can even restore old settings

Each of these are freely available shareware files that you can find through various Internet Web sites. Each of these offers slightly different features, but their main purpose is to keep track of Registry changes and backups under your control.

RegClean

For the timid or impatient (and I don't blame you one bit — the Windows 95, 98, and NT Registry files are scary at best when you get into them), Microsoft now offers for downloading from their Web site a little application called RegClean (Figure 8-36). It seemingly miraculously scours your Registry data for duplicate and wrong entries and offers to remove them for you. It also saves what it removes into a unique file so you can merge the data back into the

Registry at any time later if you want to. Pretty slick. How effective it is may be hard to tell, except that the program generates specific .REG files containing the items that it removes or changes, so you can replace what RegClean takes out or changes if you need to. So far, I have not had to put anything back that it removes, and it does not remove all that much at any one time. Other tools are likely more effective.

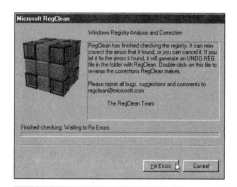

Figure 8-36 *Microsoft's RegClean after checking the Registry for errors*

ScanRegW

ScanRegW is new in Windows 98, and more or less replaces RegClean. It is run automatically by Windows at bootup, if the system is shutdown improperly, or if the Registry is deemed corrupt as Windows boots and runs. At least this program does more for us than RegClean does, because it can check for and fix some corruptions of the Registry, and does it for you.

You can invoke the program yourself, it lives in the \Windows folder as SCANREGW.EXE. It will perform a quick check and then give you an option to backup the Registry files (again if already done so today.) It makes a backup of your Registry files and stores it in \Windows\SYSBCKUP, where up to nine previous backups are kept. In the event that ScanRegW cannot use the most recent version to restore the Registry after a crash, it will have other versions to revert back to, hoping to find a good one to use. This program really has no user interface, except for a few small popup dialog boxes that appear (and are hard to capture and do not convey much information) or a quick status screen that appears during bootup if the program is set to be run because Windows discovered a crash.

Remove-IT's Clean-IT

Clean-IT is a tool that is probably more like what Microsoft's RegClean ought to be, and then some. In Figure 8-37 you can see a small bit of the junk that Clean-IT has found in the Registry that RegClean did not. Being much more thorough at not only cleaning up the Registry, but other foibles of Windows and applications that did not uninstall cleanly, this is a definite winner of a utility to have around.

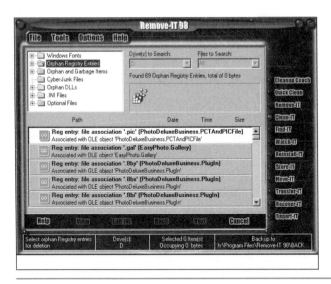

Figure 8-37 *Clean-IT with a listing of several Registry keys that can be removed*

Norton Utilities WinDoctor

If you don't already know about the Norton Utilities, or you do and think you have no business messing with, heaven forbid, a (dweeby, geeky, oh-my-gawd it's technical) *utility* program — think again! This Norton package has matured from the good old days of absolute disk sectors, bytes, hex cluster numbers, and Master Boot Records (well, they're still there . . .) — but under very approachable and helpful screens and dialog boxes that make for a no-mistakes PC technical experience.

The disk testing and optimizing utility alone is impressive, but add to the suite the new WinDoctor feature, and you're ready to tackle some of the toughest PC problems, specifically the Registry. If the display from WinDoctor in Figure 8-38 looks similar to the one of Figure 8-37 for gg, it should, however I think Clean-IT found a little more than WinDoctor shows — running on the same system at the same time. Both cleaned up the system pretty well, though there are things that WinDoctor didn't seem to touch that Clean-IT does — and Clean-IT will make backups in case you let it go too far.

Figure 8-38 *Norton WinDoctor with a listing of several Registry keys that can be removed*

General Windows Configuration Tools

TweakUI (Figure 8-39) is a free utility, available from Microsoft's Web site alone or within the entire suite of Windows 95 add-ins called PowerToys. It is also available in Windows 98. Its main purpose — or most popular use, anyway — is to let you turn off many of the annoying little features Microsoft added to the shortcut icons and titles (you know, "Shortcut to" and that ugly little arrow in the corner of the icon!). It also lets you control some of the desktop appearance, document and run history logs, and control aspects of how Windows 95 and 98 boot up. Kudos to Microsoft for this handy little gem.

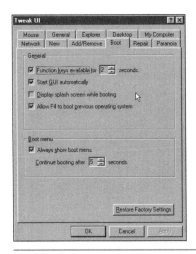

Figure 8-39 *Microsoft's TweakUI Boot features tab showing some of the things you can change about how Windows 95/98 appears at bootup*

Miscellaneous Utilities

It seems we're always looking for something new to play with on our PCs, and most often I find interesting little things around the Net that intrigue me. The following is a list of freely available, Windows shareware utilities that you can find through various Internet Web sites.

- **Barry Press Utilities**: A collection of utilities for Windows 95/98

- **DLLMaster**: Displays lists of various Windows tasks, hidden windows, processes, loaded DLLs and VXDs. One of the must-have utilities for seeing what's really going on in Windows 95/98

- **OnTrack Y2K Advisor**: Check your computer BIOS for Year 2000 compatibility at http://www.ontrack.com

- **Performance 95**: View your system's RAM and CPU usage, including threads and program IDs at http://www.bonamisoftware.com

- **SpinRite**: The ultimate disk drive test tool from Steve Gibson. It's not free but is available easily through http://www.grc.com

- **TaskPro**: An alternate that may be preferable to DLLMaster, TaskPro is another one of the must-have utilities for seeing what's really going on in Windows 95/98. It too displays lists of various Windows tasks, hidden windows, processes, loaded **DLLs** and **VXDs,** and it lets you kill off processes you don't want to leave running — much more in depth than Windows' own Task Manager

- **TestCom**: A serial (COM) port analyzer

- **Winzip32**: Choose the zip utility you want, but there must be a reason that WinZip appears to be the most popular shareware program around for archiving and decompressing files for local storage or sharing between users

If your hardware configuration is not in question, certainly what is running on your machine may be. The Barry Press utilities offer a few cute widgets to play with. One of the most valuable is call DLLMAN and is used to tell you what DLLs are needed for any EXE file you select — very handy if you get the "a required DLL is missing" error message when trying to run a program.

DLLMaster and TaskPro are equally among my favorites for showing what Windows tasks and drivers are loaded and running on your system. If you think this may be unrevealing, run your Web browser, then TaskPro, and notice just how many things a program like Netscape loads into memory! Performance 95 is somewhat similar in that it indicates which EXE files (and some DLLs) are running, and how much memory and CPU time each consumes. They're great for looking at runaway or troublesome applications.

Steve Gibson's SpinRite is a must-have to keep your disk drives in top shape. It's DOS-based and may not be as elegant as Norton's stuff, but it is *good* at testing things few people but the disk factory will handle. The OnTrack DataAdvisor falls onto this list as another must if all else fails and you absolutely, positively must recover data from a crashed, burned, mangled or dead hard drive. TestCom shows up as a cute little DOS-based tool to help you determine what's up or not with your COM ports.

Getting Better Technical Support

Calling, e-mailing, or faxing for technical support may be something we have come to dread in our experience with PC hardware and software. It takes a lot of patience waiting through phone queues and time zones. The quest for technical support also requires a considerable amount of information exchange. Indeed, the lack of information—by lack of experience, awareness, or the proper tools—creates a technical support bottleneck at all stages of the process. If you are paying for technical support by a pay-per-call service or a service contract, getting the best service for your money is critical. Books such as this one and well-chosen software tools can take a lot of pressure off of everyone along the way.

We expect technical support people to be familiar with almost every aspect of PCs, from hardware to software. Indeed, this is not very practical or even possible given the thousands of systems and programs in use. Those people who have become quite experienced and accomplished at providing technical support in one way or another are often elevated to design and development or management positions. The better someone is at technical support, the less time that person spends doing it. With luck, he or she will be able to share and promote greater expertise among others. Some of us even begin to write books to share what we know.

Technical support people, and perhaps all too often system and program developers, expect users to be more familiar with their PCs and software than they are or can be. Obviously, this is not always going to be the case, and it may never be. Users should simply be able to use their systems and programs, through good design, planning, and training on these items, and not have to be able to design, build, or program them. (But if you try it, you might find it enjoyable and worthwhile!)

Using Tools to Help Tech Support

The information provided by the tools I've highlighted in this chapter and the configuration details I've been discussing, are essential for effective technical support — even the support of software problems. Keeping your system inventory current and having a report of your current hardware and DOS and Windows configuration information will save you time in the technical support process. Certainly, the more you know about your PC, the more you'll be able to get from the services you request to support it.

Your knowledge will help you determine if you're a satisfied customer, or if you need to seek out another service to help you. Because you picked up this book, you were obviously interested in becoming more familiar with your PC. You either want to support yourself directly or determine if you're getting the right support. When you know more, hopefully you'll share the information with others. You'll begin to find that users helping other users creates a strong support network.

In addition to all of this technical information, you should be able to reproduce the conditions under which a problem occurs, and you should be able to communicate this effectively as well. If your problem is that your printer doesn't print, the support process takes longer than it has to. You'll be encouraged to check the basics: Is the printer plugged in? Is it turned on? Is it connected to your computer? Is your software configured properly? A little system information, and running a diagnostic program such as PC-Doctor or RCR and System Monitor, can help pinpoint the possible causes of your problem and get you on the right track to a solution much faster.

If You Don't Want to Fool with the Tools

The burden of technical support — getting it and giving it — can be significantly relieved if all parties involved are adequately prepared and cooperative. The technical support person should be able to define the types of information needed in order to help resolve a problem. PCs are complex systems. A lot of aspects of them interact, and, yes, conflict at times. Sorting all this out, if you haven't been able to do it with the help of this book, takes you another level deeper into the system details. You can be prepared for this, which will save time and help you determine if you're getting the right help.

Being able to fax or e-mail this information to the support department is more effective. But, what if you could simply push a button on your electronic desktop — an application dialog or a widget on a Web site — and have your system information collected and sent off to the support center of your choice, without ever seeing any references to IRQs, Plug and Play, hexadecimal addresses, and so on? You'll find this type of access to support becoming more and more popular as technical support shifts to online/electronic means.

Part of the history of this book project dates back to 1994-1995 when I helped bring the concept of electronic technical support out of the drudgery of running software, printing things out for faxing, or capturing files, attaching them to e-mail, and so on. We created software that acted like a support technician to gather pertinent data without actually being at the system — truly "push a button, get help" was the motto of the day. Back then, the Internet was not nearly what it is today. Back then, just a couple of short years ago, far fewer people had modems, and even fewer of us were "on the Internet" much less knew what it was. Making the concept work was not a problem, but getting people and systems connected was.

Today, millions of us use the Internet—perhaps the single most popular reason people buy computers now. Thus, every system sold has or will have a modem or some form of connectivity to the outside world in it eventually. With this connectivity and ample communications and CPU performance, seeking and delivering technical support electronically will start to become commonplace. Today, we have Web sites to visit that are little more than easily accessible versions of the forums and special-interest-group clubs of the old online services. The next iteration of electronically available support will allow users to submit requests for help directly to vendor help desks, complete with system information, and perhaps with interactive, remotely driven diagnostics. Behind the scenes, artificial intelligence engines, fed by system diagnostic information and technical expertise, will be able to more accurately and efficiently deliver solutions to your desktop—automatically—no waiting on hold, no multilevel phone system navigation, no Twenty Questions about you and your PC.

Security: How Much Can Electronic Support Do?

We're concerned about the security of our PC systems and the personal and business information they contain. How is this addressed by electronic or remote control support? What information can people using remote support software get off of our PCs?

Having addressed this issue as a designer of remote support tools, the answers are somewhat rhetorical, for all of the possible considerations: What do you know about the person that comes to your desktop at work, or that you leave the system with at a repair shop? What really happens to that old hard drive they just replaced? Do you clean out your browser and temp file cache often? Have you any idea what the network system operators at work or at the online services can see if they watch your online traffic? Do you give your credit card number over the phone?

Okay, so now you have an idea where all this might lead. With conventional support means, that is, someone physically has their hands on your PC, often as not without you able to look over their shoulder or to know what they are really doing — you may be *more* vulnerable and helpless to protect your system than if you let someone connect to it electronically. Electronically, in the comfort of your own office or cubicle, if you suspect something unusual is going on, you can unplug the connection or turn the system OFF. That's tough to do when the PC is ten miles away in the backroom of some computer store or in the neighbor's garage.

As for the benefits and limitations of what can be done with electronic support, suffice it to say that most of the work is simply information gathering — collecting configuration details or diagnostic results. If some form of remote control is performed, only some aspects of configuration can be affected, limited to that which you can or cannot do in the Windows or DOS environment anyway. As many of us doing PC support have found, this is often quite enough to address over 50 percent, and maybe as much as 80 percent, of the PC problems most of us have.

Unfortunately, even with Plug and Play, reconfiguration of hardware, which may be necessary as upgrades and add-ons are installed, cannot be done without shutting the system down or getting to the CMOS setup parameters. Since there is no way to have connectivity to boards, or even the keyboard and monitor when the system is shutdown or in CMOS setup menus, some direct physical hands-on work may still be required.

That said, it's about time that advancements in technology become able to help fix themselves rather than relying so much on people learning and doing the same things over and over again — 50 million times.

Summary

In closing our configuration management processes with this chapter, it's safe to say that I've covered a lot of ground in a short time. I've reviewed a lot of material that has taken many years for many people to accumulate, study, understand, and apply in daily practice, or through handy and essential software tools. You've seen how software and hardware can complement each other, and even how different types of software can be combined to make our PC configuration management quite complete, up to and including preparations for and transitions to new hardware and operating systems. Maybe you've learned something about this complex toaster, and you're better prepared to "make toast" and enjoy the rest of your day.

As with everything else in this fast-paced PC market, you can expect new systems and software revisions to be available that may supersede some of the examples shown in this book. I'll try to keep pace with these developments and consider any and all input to the configuration process for future revisions to this work—perhaps even to some of the featured software tools. The PC business thrives on real-user ideas and needs. No idea, no conflict, no problem goes unheard if you make it known to the right people the right way.

Keep in touch, and happy bits!

Appendix A

System Configuration Detail List

Update the following list, or keep a printed or file copy of the system information reported by a utility program such as PC-Doctor, Manifest, Norton's System Information, or MSD. This information is critical when you request technical support.

Record the IRQ, DMA, and I/O address assignments, as well as the make, model, version, and type for each device in your system. Also record jumper and switch settings for the system board and each add-in board, disk drive, and so on.

Configuration Item	Item Details
System BIOS:	
CPU:	
Math Chip:	
CPU Speed:	
Bus Types:	
Total RAM:	
External Cache Size:	
Diskette Drives:	
Hard Drive Adapter Type:	
Hard Drive #1:	

Continued

Configuration Item	Item Details
Hard Drive #2:	
Hard Drive #3:	
Hard Drive #4:	
SCSI Adapter:	
SCSI Devices:	
Disk Compression:	
Video Adapter:	
Video BIOS Version:	
Operating System:	
User Interfaces:	
COM Port #1:	
COM Port #2:	
COM Port #3:	
COM Port #4:	
LPT Port #1:	
LPT Port #2:	
LPT Port #3:	
Mouse Type:	
Sound Card:	
Network Adapter:	
Modem:	
USB Devices:	
FireWire Devices:	
Other:	

Keep a backup file or printed copy of the following information and files:

- AUTOEXEC.BAT
- CONFIG.SYS
- WIN.INI
- SYSTEM.INI
- MSDOS.SYS (for Windows 95 and Windows 98)

Appendix B

Standards and Participating Organizations

The table below represents a majority of the official industry standards organizations that affect the PC industry. If you are a hardware designer or software programmer and need specific technical information about a technical specification or standard, these are the places to look. While the information available from these organizations is exceptionally detailed and theoretical, it is not generally useful for end-user tasks with PCs. These organizations do not maintain information about finished goods or vendor products.

If you are looking for less technical information, consult the bibliography references listed in Appendix C. If you are looking for vendor-specific information, you will find that most vendors provide direct end-user support on CompuServe, America Online, and Web sites on the Internet. Many vendors are listed in catalogs and magazines as well.

Organization	Type of Organization or Information	Electronic Information Resources
ANSI American National Standards Institute 1430 Broadway New York, NY 10018 212-354-3300 212-398-0023 (fax)	Computer, Electronic, and other US standards	

ATA
AT-Attachment Committee/
Small Form Factor Committee
	IDE disk drive specifications	subscribe to ATA mailing
		list through:
		`Majordomo@dt.`
		`wdc.com`

CCITT International Telecommunications Union Place de Nations Ch-1211 Geneva 20 Switzerland 41-22-99-51-11 41-22-33-72-56 (fax)	Modem and telephony specifications	
Information Gatekeepers, Inc. 214 Harvard Avenue Boston, MA 02134 617-232-3111 617-734-8562 (fax)		

DMTF
Desktop Management Task Force
JF2-51
2111 Northeast 25th Street
Hillsboro, OR 97124
503-696-9300
	DMTF/DMI Workstation and
	Network management
	specifications
		`ftp.intel.com/`
		`pub/IAL`
		`www.intel.com`

EIA Electronics Industry Association Global Engineering Documents 2805 McGaw Avenue Irvine, CA 92714 714-261-1455 714-261-7892 (fax) 800-854-7179 (order info)	Computer and Electronics standards	`www.eia.org`

Organization	Type of Organization or Information	Electronic Information Resources
EPA Energy Star (MC:6202J) Washington, D.C. 20460 202-233-9114 202-233-9578 (fax)	Computers Program, Energy Star compliance	`www.epa.gov/ appdstar/esoe/ pclist.html`
FireWire IEEE-1394	Apple's multimedia interconnect standard	`http://developer. apple.com/ hardware/ FireWire/`
IEEE Institute of Electrical and Electronic Engineers The Standards Department 445 Hoes Lane P.O. Box 1331 Piscataway, NJ 08855-1311 201-562-3800 201-562-1571 (fax)	Computer and Electronics standards	`www.ieee.org`
Intel Corp. 5200 NE Elam Young Parkway Hillsboro, OR 97124-6497 503-696-2000	PCI, Plug and Play, Advanced Power Management specifications	`ftp.intel.com` `www.intel.com`
Microsoft Corp. 1 Microsoft Way Redmond, WA 98052 206-882-8080	Plug and Play, PC95, PC97, PC99, Advanced Power Management specifications	`www.microsoft.com` `ftp.microsoft.com`
PCI Peripheral Component Interconnect PCI Special Interest Group M/S HF3-15A 5200 NE Elam Young Parkway Hillsboro, OR 97124-6497 503-696-2000	System bus, built-in and add-in card specifications	`www.intel.com` `ftp.intel.com`

Continued

Organization	Type of Organization or Information	Electronic Information Resources
PCMCIA (aka PC Card) Personal Computer Memory Card Industry Association 1030 East Duane Avenue Suite G Sunnyvale, CA 94086 408-720-0107 408-720-9416 (fax)	Portable and desktop system add-in devices and cards	Internet news: `alt.periphs.pcmcia` `www.pc-card.com`
Plug and Play	Plug and Play specifications	`ftp.microsoft. com/developr/ drg/Plug-and- Play/Pnpspecs`
SCSI Small Computer Systems Interface	SCSI, SCSI-2 and SCSI-3 specs	subscribe to SCSI mailing list through: `scsiadm@ witchitaks.ncr.com`
Underwriters Labs, Inc. Underwriters Laboratory Standards 1655 Scott Blvd. Santa Clara, CA 95131 408-985-2400	Electrical and safety testing	`www.ul.com`
USB Universal Serial Bus	USB info, specifications, product manufacturers lists.	`www.usb.org`
VESA Video Electronics Standards Association 2150 North First Street San Jose, CA 95131-2029 408-435-0333 408-435-8225 (fax)	Video BIOS Enhancements, (VBE), Local Bus	`www.vesa.org`

Appendix C

Reference Materials

You will find the following books most helpful in your pursuit of the operational and functional aspects of PC systems, including repair and upgrade techniques.

Title	Author(s)	Publisher
Troubleshooting Your PC, 4E	Todd Aspinwall	MIS:Press/IDG Books Worldwide
Inside the IBM PC	Peter Norton	Brady/Prentice-Hall
Upgrading and Repairing PCs	Scott Mueller	Que Education & Training
System BIOS for IBM PCs, Compatibles, and EISA Computers	Phoenix Technologies, Ltd.	Addison-Wesley
Technical Reference, Personal Computer XT and Portable Personal Computer and *Technical Reference, Personal Computer AT*	IBM Corporation	IBM Corporation
DOS Programmer's Reference	Terry R. Dettman	Que Education & Training
Hardware Design Guide for Microsoft Windows 95		Microsoft Press
Inside the Windows 95 Registry	Ron Perrusha	O'Reilly & Associates
The Windows 95 Registry	John Woram	MIS:Press
Windows 95 Registry Troubleshooting	Rob Tidrow	New Riders
PCI System Architecture	Tom Shanley, Don Anderson	Mindshare, Inc.
Plug and Play System Architecture	Tom Shanley	Mindshare, Inc.

The technical reference manuals from IBM may be out of print, but they may be available from a technical library or friend.

Appendix D

About the CD-ROM

This appendix provides a brief description of each utility on the CD-ROM, along with instructions for installation and use. Refer to Chapter 8 for advice on how to make best use of utility software in general. I appreciate the generosity of the software providers who have allowed me to share these products with you, and I hope that you will, too.

About the Software

I have chosen products that suit occasional use and still provide adequate functionality within the context of this book. This includes unregistered shareware, evaluation versions of commercial software, as well as a suitable assortment of freeware — all common practice with book distributions of software.

Please feel free to use this software for your own personal use as much as you want or is reasonably spelled out in the license agreements. If you enjoy it and it has value to you, or you need to use it in the course of making a living or a profit, do yourself and the software authors a favor and register or buy full versions.

Demonstration software is a good means to give you a sample of how well the author's technology can work for you. Shareware is created by individuals, hobbyists mostly, who typically do not create software for a living, but who would like to recover some of the costs of the tools that helped make the software.

Copying These Programs to Other Disks

CD-ROM files by their nature are marked with the Read-Only file attribute. This and similar attributes are copied to other media along with the files.

If you ever wish to delete or move these files from the destination to which you copied them, you will need to remove the Read-Only attribute. There are two ways to do this.

To remove the Read-Only file attribute using DOS:

- From a DOS prompt, use the DOS ATTRIB program (typically found in `C:\DOS` or `C:\WINDOWS\COMMAND`:

  `ATTRIB -R filename.ext [Enter]`

To remove the Read-Only file attribute using Windows 95/98 Explorer:

1. Navigate to the file's destination drive and subdirectory.
2. Right-click the filename of interest
3. Select Properties from the menu shown.
4. In the Properties dialog box, clear the Read-Only and other attributes that may prevent you from deleting or moving the file(s).

To view files with System or Hidden attributes set:

1. If a file has somehow also acquired the System or Hidden attribute, change the default settings for Explorer by selecting View ➪ Folder Options from the Explorer menu bar.
2. Select the View tab, and select Show all files.
3. You may also wish to clear the Hide MS-DOS file extensions check box to see the entire filename with extensions for all files.
4. Close the View dialog box and then refresh your display to see all the files.

File Descriptions

Here are some acknowledgments of and background information about the programs provided on our CD-ROM. There are also notes about how to copy or install and use the software provided. Please read the following descriptions before installing or using these utilities and programs. This way you will know what the program can do for you, what system requirements may affect your use, whether it is a full and free program or a demo of a more capable system, and how best to get started using the program.

Norton Utilities Trial Version

CD-ROM directory: \Symantec NU
Main program file: SETUP.EXE
Installation and use: Hard drive; Windows 95, 98. Run SETUP.EXE under Windows to install the software. Reboot is recommended/required for full program functionality.
Author/Publisher: Symantec Corp.
Vendor Web site: www.symantec.com
Availability: Online, retail
Type: Demonstration

This is a 30-day trial version of the venerable Norton Utilities. It is a near full-featured product, with the exception of the NDIAGS.EXE program, which is a DOS-only program and not enabled in this demo.

PC-Doctor from Watergate Software

CD-ROM Directory: \PCDR
Main program file: PCDR.EXE
Installation and use: Hard drive or diskette; DOS, with appropriate ASPI, CD-ROM, network and/or sound card drivers loaded as may be needed for specific devices.

Author/Publisher: Watergate Software
Web site: www.ws.com
Availability: www.jdr.com
Type: Functional demonstration providing system information only

PC-Doctor is a most complete source of information about PC system IRQ and DMA assignments and general system contents. It covers more hardware better than any other piece of independently developed software on the market.

Some very skilled, clever, imaginative, and just plain excellent people at Watergate create these products and continue their development on a regular basis to meet the demands of an ever-changing industry.

PC-Doctor is a diagnostic program used by many PC manufacturers, end-users, and service departments. The evaluation version of PC-Doctor for DOS gives you access to the in-depth system information available through this program. The System Information provided identifies the hardware, the memory use, and the IRQ, DMA and I/O addresses used by the components in your PC system. This information is quite valuable towards establishing a proper PC configuration, and troubleshooting a questionable system.

PC-Doctor Parallel Port Loopback Plug

In order to accurately detect data and IRQ activity on parallel ports, most diagnostic programs require that a specially wired test connector be attached to all parallel (LPT) ports of interest.

This connector is very simple to make from commonly available parts: a male DB-25 data plug (male connector) and five short pieces of wire. Many computer stores and electronics stores such as Radio Shack carry these plugs in do-it-yourself form with small crimp-on pins that may be inserted into the connector body. More technical users will probably be able to dig into their "junk box" and come up with the necessary parts in a few minutes. If you have more than one parallel port in your system, make one loopback plug for each port so you only have to run the IRQ/DMA test once to detect the IRQs and any conflicts.

The wiring of the connector should be as follows:

Pin 1 connected to Pin 13

Pin 2 connected to Pin 15

Pin 10 connected to Pin 16

Pin 11 connected to Pin 17

Pin 12 connected to Pin 14

The Rosenthal Utilities

CD-ROM Directory: \R-UTIL

Main program file(s): CLEANER.EXE, R-FORMAT.EXE, RCR.EXE, RSW.EXE, SYSMON.EXE, UNINSTAL.EXE, UN_DUP.EXE, VIRSIM.COM, VSIM_A.COM, R-Y2KFIX.EXE

Installation and use: Hard drive or diskette; DOS

Author/Publisher: Doren Rosenthal

Web site: www.slonet.org/~doren

Availability: Online

Type: Shareware

I almost can't thank Doren enough for not only validating this work, but for the kindred spirit discussions by phone and email about PC resource detection and troubleshooting. At the last minute, he rushed me the hardware-based IRQ and DMA display board he has available also. I'm very impressed and thankful to have it in my PC-guru arsenal of goodies. You can find Doren on the Web at the Web site above.

Doren Rosenthal offers his Shareware utilities for your enjoyment. If you like them, please register them! A brief description of each of them appears below:

CLEANER.EXE: The Disk Drive Cleaner, used in conjunction with a special media cleaning diskette, helps safely and effectively remove debris from the delicate read/write heads of diskette drives. This helps prevent data loss, unreliable performance, and errors often traced to microscopic foreign particles, dirt, dust, oxides, and smoke that accumulate on drive heads. Preventive maintenance takes less than four minutes. It supports standard diskette drives as well as commercial automatic mass disk duplicators.

R-FORMAT: R-Format replaces the standard diskette format so it no longer hangs the system during start-up when the diskette is left in the A: drive. An embedded graphic and text message of your choice is displayed and the system then boots normally. The disk otherwise functions normally. The example graphic file, R-FORMAT.PCX, may be replaced with your own. This program may be run under DOS or Windows.

R-Y2KFIX: With the Rosenthal Year 2000 Fix and CMOS/Clock Battery Monitor, Year 2000 compliance is enforced each time system power is restored. Tests and adjustments are performed independent of ROM BIOS, Real-Time clock (hardware), or system clock (virtual) versions. Progression including leap years is verified and a millennium counter displayed. R-Y2KFix is provided as a FREE bonus to non-commercial private users just for trying "The Rosenthal Utilities." Please enjoy it with Doren's compliments as thanks for all the encouragement and support users have shown over the years. This program is *not* a TSR (terminate-and-stay-resident) utility, but it is intended to be included in your **AUTOEXEC.BAT** file to be effective, even for use with Windows 3.*x*, Windows 95, or Windows 98.

RCR.EXE: The Rosenthal Conflict Resolver provides hardware and software diagnostics to identify, resolve, and prevent all PC system DMA and IRQ conflicts for DOS, Windows 3.*x*, Windows 95, Windows 98, Windows NT and OS/2. From the earliest PCs to today's most sophisticated Plug-and-Play components, all are supported — even when systems mix old and new technologies. This program is a TSR (terminate-and-stay-resident) utility that should be included in your AUTOEXEC.BAT file, even for use with Windows 3.*x*, Windows 95, or Windows 98. RCR may be run inside Windows to view IRQ and DMA activity detected by the resident portion of the program. It causes no known conflicts or problems with Windows.

RSW.EXE: This System Workout repeatedly exercises thousands of low-level tests. System Workout confirms the reliable performance of new or upgraded systems and/or when changes are made like installing new hardware or software. Especially difficult problems like intermittent, marginal performance errors and conflicts are revealed. This program is intended to be run from DOS only, with any required DOS-level drivers installed (mouse, sound card, CD-ROM, and so on).

SYSMON.EXE: The Rosenthal System Monitor provides professional diagnostics that are automatic enough for beginners. SYSMON evaluates your hardware and configuration each day during start-up and maintains a diary log of changes to identify and quickly resolve future hardware/software conflicts. This program is a TSR (terminate-and-stay-resident) utility that should be included in your AUTOEXEC.BAT file, even for use with Windows 3.*x*, Windows 95, or Windows 98. SYSMON creates a log file of system changes at each bootup. It causes no known conflicts or problems with Windows.

UN_DUP.EXE: Duplicate files waste valuable disk space, so "Rosenthal Un_Dup" finds any files that are redundant and may be removed. The path statement is optimized and directed to the remaining identical files. Files must be identical in name, size, and contents to be considered duplicates. This is a DOS program.

UNINSTAL.EXE: Rosenthal UnInstall tracks installations to both remove unwanted additions and restore things that have been changed. It automatically removes unwanted files and directories, and restores modified Windows and DOS programs, files, directories, the Windows Registry (USER.DAT and SYSTEM.DAT) and system files (AUTOEXEC.BAT, CONFIG.SYS, WIN.INI, SYSTEM.INI. This program is a TSR (terminate-and-stay-resident) utility that should be included in your AUTOEXEC.BAT file, even for use with Windows 3.x, Windows 95, or Windows 98. It causes no known conflicts or problems with Windows.

VIRSIM.COM and **VIRSIMA.COM**: The Virus Simulator from Rosenthal Engineering is an absolute necessity for anyone seriously interested in defending against viruses. Government agencies, business, security consultants, law enforcement, institutions, and system administrators employ Virus Simulator when conducting internal security audits and training. This program may be run in DOS or Windows with your virus protection program active to test its capabilities.

The latest versions of these utilities are always available at Doren's Web site.

WinZip

CD-ROM Directory: \WINZIP
Main program file: SETUP.EXE
Installation and use: Hard drive; Windows 3.x, Windows 95, or Windows 98 — run executable file to install.
Author/Publisher: Nico Mak Computing, Inc.
Vendor Web site: www.winzip.com
Availability: Online
Type: Fully functional, unregistered

WinZip brings the convenience of Windows to the use of Zip files and other popular file archive and compression formats. The optional wizard interface makes unzipping easier than ever. WinZip features built-in support for popular Internet file formats, including TAR, gzip, Unix compress, UUencode, BinHex, and MIME. ARJ, LZH, and ARC files are supported via external programs. WinZip interfaces to most virus scanners. Please see the documentation on the CD-ROM for installation and usage documentation.

WinRescue 95

CD-ROM Directory: \RESCUE95
Main program file: RESCUE95.EXE
Installation and use: Hard drive; Windows 95. Run SETUP.EXE from \Rescue95 to install.
Author/Publisher: Ray Geide
Vendor Web site: www.superwin.com
Availability: Online
Type: Fully functional shareware, unregistered

WinRescue 95 protects the Registry by backing up and restoring the Registry and initialization files of Windows 95. A special feature cleans up the Registry and compacts it. Highly recommended protection if you are going to be working with your Windows configurations.

WinRescue 98

CD-ROM Directory: \RESCUE98
Main program file: RESCUE98.EXE
Installation and use: Hard drive; Windows 98. Run SETUP.EXE from \Rescue98 to install.
Author/Publisher: Ray Geide
Vendor Web site: www.superwin.com

Availability: Online
Type: Fully functional shareware, unregistered

Specially adapted to Windows 98, WinRescue 98 provides the Registry backup features of WinRescue 95 and adds user-designated files to Registry backups during start-up.

Glossary

8086 An Intel 8-bit external, 16-bit internal data bus microprocessor capable of addressing up to 1MB of memory and operating at speeds up to 10MHz. Its companion numerical coprocessor or math chip is the 8087. The 8086 is found in the IBM PS/2 Models 25 and 30 and some clones.

8088 An Intel 8-bit internal, 8-bit external data bus microprocessor capable of addressing up to 1MB of memory and operating at speeds up to 10MHz. This chip is used in the IBM PC, XT, and compatible clone systems. Its companion numerical coprocessor or math chip is the 8087.

80286 An Intel 16-bit internal and external data bus microprocessor capable of addressing up to 16MB of memory and operating at speeds up to 12MHz. Some non-Intel equivalents may run at 16MHz. This chip's first use in PC systems was in the IBM PC/AT. Its companion numerical coprocessor or math chip is the 80287.

80386DX An Intel 32-bit internal and external data bus microprocessor capable of addressing up to 4GB of memory and operating at speeds up to 33MHz. Some non-Intel equivalents may run at 40MHz. This chip's first use in PC/AT-compatible systems was by COMPAQ. Its companion numerical coprocessor or math chip is the 80287 in some systems, otherwise the 80387.

80386SX An Intel 32-bit internal and 16-bit external data bus microprocessor capable of addressing up to 32MB of memory and operating at speeds up to 25MHz. Its companion numerical coprocessor or math chip is the 80387SX.

80486DX An Intel 32-bit internal and external data bus microprocessor capable of operating at speeds up to 50MHz. This processor contains an internal math coprocessor (floating point processor) and an 8K internal instruction cache.

80486DX2 An Intel 32-bit internal and external data bus microprocessor capable of operating at speeds up to 66MHz internally due to a doubling of the external clock speed. This processor contains an internal math coprocessor (floating point processor) and an 8K internal instruction cache.

80486DX4 An Intel 32-bit internal and external data bus microprocessor capable of operating at speeds up to 100MHz internally due to internal multiplication (tripling) of the external clock speed. This processor contains an internal math coprocessor (floating point processor) and an 8K internal instruction cache.

80486SX An Intel 32-bit internal and external data bus microprocessor capable of operating at speeds up to 25MHz. It does not provide the internal floating point processor or the 8K cache of the 80486DX.

80486SX2 An Intel 32-bit internal and external data bus microprocessor capable of operating at speeds up to 50MHz internally due to doubling of the external clock speed. It does not provide the internal floating point processor or the 8K cache of the 80486DX.

ACPI (Advanced Configuration and Power Interface) A standard specification and method for monitoring system activity and control of system configurations with power applied to or removed from system components, or switched to other components, depending on power states. Accommodates different modes of Sleep, Suspend, and Full-On system readiness of many system components.

Adapter card A plug-in card used to exchange signals between the computer and internal or external equipment.

Add-in card *See* Adapter card.

Address A location in memory or on a hardware bus of either a specific piece of data or a physical hardware device.

Advanced Power Management A standard specification and method for monitoring system activity and control of power applied to or removed from system components, accommodating different modes of Sleep, Suspend, and Full-On system readiness. Sleep mode allows for maintaining current system activity with reduced power consumption, such as having disk drives and displays powered OFF but the CPU and memory retaining the last activities. Suspend mode allows for maintaining minimal, if any, current system activity with no power consumption. APM has been superceded by ACPI. Both are expected to be replaced by new power management standards currently under development.

ANSI (American National Standards Institute) A governing body managing specifications for the computer industry and other disciplines. In terms of computing, ANSI maintains a set of standards for the coding and displaying of computer information, including certain "escape sequences" for screen color and cursor positioning. A device-driver file, ANSI.SYS, can be loaded in your PC's CONFIG.SYS file so that your screen can respond properly to color and character changes provided from programs or terminal sessions between computers.

Archive attribute   *See* **Attributes.**

ASCII (American Standard Code for Information Interchange) ASCII defines the numerical or data representation of characters and numbers and foreign language characters in computer data storage, text files, and display. There are 128 predefined characters, numbered 0–127, representing the alphabet, numbers, and data-terminal control functions that nearly any computer system will interpret properly. ASCII characters are represented or transferred in decimal or hexadecimal numeric representations, from 0–255 (decimal) or 00–FFh (hex). The upper 128 characters (128–255) vary between computer systems and languages and are known as the symbol set. IBM defined these as Extended ASCII characters, which include a variety of lines and boxes for pseudo-graphical screen displays. ASCII also defines the format of text files. ASCII text files generated on PCs differ slightly from the original ASCII standard and may appear with extra lines on other computer systems.

AT A model series of the IBM PC family known as Advanced Technology. This series includes those systems that use the 80286 microprocessor chip. The AT classification has been applied to 80386- and 80486-based systems that offer basic compatibility with and enhancements over the original specification.

ATA (AT-Attachments) An industry-wide specification for the interfacing of devices, typically hard disk drives, to the PC/AT standard data bus.

AT-compatible A description of a personal computer system that provides the minimum functions and features of the original IBM PC/AT system and is capable of running the same software and using the same hardware devices.

Attributes Every DOS file entry, including subdirectories, is accompanied by an attribute byte of information that specifies whether the file is read-only, hidden, system, or archived. Read-only indicates that no program operation should erase or write-over a file with this attribute. Hidden indicates that the file should not be displayed or used in normal DOS DIR, COPY or similar operations. The system attribute indicates that a file belongs to the operating system, which typically applies only to the hidden DOS files IO.SYS or IBMBIO.COM, and MSDOS.SYS or IBMDOS.COM files. The archive attribute indicates that a file has been changed since the last backup, or that it should be backed up during the next backup session. Backup operations clear this attribute.

AUTOEXEC.BAT file An ASCII text file that may contain one or more lines of DOS commands that you want executed every time you boot up your PC. Also known as just the autoexec file, this file can be customized using a text editor program so that you can specify a DOS prompt, set a drive and directory path to be searched when you call up programs, or load terminate-and-stay resident (TSR) programs that you want to have available all of the time.

Base address The initial or starting address of a device or memory location.

Base memory *See* DOS memory.

Batch file or BATch file An ASCII text file that may contain one or more lines of DOS commands that you want to execute by calling for one file, the name of the batch file, rather than keying them in individually. Also known as bat files, these files can be customized using a text editor program so that you can specify a DOS prompt, set a drive and directory path to be searched when you call up programs, or load and execute specific programs. Batch files are used extensively as shortcuts for routine or repetitive tasks or those that you just don't want to have to remember each step for. These files always have the extension .BAT, as required by DOS.

BIOS (Basic Input/Output System) The first set of program code to run when a PC system is booted up. The BIOS defines specific addresses and devices and provides software interface services for programs to use the equipment in a PC system. The PC system BIOS resides in a ROM chip on the system board. BIOSs also exist on add-in cards to provide additional adapter and interface services between hardware and software.

Bit   A bit is the smallest unit of information or memory possible in a digital or computer system. A bit has only two values: 1, or on, and 0, or off. A bit is the unit of measure in a binary (1/0) system. It might be thought of as a binary information term. A bit is one of 8 pieces of information in a byte, one of 16 pieces in a word (16-bit words), or one of 4 pieces in a nibble (half a byte.)

Built-in command   A command or service that loads with and is available as part of the DOS command processor program, COMMAND.COM. DIR, COPY, DEL, TYPE and CLS are examples of some internal DOS commands. *See also* **Internal command** and your DOS manual.

Burn-in   The process of running diagnostic or repetitive test software on some or all components of and in a PC system for an extended period of time under controlled conditions. This process helps verify functionality and sort out weak or defective units before they are delivered or used under normal working conditions.

Bus   An internal wiring configuration between the CPU and various interface circuits carrying address, data, and timing information required by one or more internal, built-in, add-in or external adapters and devices.

Byte   The common unit of measure of memory, information, file size, or storage capacity. A byte consists of 8 bits of information. There are typically two bytes to a word (typically 16 bits) of information. 1,024 bytes is referred to as a kilobyte or K, and contains 8,192 bits of information.

Cache   A reserved storage area used to hold information enroute to other devices, memory, or the CPU. Information that is called for during a disk-read operation can be read into a cache with additional information "stock-piled" ahead of time so that it is available for use faster than having to wait for a disk's mechanical and electronic delays. Caching is becoming common between disks and the computer data bus or CPU and between the memory and CPU to speed up a system's operation. Some CPU chips and controller cards include caching as part of their design.

CGA (Color Graphics Adapter) The first IBM-PC color display system, providing low-resolution (320 × 200) color graphics and basic text functions.

Cluster The smallest unit of measure of disk storage space under PC- or MS-DOS. A cluster typically consists of four or more sectors of information storage space and contains 2,048 or more bytes of storage capacity.

CMOS clock A special clock chip that runs continuously, either from the PC system power supply or a small battery, providing date and time information.

CMOS RAM A special memory chip used to store system configuration information. Rarely found in PC or XT models and usually found in 286 or higher models.

CMOS setup The process of selecting and storing configuration (device, memory, date, and time) information about your system for use during bootup. This process may be done through your PC's BIOS program or an external (disk-based) utility program.

Communications program An application program that is used to simulate a computer data terminal when communicating with a computer at another location by modem or data communication line. Such programs often provide color display features, modem command setups, telephone number dialing directories, and script- or batch-file-like automatic keystroke and file transfer functions.

CONFIG.SYS An ASCII text file that may contain one or more lines of special DOS commands that you want executed every time you boot up your PC. Also known as the config file, this file can be customized using a text editor program, so that you can specify one or more items specific to how your system should operate when it boots up. You may specify device drivers (with DEVICE=) such as memory management programs, disk caching, and RAM disks; the number of files and buffers you want DOS to use; and the location, name and any special parameters for your command processor (usually COMMAND.COM), among other parameters. Refer to your DOS manual or device driver software manual for specific information.

Conventional memory Also known as DOS memory, this is the range of your PC's memory from 0–640K where device drivers, DOS parameters, the DOS command processor (COMMAND.COM), your applications programs and data are stored when you use your computer. *See* **Extended, Expanded, Video, High,** and **Upper memory.**

CPU (Central Processing Unit) The main integrated circuit chip, processor circuit or board in a computer system. For IBM PC-compatible systems, the CPU may be an Intel or comparable 8088, 8086, 80286, 80386 (SX or DX), 80486 (SX or DX), Pentium, NEC V20 or V30, or other manufacturer's chip.

Current directory This is the subdirectory you or a program has last selected to operate from that is searched first before the DOS PATH is searched when calling a program. *See also* **Current disk drive** and **Logged drive.**

Current disk drive The drive that you have selected for DOS and programs to use before searching the specified drives and directories in the DOS PATH (if any is specified). This may also be the drive indicated by your DOS prompt (typically C>, or C:\>, or similar) or that you have selected by specifying a drive letter followed by a colon and the Enter key, as in A: Enter. This is also known as the logged drive.

Defragment The process of reorganizing disk files so that they occupy contiguous sectors and clusters on a disk. This is done to reduce the access time (movement of the data read/write heads) needed to read a single data file.

Device driver A special piece of software required by some hardware or software configurations to interface your computer to a hardware device. Common device drivers are ANSI.SYS, used for display screen control; RAMDRIVE.SYS, which creates and maintains a portion of memory that acts like a disk drive; and HIMEM.SYS, a special device driver used to manage a specific area of extended memory called the high memory area (HMA). Device drivers are usually intended to be used in the CONFIG.SYS file, preceded by a DEVICE= statement.

DIMM (Dual In-line Memory Module) A high-density memory packaging system consisting of 168 pins similar to the edge connector used on larger printed circuit cards. DIMM is used in addition to or in place of SIMM memory design.

DIN connector A circular multiwire electronic connector based on international (German) standards. Available in normal and miniature sizes with 3 to 7 connection pins. The PC uses 5-pin normal and 6-pin mini DIN connectors for keyboards, and 6-pin mini-DIN connectors for pointing devices.

DIP switch   A small, board-mounted switch assembly resembling a DIP integrated circuit (IC) package in size and form. Used for the selection of system addresses and options.

Directory   File space on disks used to store information about files organized and referred to through a directory name. Each disk has at least one directory, called the root directory, which is a specific area reserved for other file and directory entries. A hard disk root directory may contain up to 512 other files or directory references, limited by the amount of disk space reserved for root directory entries. The files and directories referred to by the root directory may be of any size up to the limit of available disk space. Directories may be thought of as folders or boxes, as they may appear with some graphical user-interfaces, although they are not visually represented that way by DOS. See Root directory and Subdirectories. All directories, except for the root directory, must have a name. The name for a directory follows the one- to eight-character restrictions that apply to filenames for DOS-only systems. Windows 95 and higher systems enjoy both longer file and directory names.

Disk cache   A portion of memory set aside to store information that has been read from a disk drive. The disk cache memory area is reserved and controlled by a disk caching program that you load in CONFIG.SYS or AUTOEXEC.BAT. The caching program intercepts a program or DOS request for information from a disk drive, and reads the requested data, plus extra data areas, so that it is available in memory, which is faster than a disk drive. This is commonly referred to as read-ahead caching. The cache may also be used for holding information to be written to disk, accepting the information faster than the disk can accept it and then writing the information to disk a short time later.

Disk drive adapter   A built-in or add-in card interface or controller that provides necessary connections between the computer system I/O circuits and a disk drive.

DLL (Dynamically Linked Library)   A file containing executable program functions that are invoked from another program. DLLs may be shared among many applications and are used only when a program requires the functions contained within, reducing program memory and disk space requirements by eliminating duplication of program elements and file size.

DMA (Direct Memory Access) A method of transferring information between a computer's memory and another device, such as a disk drive, without requiring CPU intervention.

DOS (disk operating system) A set of software written for a specific type of computer system, disk, file and application types to provide control over disk storage services and other input and output functions required by application programs and system maintenance. All computers using disk drives have some form of disk operating system containing applicable programs and services. For IBM-PC-compatible computers, the term DOS is commonly accepted to mean the computer software services specific to PC systems.

DOS memory Temporary memory used for storage of DOS boot and operating system information, programs, and data during the operation of your computer system. DOS memory occupies up to the first 640K of Random Access Memory (RAM) space provided in your system's hardware. This memory empties out or loses its contents when your computer is shut off.

DOS system diskette A diskette formatted for use with DOS-based PCs and file system that also contains the two DOS-system hidden files and COMMAND.COM to allow booting up your system from a diskette drive.

DRAM (Dynamic Random Access Memory) Relatively slow (50 to 200 nSec access time) economical memory integrated circuits. These require a periodic refresh cycle to maintain their contents. Typically used for the main memory in the PC system, but occasionally also used for video memory. *See also* **RAM** and **SRAM.**

Drive The mechanical and electronic assembly that holds disk storage media and provides the reading and writing functions for data storage and retrieval.

EGA (Enhanced Graphics Adapter) A color graphics system designed by IBM, providing medium-resolution text and graphics, compatible also with monochrome text and CGA displays.

EISA (Extended Industry Standard Architecture) The definition of a PC internal bus structure that maintains compatibility with IBM's original PC, XT, and AT bus designs (known as the ISA, or Industry Standard Architecture) but offering considerably more features and speed between the computer system and adapter cards, including a definition for 32-bit PC systems that do not follow IBM's MCA (MicroChannel Architecture).

EMM (Expanded memory manager) The term is often given to memory management software (such as EMM386 or QEMM) and is also used to refer to the physical Expanded memory chips and cards. See also **Expanded memory.**

EMS (Expanded memory specification) The IBM-PC industry standards for software and memory hardware that make up expanded memory.

Environment An area of memory set up and used by the DOS software to store and retrieve a small amount of information that can be shared or referred to by many programs. Among other information that the DOS environment area could hold are the PATH, current drive, PROMPT, COMSPEC, and any SET variables.

ESDI (Enhanced Small Device Interface) A standards definition for the interconnection of older high-speed disk drives. This standard is an alternative to earlier MFM, coincident applications of SCSI, and recent IDE drive interfaces.

Executable file A program file that may be invoked from the operating system. DLLs and overlay files also contain executable program information, but their functions must be invoked from within another program.

Expanded memory This is an additional area of memory created and managed by a device driver program using the Lotus-Intel-Microsoft Expanded Memory Specification, known also as LIMS-EMS. There are three common forms of EMS; that conforming to the LIMS-EMS 3.2 standard for software-only access to this memory, LIMS-EMS 4.0 in software, and LIMS-EMS 4.0 in hardware. With the proper hardware, this memory may exist and be used on all PC systems, from PCs to 486 systems. Expanded memory may be made up of extended memory (memory above 1MB) on 386 and 486 systems, or it may be simulated in extended memory on 286 systems. LIMS-EMS 3.2, 4.0 (software) and 4.0 (hardware) are commonly used for additional data storage for spreadsheets and databases. Only LIMS-EMS conforming to the 4.0 standard for hardware may be used for multitasking. Expanded memory resides at an upper memory address, occupying one 64K block between 640K and 1MB. The actual amount of memory available depends on your hardware and the amount of memory you can assign to be expanded memory. The 64K block taken up by expanded memory is only a window or port giving access to the actual amount of EMS available. There may be as little as 64K or as much as 32MB of expanded memory.

Extended memory This is memory in the address range above 1Mb, available only on 80286 or higher systems. It is commonly used for RAM disks, disk caching, and some applications programs. Using a special driver called HIMEM.SYS or similar services provided with memory management software, the first 64K of extended memory may be assigned as a high memory area, which some programs and DOS can be loaded into.

External command A program or service provided as part of DOS that exists as separate programs on disk rather than built into the COMMAND.COM program that loads when you boot up your system. These programs have .COM or .EXE extensions. Some of these are FORMAT.COM, DISKCOPY.COM, DEBUG.EXE, LABEL.COM, MORE.COM, and PRINT.COM.

FDISK A special part of the hard disk formatting process required to assign and establish usable areas of the disk as either bootable, active, data-only for DOS, or as non-DOS for other operating system use. The FDISK process is to be performed between the low-level format and the DOS format of a hard disk prior to its use.

FIFO or FIFO buffering First-in, first-out. A small-capacity data storage element, memory or register that holds data flowing between a source and a destination. The data flow moves in the order in which it is received and cannot be accessed directly or randomly as with normal memory storage. A FIFO is commonly used in serial communication (COM) ports to retain data while applications software and storage devices catch up to and can store the incoming stream of data.

File An area of disk space containing a program or data as a single unit, referred to by the DOS file directory. Its beginning location is recorded in the file directory, with reference to all space occupied by the file recorded in the DOS file allocation table (FAT). Files are pieces of data or software that you work with on your computer. They may be copied, moved, erased, or modified, all of which is tracked by DOS for the directory and FAT.

File Allocation Table   This is DOS's index to the disk clusters that files or FAT and directories occupy. It provides a table or pointer to the next disk cluster a file occupies. There are two copies of the FAT on a disk, for reliability. When files are erased, copied, moved, reorganized, or defragmented, the FAT is updated to reflect the new position of files or the availability of empty disk space. Files may occupy many different cluster locations on disk, and the FAT is the only reference to where all of the file pieces are.

File attributes   *See* **Attributes.**

Flag   A hardware bit or register, or a single data element in memory that is used to contain the status of an operation, much like the flag on a mailbox signals the mail delivery person that you have an item to be picked up.

Format   The process of preparing a disk (floppy or hard) with a specific directory and file structure for use by DOS and applications programs. Formatting may consist of making the disk usable for data storage only, providing reserved space to make the disk bootable later on, or making the disk bootable, including the copying of the DOS hidden files and COMMAND.COM. FORMAT is the final process of preparing a hard disk, preceded by a low-level format and FDISK. All disk media require a format. RAM or virtual disks do not require formatting. Formatting, unless performed with certain types of software, erases all data from a disk.

Gigabyte or GB   A unit of measure referring to 1,024MB or 1,073,741,824 bytes of information, storage space or memory. Devices with this capacity are usually large disk drives and tape backup units with 1.2 to well over 12GB of storage area.

Hardware interrupt   A signal from a hardware device connected to a PC system that causes the CPU and computer program to act on an event that requires software manipulation, such as controlling mouse movements, accepting keyboard input, or transferring a data file through a serial I/O port.

Hexadecimal   A base-16 numbering system made up of 4 digits or bits of information, where the least significant place equals one and the most significant place equals eight. A hexadecimal, or hex, number is represented as the numbers 0–9 and letters A–F, for the numerical range 0–15 as 0–F. A byte of hex information can represent from 0 to 255 different items, as 00 to FF.

Hidden file *See* **Attributes.**

High memory area or HMA A 64K region of memory above the 1MB address range created by HIMEM.SYS or a similar memory utility. The HMA can be used by one program for program storage, leaving more space available in the DOS or the low memory area from 0 to 640K.

Host adapter A built-in or add-in card interface between a device, such as a SCSI hard disk or CD-ROM drive, and the I/O bus of a computer system. A host adapter typically does not provide control functions, instead acting only as an address and signal conversion and routing circuit.

IBM-PC-compatible A description of a personal computer system that provides the minimum functions and features of the original IBM PC system and is capable of running the same software and using the same hardware devices.

IDC (Insulation displacement connector) The type of connector found on flat ribbon cables, used to connect I/O cards and disk drives.

IDE (Integrated Drive Electronics) A standards definition for the interconnection of high-speed disk drives in which the controller and drive circuits are together on the disk drive and interconnect to the PC I/O system through a special adapter card. This standard is an alternative to earlier MFM, ESDI, and SCSI drive interfaces, and it is also part of the ATA-standard.

Interlaced operation A method of displaying elements on a display screen in alternating rows of pixels (picture elements) or scans across a display screen, as opposed to noninterlaced operation, which scans each row in succession. Interlacing often indicates a flickering or blinking of the illuminated screen.

Interleave The property, order, or layout of data sectors around disk cylinders to coincide with the speed of drive and controller electronics so that data can be accessed as quickly as possible. An improper interleave can make a sector arrive too soon or too late at the data heads, and thus be unavailable when the drive and controller are ready for it, slowing disk system performance. An optimal interleave will have the rotation of the disk, placement of a data sector and electronics coincident so there is little or no delay in data availability. Interleave is set or determined at the time of a low-level format, which sets the order of the data sectors. Re-interleaving consists of shuffling data sectors to a pattern optimal for best performance.

Internal command   A command that loads with and is available as part of the DOS command processor program, COMMAND.COM. DIR, COPY, DEL, TYPE, and CLS are examples of some internal DOS commands. The same as Built-in command. Also see your DOS manual.

Interrupt   *See* **Hardware interrupt, IRQ**, and **Software Interrupt.**

I/O or input/output   The capability or process of software or hardware to accept or transfer data between computer programs or devices.

IPX   A device driver-type TSR program that interfaces a network interface card to the operating system.

IRQ (Interrupt request)   This is a set of hardware signals available on the PC add-in card connections that can request prompt attention by the CPU when data must be transferred to/from add-in devices and the CPU or memory.

ISA (Industry Standard Architecture)   The term given to the IBM PC, XT, and AT respective 8- and 16-bit PC bus systems. Non-32-bit, non–IBM MicroChannel Architecture systems are generally ISA systems.

ISDN (Integrated Services Digital Network)   A technique of providing high-speed digital communications over conventional telephone wires, using signaling above and different from voice-range frequencies. ISDN uses three different signal channels over the same pair of wires, one D-channel for digital signaling such as dialing and several enhanced but seldom used telephone calling features, and two B-channels, each capable of handling voice or data communications up to 64 kilobits per second. ISDN lines may be configured as Point-to-Point (both B-channels would connect to the same destination) or Multi-Point (allowing each B-channel to connect to different locations), and Data+Data (B-channels can be used for data-only) or Data+Voice where either B-channel may be used for data or voice transmission. Interconnection to an ISDN line requires a special termination/power unit, known as an NT-1 (network termination 1), which may or may not be built into the ISDN "modem" or router equipment at the subscriber end. An ISDN "modem" may be used and controlled quite similarly to a standard analog modem, and may or may not also provide voice-line capabilities for analog devices. An ISDN router must be configured for specific network addresses and traffic control, and may or may not provide voice/analog line capabilities.

ISO (International Standards Organization) A multifaceted, multinational group that establishes cross-border/cross-technology definitions for many industrial and consumer products. Related to the PC industry, it helps define electronic interconnection standards and tolerances.

Kilobyte or K A unit of measure referring to 1,024 bytes or 8,192 bits of information, storage space, or memory.

Label or Volume label A 1- to 11-character name recorded on a disk to identify it during disk and file operations. The volume label is written to disk with the DOS LABEL or FORMAT programs or with disk utility programs. This may be confused with the paper tag affixed to the outside of a diskette.

LAN (Local area network) An interconnection of systems and appropriate software that allows the sharing of programs, data files, and other resources among several users.

LCD (Liquid crystal display) A type of data display that uses microscopic crystals, which are sensitive to electrical energy to control whether they pass or reflect light. Patterns of crystals may be designed to form characters and figures, as are the small dots of luminescent phosphor in a CRT (display monitor or TV picture tube.)

LIMS (Lotus-Intel- Microsoft Standard) *See* **Expanded memory.**

Local Bus A processor to I/O device interface alternative to the PC's standard I/O bus connections, providing extremely fast transfer of data and control signals between a device and the CPU. It is commonly used for video cards and disk drive interfaces to enhance system performance. Local Bus is a trademark of the Video Electronics Standards Association.

Logged drive The disk drive you are currently displaying or using, commonly identified by the DOS prompt (C> or A:\>). If your prompt does not display the current drive, you may do a DIR or DIR/p to see the drive information displayed.

Logical devices   A hardware device that is referred to in DOS or applications by a name or abbreviation that represents a hardware address assignment, rather than by its actual physical address. The physical address for a logical device may be different. Logical device assignments are based on rules established by IBM and the ROM BIOS at bootup.

Logical drive   A portion of a disk drive assigned as a smaller partition of a larger physical disk drive. Also a virtual or nondisk drive created and managed through special software. RAM drives (created with RAMDRIVE.SYS or VDISK.SYS) or compressed disk/file areas (such as those created by Stacker, DoubleDisk, or SuperStor) are also logical drives. A 40MB disk drive partitioned as drives C: and D: is said to have two logical drives. That same disk with one drive area referred to as C: has only one logical drive, coincident with the entire physical drive area. DOS may use up to 26 logical drives. Logical drives may also appear as drives on a network server or mapped by the DOS ASSIGN or SUBST programs.

Logical pages   Sections of memory that are accessed by an indirect name or reference rather than by direct location addressing, under control of a memory manager or multitasking control program.

Loopback plug   A connector specifically wired to return an outgoing signal to an input signal line for the purpose of detecting if the output signal is active or not, as sensed at the input line.

Lower memory   *See* DOS memory.

MCA (MicroChannel Architecture)   IBM's system board and adapter card standards for the PS/2 (Personal System/2) series of computers. This is a non-ISA bus system requiring the use of different adapter cards and special configuration information than are used on early PC-, XT-, and AT-compatible systems.

MCGA (Multi-Color Graphics Array)   An implementation of CGA built into IBM PS/2 Model 25 and 30 systems using an IBM analog monitor and providing some enhancements for higher resolution display and grey-scale shading for monochrome monitors.

MDA (Monochrome Display Adapter)   The first IBM PC video system, providing text-only on a one-color (green or amber) display. If you have one of these adapters, you own an antique!

Megabyte or MB A unit of measure referring to 1,024K or 1,048,576 bytes of information, storage space, or memory. One megabyte contains 8,388,608 bits of information. One megabyte is also the memory address limit of a PC- or XT-class computer using an 8088, 8086, V20, or V30 CPU chip. 1MB is 0.001GB.

Megahertz or MHz A measure of frequency in millions of cycles per second. The speed of a computer system's main CPU clock is rated in megahertz.

Memory Computer information storage area made up of chips (integrated circuits) or other components, which may include disk drives. Personal computers use many types of memory, from dynamic RAM chips for temporary DOS, extended, expanded, and video memory to static RAM chips for CPU instruction caching to memory cartridges and disk drives for program and data storage.

Memory disk *See* **RAM disk.**

Microchannel An I/O card interconnection design created by IBM for use in the IBM PS/2 series systems.

Microprocessor A computer central processing unit contained within one integrated circuit chip package.

MIDI (Musical Instrument Device Interface) An industry standard for hardware and software connections, control, and data transfer between like-equipped musical instruments and computer systems.

Motherboard The main component or system board of your computer system. It contains the necessary connectors, components, and interface circuits required for communications between the CPU, memory, and I/O devices.

Network interface card or NIC An add-in card or external adapter unit used to connect a workstation (PC system) to a common network or distribution system.

Nibble A nibble is one-half of a byte, or 4 bits, of information.

Noninterlaced operation A method of displaying elements on a display screen at a fast rate throughout the entire area of the screen, as opposed to interlaced operation, which scans alternate rows of display elements or pixels, the latter often indicating a flickering or blinking of the illuminated screen.

Null modem A passive, wire-only data connection between two similar ports of computer systems, connecting the output of one computer to the input of another, and vice versa. Data flow control or handshaking signals may also be connected between systems. A null modem is used between two nearby systems much as you might interconnect two computers at different locations by telephone modem.

Offsets When addressing data elements or hardware devices, often the locations that data is stored or moved through are in a fixed grouping, beginning at a known or base address, or segment of the memory range. The offset is that distance, location, or number of bits or bytes that the desired information is from the base or segment location. Accessing areas of memory is done with an offset address based on the first location in a segment of memory. For example, an address of 0:0040h represents the first segment, and an offset of 40 bytes. An address of A:0040h would be the 40th (in hex) byte location (offset) in the tenth (Ah) segment.

Operating system *See* DOS (disk operating system).

Overlays A portion of a complete executable program, existing separately from the main control program, that is loaded into memory only when it is required by the main program, thus reducing overall program memory requirements for most operations. Occasionally, overlays may be built into the main program file, but they are also not loaded into memory until needed.

Page frame The location in DOS/PC system memory (between 640K and 1MB) where the pages or groups of expanded memory are accessed.

Parallel I/O A method of transferring data between devices or portions of a computer where 8 or more bits of information are sent in one cycle or operation. Parallel transfers require 8 or more wires to move the information. At speeds from 12,000 to 92,000 bytes per second or faster, this method is faster than the serial transfer of data where one bit of information follows another. Commonly used for the printer port on PCs.

Parallel port A computer's parallel I/O (LPT) connection, built into the system board or provided by an add-in card.

Parameter Information provided when calling or within a program specifying how or when it is to run with which files, disks, paths, or similar attributes.

Parity A method of calculating the pattern of data transferred as a verification that the data has been transferred or stored correctly. Parity is used in all PC memory structures, as the 9th, 17th, or 33rd bit in 8-, 16-, or 32-bit memory storage operations. If there is an error in memory, it will usually show up as a parity error, halting the computer so that processing does not proceed with bad data. Parity is also used in some serial data connections as an eight or ninth bit to insure that each character of data is received correctly.

Partition A section of a hard disk drive typically defined as a logical drive, which may occupy some or all of the hard-disk capacity. A partition is created by the DOS FDISK or other disk utility software.

Path A DOS parameter stored as part of the DOS environment space, indicating the order and locations DOS is to use when you request a program to run. A path is also used to specify the disk and directory information for a program or data file.

PC The first model designation for IBM's family of personal computers. This model provided 64 to 256K of RAM on the system board, a cassette tape adapter as an alternative to diskette storage, and five add-in card slots. The term generally refers to all IBM PC–compatible models and has gained popular use as a generic term referring to all forms, makes, and models for personal computers.

PC compatible *See* **IBM-PC-compatible** and **AT-compatible.**

PCMCIA (Personal Computer Memory Card Industry Association)
An I/O interconnect definition used for memory cards, disk drives, modems, network and other connections to portable computers.

Pentium A 64-bit Intel microprocessor capable of operating at 60–266+MHz, containing a 16K instruction cache, floating point processor, and several internal features for extremely fast program operations.

Pentium II A 64-bit Intel microprocessor capable of operating at 200–450+MHz, containing a 16K instruction cache, floating point processor, and several internal features for extremely fast program operations. Packaged in what is known as Intel's Slot 1 module, containing the CPU and local chipset components.

Peripheral component interconnect or PCI An Intel-developed standard interface between the CPU and I/O devices providing enhanced system performance. PCI is typically used for video and disk drive interconnections to the CPU.

PGA, PGC or Professional Graphics Adapter, Professional Graphics Controller, Professional Color Graphics System This was an interim IBM high-resolution color graphics system in limited distribution between EGA and VGA.

Plug and Play A standard for PC BIOS peripheral and I/O device identification and operating system configuration established to reduce the manual configuration technicalities for adding or changing PC peripheral devices. Plug-and-Play routines in the system BIOS work with and around older, legacy or otherwise fixed or manually configured I/O devices and report device configuration information to the operating system. (The operating system does not itself control or affect PnP or I/O device configurations.)

PnP *See* **Plug and Play.**

Pointing device A hardware input device, a mouse, trackball, cursor tablet, or keystrokes used to direct a pointer, cross-hair or cursor position indicator around the area of a display screen to locate or position graphic or character elements or select position-activated choices (buttons, scroll bar controls, menu selections, and so on) displayed by a computer program.

Port address The physical address within the computer's memory range that a hardware device is set to decode and allow access to its services through.

POST (Power On Self Test) A series of hardware tests run on your PC when power is turned on to the system. POST surveys installed memory and equipment, storing and using this information for bootup and subsequent use by DOS and applications programs. POST will provide either speaker beep messages, video display messages, or both if it encounters errors in the system during testing and bootup.

RAM (Random Access Memory) A storage area that information can be sent to and taken from by addressing specific locations in any order at any time. The memory in your PC and even the disk drives are a form of random access memory, although the memory is most commonly referred to as the RAM. RAM memory chips come in two forms, the more common Dynamic RAM (DRAM), which must be refreshed often to retain the information stored in it, and Static RAM, which can retain information without refreshing, saving power and time. RAM memory chips are referred to by their storage capacity and maximum speed of operation in the part numbers assigned to them. Chips with 16K and 64K capacity were common in early PCs, as were 256K and 1MB chips in the early 1990s, but 8, 16, 32 and 64MB RAM components are now more common.

RAM disk or RAM drive A portion of memory assigned by a device driver or program to function like a disk drive on a temporary basis. Any data stored in a RAM drive exists there as long as your computer is not rebooted or turned off.

ROM (Read-Only Memory) This is a type of memory chip that is preprogrammed with instructions or information specific to the computer type or device it is used in. All PCs have a ROM-based BIOS that holds the initial bootup instructions that are used when your computer is first turned on or when a warm-boot is issued. Some video and disk adapters contain a form of ROM-based program that replaces or assists the PC BIOS or DOS in using a particular adapter.

ROM BIOS The ROM-chip based start-up or controlling program for a computer system or peripheral device. *See also* **BIOS** and **ROM.**

Root directory The first directory area on any disk media. The DOS command processor and any CONFIG.SYS or AUTOEXEC.BAT file must typically reside in the root directory of a bootable disk. The root directory has space for a fixed number of entries, which may be files or subdirectories. A hard disk root directory may contain up to 512 files or subdirectory entries, the size of which is limited only by the capacity of the disk drive. Subdirectories may have nearly unlimited numbers of entries.

SCSI (Small Computer System Interface) An interface specification for interconnecting peripheral devices to a computer bus. SCSI allows for attaching multiple high-speed devices such as disk and tape drives through a single 50-pin cable.

Segments A method of grouping memory locations, usually in 64K increments or blocks, to make addressing easier to display and understand. Segment 0 is the first 64K of RAM in a PC. Accessing areas of memory within that segment is done with an offset address based on the first location in the segment. An address of 0:0040h would be the 40th (in hex) byte location in the first 64K of memory. An address of A:0040h would be the 40th (in hex) byte location in the tenth (Ah) 64K of memory.

Serial I/O A method of transferring data between two devices one bit at a time, usually within a predetermined frame of bits that makes up a character, plus transfer control information (start and stop or beginning and end of character information). Modems and many printers use serial data transfer. One-way serial transfer can be done on as few as two wires, with two-way transfers requiring as few as three wires. Transfer speeds of 110,000 to 115,000 bits (11,000 to 11,500 characters) per second are possible through a PC serial port.

Serial port A computer's serial I/O (COM) connection, built into the system board or provided by an add-in card.

Shadow RAM A special memory configuration that remaps some or all of the information stored in BIOS and adapter ROM chips to faster dedicated RAM chips. This feature is controllable on many PC systems that have it, allowing you to use memory management software to provide this and other features.

SIMM (Single Inline Memory Module) A dense memory packaging technique with small memory chips mounted on a small circuit board that clips into a special socket.

Software Interrupt A (non-hardware) signal or command from a currently executing program that causes the CPU and computer program to act on an event that requires special attention, such as the completion of a routine operation or the execution of a new function. Many software interrupt services are predefined and available through the system BIOS and DOS, while others may be made available by device driver software or running programs. Most disk accesses, keyboard operations, and timing services are provided to applications through software interrupt services.

SRAM (Static Random Access Memory) Fast access (less than 50 nanoseconds), somewhat expensive, memory integrated circuits that do not require a refresh cycle to maintain their contents. Typically used in video and cache applications. *See also* **DRAM** and **RAM**.

ST506/412 The original device interface specification for small hard drives, designed by Seagate and first commonly used in the IBM PC/XT.

Subdirectory A directory contained within the root directory or in other subdirectories, used to organize programs and files by application or data type, system user, or other criteria. A subdirectory is analogous to a file folder in a filing cabinet or an index tab in a book.

Surface scan The process of reading and verifying the data stored on a disk to determine its accuracy and reliability, usually as part of a utility or diagnostic program's operation to test or recover data.

System attribute or system file *See* Attributes.

TSR (Terminate-and-stay-resident program) Also known as a memory-resident program. A program that remains in memory to provide services automatically or on request through a special key sequence (also known as hot keys). Device drivers (MOUSE, ANSI, SETVER) and disk caches, RAM disks, and print spoolers are forms of automatic TSR programs. SideKick, Lightning, and assorted screen-capture programs are examples of hot-key–controlled TSR programs.

Twisted-pair cable A pair of wires bundled together by twisting or wrapping them around each other in a regular pattern. Twisting the wires reduces the influx of other signals into the wires, preventing interference, as opposed to coaxial (concentric orientation) or parallel wire cabling.

UAR/T (Universal Asynchronous Receiver/Transmitter) This is a special integrated circuit or function used to convert parallel computer bus information into serial transfer information and vice versa. A UAR/T also provides proper system-to-system online status, modem ring and data carrier detect signals, as well as start/stop transfer features. The most recent version of this chip, called the 16550A, is crucial to high-speed (greater than 2,400 bits per second) data transfers under multitasking environments.

Upper memory and upper memory blocks Memory space between 640K and 1MB that may be controlled and made available by a special device or UMB (EMM386.SYS, QEMM386, 386Max, and so on) for the purpose of storing and running TSR programs and leaving more DOS RAM (from 0 to 640K) available for other programs and data. Some of this area is occupied by BIOS, video, and disk adapters.

V20 An NEC clone of the Intel 8088 8-bit internal and external data bus microprocessor capable of addressing up to 1MB of memory and operating at speeds up to 10 MHz. NEC has optimized several of the internal microcode commands so this CPU chip can perform some operations faster than the Intel chip it can be used in place of. Its companion numerical coprocessor or math chip is the 8087. This chip can generally be used in any PC or XT system that uses an 8088 chip.

V30 An Intel 16-bit internal, 8-bit external data bus microprocessor capable of addressing up to 1MB of memory and operating at speeds up to 10MHz. NEC has optimized several of the internal microcode commands so this CPU chip can perform some operations faster than the Intel chip it can replace. Its companion numerical coprocessor or math chip is the 8087. This chip can only be used in IBM PS/2 Models 25 and 30 and in some clones.

Variable Information provided when calling or within a program specifying how or when it is to run with which files, disks, paths, or similar attributes. A variable may be allowed for in a batch file, using %1 through %9 designations to substitute or include values keyed-in at the command line when the Batch file is called.

VGA (Video Graphics Array) A high-resolution text and graphics system supporting color and previous IBM video standards using an analog-interfaced video monitor.

Video adapter card The interface card between the computer's I/O system and the video display device.

Video memory Memory contained on the video adapter dedicated to storing information to be processed by the adapter for placement on the display screen. The amount and exact location of video memory depends on the type and features of your video adapter. This memory and the video adapter functions are located in upper memory between 640K and 832K.

Virtual disk *See* **RAM disk.**

Virtual memory   Disk space allocated and managed by an operating system that is used to augment the available RAM memory, and is designed to contain inactive program code and data when switching between multiple computer tasks.

XMS (Extended Memory Specification)   A standard that defines access and control over upper, high, and extended memory on 286 and higher computer systems. XMS support is provided by loading the HIMEM.SYS device driver or other memory management software that provides XMS features.

XT   The second model of IBM PC series provided with "extended technology" allowing the addition of hard disks and eight add-in card slots. The original XT models had between 64K and 256K of RAM on board, a single floppy drive, and a 10MB hard disk.

Index

IDG BOOKS WORLDWIDE, INC.

END-USER LICENSE AGREEMENT

READ THIS. You should carefully read these terms and conditions before opening the software packet(s) included with this book ("Book"). This is a license agreement ("Agreement") between you and IDG Books Worldwide, Inc. ("IDGB"). By opening the accompanying software packet(s), you acknowledge that you have read and accept the following terms and conditions. If you do not agree and do not want to be bound by such terms and conditions, promptly return the Book and the unopened software packet(s) to the place you obtained them for a full refund.

1. **License Grant.** IDGB grants to you (either an individual or entity) a nonexclusive license to use one copy of the enclosed software program(s) (collectively, the "Software") solely for your own personal or business purposes on a single computer (whether a standard computer or a workstation component of a multiuser network). The Software is in use on a computer when it is loaded into temporary memory (RAM) or installed into permanent memory (hard disk, CD-ROM, or other storage device). IDGB reserves all rights not expressly granted herein.

2. **Ownership.** IDGB is the owner of all right, title, and interest, including copyright, in and to the compilation of the Software recorded on the disk(s) or CD-ROM ("Software Media"). Copyright to the individual programs recorded on the Software Media is owned by the author or other authorized copyright owner of each program. Ownership of the Software and all proprietary rights relating thereto remain with IDGB and its licensers.

3. **Restrictions On Use and Transfer.**

   (a) You may only (i) make one copy of the Software for backup or archival purposes, or (ii) transfer the Software to a single hard disk, provided that you keep the original for backup or archival purposes. You may not (i) rent or lease the Software, (ii) copy or reproduce the Software through a LAN or other network system or through any computer subscriber system or bulletin-board system, or (iii) modify, adapt, or create derivative works based on the Software.

   (b) You may not reverse engineer, decompile, or disassemble the Software. You may transfer the Software and user documentation on a permanent basis, provided that the transferee agrees to accept the terms and conditions of this Agreement and you retain no copies. If the Software is an update or has been updated, any transfer must include the most recent update and all prior versions.

4. **Restrictions On Use of Individual Programs.** You must follow the individual requirements and restrictions detailed for each individual program in Appendix D, "About the CD-ROM," of this Book. These limitations are also contained in the individual license agreements recorded on the Software Media. These limitations may include a requirement that after using the program for a specified period of time, the user must pay a registration fee or discontinue use. By opening the Software packet(s), you will be agreeing to abide by the licenses and restrictions for these individual programs that are detailed in Appendix D, "About the CD-ROM," and on the Software Media. None of the material on this Software Media or listed in this Book may ever be redistributed, in original or modified form, for commercial purposes.

5. **Limited Warranty.**

   (a) IDGB warrants that the Software and Software Media are free from defects in materials and workmanship under normal use for a period of sixty (60) days from the date of purchase of this Book. If IDGB receives notification within the warranty period of defects in materials or workmanship, IDGB will replace the defective Software Media.

(b) **IDGB AND THE AUTHORS OF THE BOOK DISCLAIM ALL OTHER WARRANTIES, EXPRESS OR IMPLIED, INCLUDING WITHOUT LIMITATION IMPLIED WARRANTIES OF MERCHANTABILITY AND FITNESS FOR A PARTICULAR PURPOSE, WITH RESPECT TO THE SOFTWARE, THE PROGRAMS, THE SOURCE CODE CONTAINED THEREIN, AND/OR THE TECHNIQUES DESCRIBED IN THIS BOOK. IDGB DOES NOT WARRANT THAT THE FUNCTIONS CONTAINED IN THE SOFTWARE WILL MEET YOUR REQUIREMENTS OR THAT THE OPERATION OF THE SOFTWARE WILL BE ERROR FREE.**

(c) This limited warranty gives you specific legal rights, and you may have other rights that vary from jurisdiction to jurisdiction.

6. **Remedies.**

(a) IDGB's entire liability and your exclusive remedy for defects in materials and workmanship shall be limited to replacement of the Software Media, which may be returned to IDGB with a copy of your receipt at the following address: Software Media Fulfillment Department, Attn.: *IRQ, DMA & I/O, 3rd Edition*, IDG Books Worldwide, Inc., 7260 Shadeland Station, Ste. 100, Indianapolis, IN 46256, or call 1-800-762-2974. Please allow three to four weeks for delivery. This Limited Warranty is void if failure of the Software Media has resulted from accident, abuse, or misapplication. Any replacement Software Media will be warranted for the remainder of the original warranty period or thirty (30) days, whichever is longer.

(b) In no event shall IDGB or the authors be liable for any damages whatsoever (including without limitation damages for loss of business profits, business interruption, loss of business information, or any other pecuniary loss) arising from the use of or inability to use the Book or the Software, even if IDGB has been advised of the possibility of such damages.

(c) Because some jurisdictions do not allow the exclusion or limitation of liability for consequential or incidental damages, the above limitation or exclusion may not apply to you.

7. **U.S. Government Restricted Rights.** Use, duplication, or disclosure of the Software by the U.S. Government is subject to restrictions stated in paragraph (c)(1)(ii) of the Rights in Technical Data and Computer Software clause of DFARS 252.227-7013, and in subparagraphs (a) through (d) of the Commercial Computer — Restricted Rights clause at FAR 52.227-19, and in similar clauses in the NASA FAR supplement, when applicable.

8. **General.** This Agreement constitutes the entire understanding of the parties and revokes and supersedes all prior agreements, oral or written, between them and may not be modified or amended except in a writing signed by both parties hereto that specifically refers to this Agreement. This Agreement shall take precedence over any other documents that may be in conflict herewith. If any one or more provisions contained in this Agreement are held by any court or tribunal to be invalid, illegal, or otherwise unenforceable, each and every other provision shall remain in full force and effect.